Anna
Visionary
Black
Feminist

Anna Julia Cooper, Visionary Black Feminist

A Critical Introduction

Vivian M. May

Foreword by Beverly Guy-Sheftall

Routledge
Taylor & Francis Group

New York   London

Photograph Permissions: The Oberlin Class of 1884 portrait of Anna Julia Cooper appears courtesy of the Oberlin College Archives, Oberlin OH. The photographs of Dunbar High School, of Cooper in her M.A. regalia, of Cooper standing by a bust of Frederick Douglass at Frelinguysen's Registrar's desk (in her parlor), and of a Frelinguysen class meeting in Cooper's home all appear courtesy of the Scurlock Studios Records, Archives Center, National Museum of American History, Smithsonian Institution. The early group portrait of Cooper seated next to Charlotte Forten Grimké, with Ella D. Barrier, Francis J. Grimké, and Fannie Shippen Smythe standing in the rear, appears courtesy of the Association for the Study of African American Life and History. The Oberlin class of 1884 reunion photograph of Cooper, Ida Gibbs Hunt, and Mary Church Terrell, taken in Cooper's home, was printed in the Washington Post April 4, 1952 page C9 alongside an article about the three women entitled "Reunited Trio Blazed a Trail": every attempt has been made to secure permissions for this image. The portrait of Cooper in her doctoral robes appeared previously in Hutchinson, page 154: every attempt has been made to secure permissions for this image.

This edition published 2012
by Routledge
2 Park Square, Milton Park, Abingdon, Oxon OX14 4RN

Simultaneously published in the USA and Canada
by Routledge
711 Third Avenue, New York, NY 10017, USA

Routledge is an imprint of the Taylor & Francis Group, an informa business

© 2007 by Taylor & Francis Group, LLC

International Standard Book Number-10: 0-415-95643-9 (Softcover) 0-415-95642-0 (Hardcover)
International Standard Book Number-13: 978-0-415-95643-7 (Softcover) 978-0-415-95642-0 (Hardcover)

Library of Congress Cataloging-in-Publication Data

May, Vivian M.
    Anna Julia Cooper, visionary Black feminist : a critical introduction / Vivian M. May.
        p. cm.
    Includes index.
    ISBN 978-0-415-95642-0 ISBN 978-0-415-95643-7
    1. Feminist theory. 2. African American philosophy. 3. Cooper, Anna J. (Anna Julia), 1858-1964. I. Title.
    HQ1190.M383 2007

305.48'8960730092--dc22
[B]   2006026826

Visit the Taylor & Francis Web site at
http://www.taylorandfrancis.com

and the Routledge Web site at
http://www.routledge.com

Contents

Preface

I was first introduced to Anna Julia Cooper well over ten years ago in two graduate seminars taught by Beverly Guy-Sheftall, "Black Women: Historical Perspectives" (Spring 1993) and "African American Feminist Thought" (Fall 1994). Both proved to be formative experiences; however, I remember that initial seminar very clearly, first because the course substantially altered my worldview and because Guy-Sheftall fostered a reflexive and politicized community of learning in which close ties and deep friendships developed that I value to this day. But what I also recall, vividly, is going to the bookstore to pick up a copy of Anna Julia Cooper's *A Voice from the South by a Black Woman of the South*. I wanted to get a head start on my reading, but little did I suspect that I would read *A Voice* in one sitting when I got home — and then re-read it the very next day, cover to cover. From the moment I opened the pages to her book, I was "bitten" by Cooper and would catch the "bug," as Beverly recently diagnosed me as having.

But at the same time that I found exhilaration in Cooper's ideas and in her ironic yet highly political writing style, I was also dismayed. In numerous undergraduate and graduate courses in feminist philosophy, existentialism, political philosophy, women's history, and African American literature, why had I not heard mention of Cooper? She belongs in all of these contexts, and more. Would I ever have encountered her work if I had not taken Guy-Sheftall's courses? I am not sure that I would have; then, as now, Cooper was under-read, marginalized, and tokenized. Today, upon encountering Cooper for the first time, students still ask to know more about who she was and inquire as to why they have not read her work in other courses. As a professor, I am happy to see new cadres of undergraduate and graduate students also getting "bitten" by Cooper; usually, they insist she should be *required* reading and hotly debate the meanings and implications of her ideas, all the while finding pleasure (and sometimes frustration) in her playful writing style and dry wit.

Despite the passion I have long had for Cooper's ideas, I put off writing about her for many years. I had a lot more to learn. First, what I knew of the field of Black feminist theorizing was too slim to do Cooper's work justice. At the same time, I was cautious of exploiting race privilege as a white feminist scholar. Therefore, I buckled down to immerse myself in African American feminist theory and literature just as I had done in a second language — French — while living in Quebec, setting aside the language of domination to engage in a different way of being in the world, a new epistemology and ontology via the tongue. As June Jordan would argue, "syntax, the structure of an idea, leads you to the world view of the speaker and reveals her values. The syntax of a sentence equals the structure of your consciousness" (*Some* 163).

Again, I return to that spring of 1993: throughout the semester, Professor Guy-Sheftall would point out work that needed to be done in African American feminist thought and history, questions that required further exploration, theorists who deserved more recognition. One afternoon, she remarked that nobody had taken up Cooper's Sorbonne thesis in any substantial way, and that though it had recently been translated into English, somebody versant in French and in Black feminist theories needed to attend to Cooper's dissertation. Since that time — since graduating and beginning my first job as a professor — I kept thinking that more Cooper scholarship would appear, that the dynamic critical conversation about Cooper that emerged in the late 1980s through much of the 1990s would continue to flourish. Fortunately, Charles Lemert and Esme Bhan's 1998 edited collection of Cooper's writings has made more of her work widely available, as does France Richardson Keller's new edition of her translation into English of Cooper's Sorbonne thesis. Hence, things are changing, though frankly more slowly than I would have thought; some exciting new works about Cooper have been published, and each year several dissertations are written that focus at least in part on her work. But still too rare is the book-length study of Cooper, and even scarcer is scholarly attention to her later writings, in particular her dissertation.

So it is, many years later, two very different "immersion" voyages into two languages/syntaxes/consciousnesses eventually led to this book. Cooper kept calling me, and finally I decided to answer; this is the book I have wanted to write for more than ten years. I hope to have done justice to the radical teacher in Cooper, as well as to the many passionate, dedicated, and critical educators to whom I remain indebted, especially Beverly Guy-Sheftall, Trudier Harris, and Geneviève Leidelinger.

Foreword

Like my former graduate student and now professor of Women's Studies, Vivian May, I have been affected in profound ways by Anna Julia Cooper's life and writings, but my introduction to her as a feminist intellectual was accidental, though surely inevitable. I was not introduced to Cooper in a women's studies or African American studies class as an undergraduate student at Spelman College or as a doctoral student in American studies at Emory University in the 1980s. Though I had read Paula Giddings's *When and Where I Enter: The Impact of Black Women on Race and Sex in America* (William Morrow, 1984), whose title came from Cooper's now better-known and even influential text *A Voice from the South* (1892), I "discovered" her in a different way some years after reading Giddings's important monograph. Many years later, when I was completing *Words of Fire: An Anthology of African American Feminist Thought* (New Press, 1995), I tried to capture the significance of our first book-length Black feminist text: "This collection of essays provides a global perspective on racism, imperialism, and colonialism; praises black achievements; advocates black women's education; and critiques black male sexism and the racism of white women" (43).

Teaching "Black Women: Historical Perspectives" and "African American Feminist Thought" for the first time in Emory's graduate program in women's studies in the early 1990s prompted me to conceptualize *Words of Fire*, the first published collection of Black feminist thought. Because there was no text for these courses, I circulated photocopied articles and began to assemble what would later become a widely used anthology for those of us who wanted to introduce our undergraduate and graduate students to a largely invisible and even maligned Black feminist intellectual tradition that began in the United States with the speeches and writings of Maria Stewart in 1832. Vivian May was enrolled in that course when I taught Anna Julia Cooper for the first time. I recall admitting to my class that I was not really "prepared" to teach Cooper since I was just beginning to "know" her, but that I hoped over time I would become more expert. Perhaps more importantly, I challenged them to become Cooper scholars and hoped that one day someone sitting in the class would become as passionate about her as I was. It was Vivian May who answered this challenge some years later, though I could not have foreseen what the impact of teaching Black feminism might have been, especially since I was honest about my being a student of Cooper myself at that point in my own professional development.

I also recall having shared with my eager students the circumstances under which Cooper came to occupy a special place in my mind and heart. Late one spring evening in Emory's Woodruff Library, while working on a paper for one of my graduate classes, I was perusing the shelves looking for a particular book by a nineteenth-century Black woman writer, Frances E. W. Harper. My fingers literally stumbled upon Cooper's *A Voice from the South*, and I can remember that moment as if it were yesterday. I pulled the book off the shelf (not remembering having read about her in Giddings's text), started reading, and finished it (as did Vivian) in a few hours. I was literally awestruck when I read Cooper's insightful and original pronouncement, which she wrote long before there was a discourse that scholars would later identify as Black feminist theory: "The Colored woman today occupies, one may say, a unique position in this country. ... She is confronted by both a woman question and a race problem, and is as yet an unknown or an unacknowledged factor in both" (*Voice* 134). I also bemoaned the fact that I was a professor at a Black women's college (Spelman) and a self-identified Black feminist, and I had never read what was perhaps the most important book in the nineteenth-century feminist canon. I remember vowing to myself on that very night that I would participate in an active way in excavating and making more visible this important but buried Black feminist intellectual tradition. Teaching African American feminist thought to graduate students at Emory and publishing *Words of Fire* was how I began.

It is impossible for me to fully capture here what Vivian May's groundbreaking scholarship on Cooper means to me, given my own efforts at illuminating the complexities of Black feminist theorizing over the past two decades. While I had intended to write a monograph on Cooper myself, perhaps a literary biography, May's book, *Anna Julia Cooper, Visionary Black*

Feminist: A Critical Introduction, has relieved me of this responsibility, and I can now rest comfortably knowing that a major contribution to the growing scholarship on Cooper is now in the public domain.[1] It is humbling to acknowledge that she has written a more compelling study of Cooper than I would have, and I believe I know why this is the case: her doctoral training in the interdisciplinary field of women's studies (such programs did not exist while I was pursuing the Ph.D.); her knowledge of French, which has enabled her to write the best analysis of Cooper's doctoral dissertation so far; her profound grasp of Black feminist theory, because of her teaching and research commitments, including her own course on "Anna Julia Cooper's Black Feminist Thought"; and her unwavering desire (I suspect) to live up to her professor's wishes that one of her students take Cooper seriously as a scholar.

With the publication of this second monograph on Cooper's writings,[2] Professor Vivian May's scholarly contributions to women's studies, Black feminist studies, and African diaspora studies are sure to be recognized by other scholars in these fields. Those of us who had the pleasure of teaching her at Emory are especially gratified and are looking forward to more articles and books. Having observed Vivian teaching at Texas Woman's University, I know that her impact on her students at Syracuse University will be equally as strong. I have also used her Introduction to Women's Studies syllabi in my rethinking of the introductory women's studies courses I teach at Spelman. When a group of us were planning the first conference on the Ph.D. in women's studies, which took place at Emory, Vivian May joined us and was crucial to our deliberations. I am also pleased that she has joined a friend and colleague of mine, Professor Chandra Talpade Mohanty, in the Women's Studies Department at Syracuse. And finally, the field of women's studies is in excellent hands because of a younger generation of scholars, like Vivian, who were affected in particular ways by their "foremothers," who've learned from our mistakes, and who are already producing significant scholarship that we would not have been able to imagine.

Beverly Guy-Sheftall

Anna Julia Cooper Professor of Women's Studies
Director, Women's Research & Resource Center
Spelman College
Atlanta, Georgia

Acknowledgments

For her ongoing passion, perceptiveness, and invaluable encouragement during this project and over the past 14 years, I would like to thank Beverly Guy-Sheftall, Anna Julia Cooper Professor of Women's Studies and founding director of the Women's Research and Resource Center, Spelman College. For their insightful suggestions, thoughtful feedback, and enthusiasm for the book, I am grateful to those whom Routledge asked to review the manuscript: Trudier Harris, J. Carlyle Sitterson Professor of English, University of North Carolina, Chapel Hill; Elizabeth V. Spelman, Barbara Richmond 1940 Professor in the Humanities and Professor of Philosophy and Women's Studies, Smith College; and Shannon Sullivan, Associate Professor of Philosophy and Women's Studies, Penn State University and Chair, Philosophy Department. My editor at Routledge, David McBride (now at Oxford University Press), provided essential help, and I appreciate his belief in the value and timeliness of this book. For their attentive work and responsiveness, thanks are also in order to many others at Routledge and Taylor & Francis, including Anna Sternoff and Sylvia Wood.

The Oberlin Class of 1884 portrait of Anna Julia Cooper appears courtesy of the Oberlin College Archives, Oberlin, Ohio. The photographs of Dunbar High School, of Cooper in her M.A. regalia, of Cooper standing by a bust of Frederick Douglass at Frelinghuysen's registrar's desk (in her parlor), and of a Frelinghuysen class meeting in Cooper's home all appear courtesy of Scurlock Studios Records, Archives Center, National Museum of American History, Smithsonian Institution. The early group portrait of Cooper seated next to Charlotte Forten Grimké, with Ella D. Barrier, Francis J. Grimké, and Fannie Shippen Smythe standing in the rear, appears courtesy of the Association for the Study of African American Life and History. The Oberlin class of 1884 reunion photograph of Cooper, Ida Gibbs Hunt, and Mary Church Terrell, taken in Cooper's home, was printed in the *Washington Post*, April 4, 1952, page C9, alongside an article about the three women entitled "Reunited Trio Blazed a Trail": every attempt has been made to secure permission to reproduce this image. The portrait of Cooper in her doctoral robes appeared previously in Hutchinson (154): every attempt has been made to secure permission to reproduce this image. Permission to copy the image from Hutchinson granted courtesy of the The Anacostia Museum & Center for African American History and Culture Library, Smithsonian Institution.

I have been fortunate to be invited to present some of my work on Cooper as the book evolved. A special thanks to Donna-Dale Marcano (assistant professor of Philosophy, Trinity College), who invited me to participate in an African American History Committee panel about Anna Julia Cooper at LeMoyne College in February 2005, and to Angela Cotten (assistant professor of Ethnic Studies, California State University Stanislaus), who invited me to participate in the "Cultural Sites of Critical Insight" conference at SUNY Stony Brook in October 2002.

Of course, I am indebted to many librarians, archivists, and editors for their behind-the-scenes labor and valuable assistance. In the Washington, D.C. area, I would like to thank Donna Wells, prints and photographs librarian, Moorland-Spingarn Research Center, Howard University; Jennifer Morris at the Anacostia Museum and Center for African American History and Culture Library, Smithsonian Institution; archivist Kay Peterson, National Museum of American History, Smithsonian Institution; Faye Haskins, photo librarian, Martin Luther King Library, Washingtoniana Division, D.C. Public Library; and James Russell, permissions editor for the Washington *Post*. At the Association for the Study of African American Life and History, I would like to thank Sylvia Cyrus-Albritton, executive director, Barbara Dunn, director of membership services, and Ja-Tun Thomas. At the Oberlin College Archives, Kenneth Grossi, associate archivist, and Tamara Martin, administrative secretary, were most obliging and efficient. At St. Augustine's College, in Raleigh, North Carolina, I am grateful to Linda Simmons-Henry, director of libraries, Marc A. Newman, vice president for institutional advancement, and Lashaunda Shaw, administrative assistant to Mr. Newman, for their help. At the Syracuse University Library, Dorcas MacDonald, librarian head, and her staff in Inter-Library Loan have been resolute in locating obscure materials. In addition, Penelope Singer, technical specialist in the Digital Imaging Service Center, helped to prepare several of the images used herein.

I value the aid and support of many others at Syracuse University. Cathryn Newton, Dean of the College of Arts and Sciences, facilitated this project both formally, through a research leave in the fall of 2005, and informally, through one-on-one conversations. Associate Dean for humanities Gerry Greenberg took the time on several occasions to answer questions and give advice when I stopped by his office. My chair, Linda Martín Alcoff, encouraged me in moments of doubt and helped immensely with a course reduction at a crucial time. Early on, my women's studies colleagues Chandra Talpade Mohanty and Gwendolyn Pough gave helpful feedback on the book proposal, as did Norman Kutcher in the History Department. Kalpana Srinivas, Assistant Chancellor, formerly senior administrator in the College of Arts and Sciences, lent a sympathetic ear and assistance. Brian Calhoun-Bryant, computer consultant in Arts and Sciences Computing Services, offered wonderful computer support (and kept his sense of humor throughout the project). And to the students in my spring 2006 seminar on Anna Julia Cooper's contributions to African American feminist thought, I continue to appreciate your keen enthusiasm for Cooper.

Without the support of friends and family, the research process would be a lonely venture indeed. Long-distance phone calls with Elizabeth West, assistant professor of English at Georgia State University and a buddy since graduate school, have been so important. To my parents and sister, thank you for countless conversations and for your unshakable affection. And to my partner, Beth, thank you for everything, every day: it is the most ordinary things in life that are the most important.

Introduction
"A Woman of Rare Courage and Conviction"[1]

Anna Julia Cooper (1858–1964; Figure 0.1) was an internationally renowned African American feminist educator, activist, orator, and scholar. She is most recognized for her important 1892 collection of essays, *A Voice from the South by a Black Woman of the South*. In *A Voice*, Cooper theorizes from her own experiences as a Black woman to highlight how race and gender politics are interlocking, to speak out against myriad forms of violence and domination, and to insist upon the right of all marginalized people to self-determination and self-definition. Highlighting how seemingly different experiences and identities are connected, Cooper insists upon an inclusive model of liberation and human rights. Refusing to accommodate history's silences and refuting

Figure 0.1 Portrait, Anna Julia Cooper, Oberlin Class of 1884. Courtesy of the Oberlin College Archives, Oberlin, Ohio.

1

the gross stereotypes of Black womanhood developed by so-called experts, Cooper raises her voice to issue a call to action and to emphasize the powerful knowledge and radical imagination that exist in the margins. Without doubt, *A Voice from the South* is a significant theoretical and political work.

However, unlike that of other major social theorists of her time, from Charlotte Perkins Gilman to W. E. B. Du Bois, the evolution of Cooper's intellectual and activist contributions has not yet been adequately considered. In other words, at the same time that more in-depth work on *A Voice from the South* is still needed, it is also the case that *A Voice* does not comprise the sum total of Cooper's work. She published several other books, essays, and pamphlets, many of which remain overlooked, as does much of her extensive work as a community activist.[2] Cooper continued to build upon and further develop many of the important concepts articulated in *A Voice* — after all, she wrote and worked well into her nineties. This book starts from the premise that her prophetic ideas, as they emerge across her body of work, deserve a closer look.

Yet the question remains: Why have Cooper's astute ideas and methods not been given the attention they deserve, since, as an educator, scholar, and activist, Cooper implemented a major challenge to the disciplining of both ideas and bodies? Does she continue to be overlooked in part because she was Black and female? Cooper faced extensive resistance on both counts throughout her lifetime: the tenacity and perniciousness of racism-sexism should not be underestimated when considering her relative marginality today, both as a theorist and as an activist. Of course, in many ways, Cooper was ahead of her time: future work by anticolonial, feminist, and Black studies scholars would provide the lenses necessary for her ideas to become, retroactively, better understood and for more of the nuances in Cooper's work to come to the fore. Yet I would argue that prescience alone cannot fully account for Cooper's undervaluation, for other public intellectuals and social theorists who were forward-thinking continue to be given far more time and attention than does Cooper.

For example, why do many of us know of Aimé Césaire's or C. L. R. James's analyses of the dialectical nature of the Haitian and French Revolutions and of an emergent transatlantic revolutionary consciousness, but not Cooper's? Although most Cooper scholarship has focused primarily on *A Voice from the South*, her 1925 Sorbonne dissertation, *L'Attitude de la France à l'égard de l'esclavage pendant la Révolution*, merits closer attention: there, Cooper offers a cross-cultural analysis of the French and Haitian revolutions and of early capitalism's dependence on slavery in the Age of Revolution. Cooper's thesis should also be included in our working conceptions of a "Paris Noir," of the Black Renaissance/Harlem Renaissance, and of an emerging international Black modernism of the 1920s, but she is rarely acknowledged in these areas of inquiry, either. Further, when considering Pan-Africanism in the United States, why do we often point to W. E . B. Du Bois or Marcus Garvey, yet rarely to Cooper, who not only spoke at the 1900 Pan-African Congress in London but was also a member of the international executive committee? As Cooper complained to Du Bois, she, and many other radical Black women, might well have participated more fully in the later congresses, except for the fact that they were mostly held during the school year, rather than in the summer break when the many African American women who worked as educators could have participated.[3]

Studies of Black modernism or of revolutionary and colonial history are not the only sites where Cooper's ideas tend to be overlooked. For instance, in exploring the history of feminist philosophy, why are feminists from Mary Wollstonecraft to Simone de Beauvoir widely cited for critiquing sexist and male-centered reason and for naming the political structures of patriarchy, but not Cooper? In *A Voice from the South* and in her later writings and speeches, Cooper argues for located and embodied forms of knowing, develops a sophisticated analysis of the workings of oppression, and calls for an intersubjective approach to ethics, but her philosophical innovations have not been adequately considered in the fields of either feminist theory or social philosophy.

To help bridge these unacceptable gaps in our scholarship, *Anna Julia Cooper, Visionary Black Feminist: A Critical Introduction* attends to Cooper's radical voice across her body of work, including *A Voice from the South*, her dissertation, letters, pamphlets, and speeches. So that contemporary readers can better appreciate the continued relevance of Cooper's insurgent ideas and defiant practices, I discuss how the contexts of constraint in which Cooper lived and worked shaped her critical strategies. I also highlight a wide range of Cooper's activist and philosophical contributions that remain overlooked. Moreover, in referring to the *visionary* nature of Cooper's ideas and practices, my intention is to build on a core theme across Cooper's work — the premise that oppressed peoples are agents both of knowledge and history, even if their agency, resistance, and alternative ways of knowing have been suppressed or denied by the powerful.

For example, Cooper opens *A Voice* by underscoring from the start Black women's "open-eyed" status, a phrase that connotes simultaneous awareness and agency, past and present (*Voice* ii). Rather than eyes lowered in submission or closed in denial, an open-eyed person is alert and perceptive—she takes in the world's ugly or denied realities as much as its wonders. Cooper also highlights this capacity in her later work. In her dissertation, for instance, she credits Toussaint Louverture's capacity to "see and foresee"[4] as key to the success of the Haitian Revolution: even if his political savvy and keen intellect were denied or dismissed by the ruling French and the elite *gens de couleur,* Louverture rejected the dominant worldview and saw another vision for himself and for Saint-Domingue, an independent nation-state where racial slavery was outlawed (*L'Attitude* 111).

Therefore, throughout *Anna Julia Cooper, Visionary Black Feminist: A Critical Introduction,* I accentuate Cooper's own "open-eyed" critical consciousness and agency across her life's work. However, in focusing on her innovations and insights, I do not want to imply that her ideas are so extraordinary as to be beyond compare or critique. Such an approach tokenizes under the guise of reverence. By contextualizing Cooper's body of work, and by illustrating how she remains relevant to contemporary political and philosophical debates, my aim is to challenge the insidious double dynamic that often hinders critical reception of minority theorists, an approach prone to biographical visibility (in which Cooper's life achievements are celebrated as without equal) twinned with theoretical obscurity (in which her theorizing at the intersection of race, gender, and nation — a major contribution — remains relatively unnoticed). I therefore underscore Cooper's astuteness as a scholar, educator, and activist not as a gesture of idolization, but to offer different ways of reading Cooper's contributions, alternative strategies for interpreting her many voices.

Cooper is too often treated as if she were simply a quaint historical figure rather than a major theorist whose voice and ideas deserve a continued hearing "at the bar," as Cooper would put it (*Voice* ii). Given that she leaves many unresolved tensions and ambiguities in her arguments, Cooper is also sometimes too quickly put aside as an elitist or accommodationist. In other words, rather than invitations to critical consciousness and action from a radical public intellectual, her interrogatory mode of writing and her intricately textured, complexly encoded voice are frequently interpreted as signs of confusion on her part or even of her having been duped by dominant discourse. Certainly, Cooper engaged with various "master narratives," such as prevailing notions of civilization, gender roles, or racial uplift; however, she eschewed mastery as an ideal altogether.

To understand this is better to appreciate how, in all of her work, Cooper shied away from hierarchy and refused to adhere to single-axis approaches to subjectivity, politics, or knowledge. As an educator, activist, and intellectual, she enacted a critical pedagogy that put the onus upon her audience to make meaning out of the multiple possibilities. Certainly, the open-eyed and open-ended pedagogy of the question is far more radical and agential than the (passive, even regurgitative) pedagogy of the simple, clear-cut answer. As Simone de Beauvoir suggests in her analysis of the workings of fascism, the loss of individual agency and collective freedom lies in great part in our failure to take up the often difficult task of questioning our everyday reality, of challenging the status quo (Beauvoir 7–73).

Thus, the intent of *Anna Julia Cooper, Visionary Black Feminist: A Critical Introduction* is not merely to document unacknowledged aspects of Cooper's ideas, but to offer different ways of reading her multivocal texts and to illustrate the implications of her theories and methods for reinterpreting our past and present. Closer examination of Cooper's body of work adds to our understanding of how marginalized groups rupture seemingly impenetrable historical and philosophical paradigms; how socially located, interdisciplinary ways of knowing hold significant implications for both knowledge and politics; and how a cross-cultural, comparative feminist framework alters conceptions of African American women's agency, history, and politics. Though these issues may seem somewhat esoteric, Cooper shows us how such questions about identity, difference, and politics are deeply salient: they inform our everyday ideas about knowledge, personhood, and the meaning of our collective experiences.

Chapter 1, "'A little more than ordinary interest in the underprivileged': Cooper's Lifelong Commitment to Liberation," offers readers unfamiliar with Cooper a biographical overview of her life as a scholar, educator, and outspoken community advocate, material that is particularly useful since the two main Cooper biographies (Hutchinson and Gabel) have gone out of print. For readers already conversant with the basic details of Cooper's life, the chapter provides experiential contexts for understanding and rethinking many of her theoretical precepts. Moreover, by highlighting how Cooper's numerous friendships bridged the public/private, political/personal divides conventionally used to measure a woman's life, I debunk claims that Cooper was a lonely, isolated individual or that her radical vision lessened over time. The chapter closes with a discussion of some of the ethical and analytical pitfalls of biography, specifically with regard to Cooper as a Black feminist public intellectual.

The core premise of chapter 2, "'Life must be something more than dilettante speculation': Cooper's Multidimensional Praxis," is twofold. First, we must look to the full range of Cooper's work as a teacher, scholar and activist to understand adequately the various dimensions of her philosophical vision and practice. Second, we must alter our working definitions of activism to uncover some of the more radical aspects of Cooper's work. I maintain that acknowledging her role as an educator at Frelinghuysen and not just at Dunbar, examining her lesser-known writings as well as her more famous ones, and attending to her advocacy and activism for equity both at home and abroad disrupt sweeping generalizations about Cooper (e.g., that she was a pawn of an elitist education, of exclusionary ideas about racial uplift, or of a white, middle-class gender ideology). Looking at the broad scope of Cooper's activism and writing and attending to the hostile contexts in which she lived and worked shift our understanding of her rhetorical strategies, cultural analyses, and philosophical premises.

Chapter 3, "'If you object to imaginary lines — don't draw them!': Cooper's Border-Crossing Methods," highlights the innovative aspects of Cooper's narrative strategies and interdisciplinary methods. Rather than being happenstance, I contend, Cooper's "riffing" from one subject to the next, and from one continent to another prefigures the disciplinary and geographic border crossing found in much contemporary feminist theory, particularly by women of color. Cooper's textual techniques are philosophically significant, particularly in how she interrupts dominant groups' willful ignorance. Through a subtle use of indirection, she questions prevailing ideas about meritocracy and the democratic social contract. Moreover, Cooper denaturalizes white superiority and argues that Black men and women are agents of knowledge, culture, and transformation. I maintain that Cooper's unruly interdisciplinary strategies comprise a methodology of dissent.

Cooper's doctoral dissertation is the central focus of chapter 4, "'Failing at the most essential provision of the revolutionary ideal': Lessons from France and Haiti's Transatlantic Struggle over Abolition and *Égalité*." Anticipating later, better-known critiques of patently biased but powerful notions of colonized people as passive recipients of reason and virtue from Europe, Cooper challenges conventional ideas about the Age of Revolution by focusing on the Haitian revolution as central, not anomalous or imitative. In her study of the interplay of Haitian and French politics, Cooper demonstrates that resistance from Haitian *gens de couleur*, free blacks, and slaves affected France's nascent democracy. She also analyzes slavery's role in the rise of capitalism and excoriates human exploitation, both in France and in Saint-Domingue: Cooper asserts that an economic dependence on slavery and an inability to confront its own colonial expansion undermined France's revolutionary potential and egalitarian ideals. Moreover, Cooper homes in on the pivotal role of diversity in politics and suggests that how a society contends with conflict and difference distinguishes democratic societies from repressive and authoritarian ones.

Chapter 5, "Mapping Sites of Power: Cooper's Redefinition of 'the philosophic mind,'" focuses on how Cooper reworks the boundaries of theoretical inquiry. First, she highlights the duplicity of widely accepted philosophical norms to show how racism and sexism infiltrate ostensibly neutral knowledge practices, shape our ideas about politics and society, and affect our notions of identity, ethics, and reason. In showing how prejudice and stereotype are equally at work in the natural and social sciences, literature, the arts, and popular culture, Cooper suggests that misrepresenting marginalized groups is an insidious tactic of domination. She connects cognitive erasure, historical silencing, and physical violation to show how domination plays out on many levels at once: it is simultaneously physical, psychological, and ideological. Moreover, by revealing an array of biases at work under the guise of objectivity, Cooper discredits predominant theories of biological determinism and argues that inequality is socially constructed and institutionalized, not inherent. She therefore underscores that self-emancipation is a precondition to radical action. Linking internal and external forms of domination, she stipulates the need to connect thought with action, a "living into" the problems that surround us, via an ethics of interdependence and an understanding of collective or reciprocal citizenship.

The concluding essay, Chapter 6, "Tracing Resistant Legacies, Rethinking Intellectual Genealogies: Reflections on Cooper's Black Feminist Theorizing," pulls out key points from across the book to highlight Cooper's contributions to Black feminist theorizing. In many respects, Cooper's work clearly fits longstanding traditions in Africana and feminist thought: exposing history's erasures or "whitewashing," refusing objectifying or pathologizing discourses, challenging sexist, ethnocentric, and racist biases embedded in ostensibly "universal" somatic and philosophical norms, exploring the contradiction of having relations of exploitation entrenched in the heart of democracy, and refusing exclusionary concepts of liberty or rights. However, rather than simply "add and stir" Cooper into existing frameworks of feminist and Africana theories and methods, new imaginaries need to be mapped out. In fact, taking Cooper seriously calls for a reconsideration of historical and theoretical genealogies across fields of inquiry. Finally, genuinely to take up Cooper's ideas and to reflect and act upon their implications requires a sustained engagement with Black feminist theorizing. Cooper's philosophical tenets and activist premises are informed by the work of African American feminists who came before her; and likewise, she helped to shape the worldview of those who followed. Cooper's work is a foundational contribution to Black feminist thought and she must be read alongside and in conversation with her sisters or "chieftains in the service," as she named them (*Voice* 140).

Anna Julia Cooper: Curriculum Vitae

Education

St. Augustine's Normal School, High School Diploma, 1877. After graduating, Cooper continued with her teaching and further studies at St. Augustine's until 1881.

Oberlin, B.A. in Mathematics, 1884.

Oberlin, M.A. in Mathematics, 1887.

La Guilde Internationale, Paris: studied French literature, history, and phonetics (summers of 1911–1913).

Columbia University: doctoral student, Romance Languages (summers of 1914–1917).

Sorbonne, University of Paris: Ph.D. in History, 1925.

Books

A Voice from the South by a Black Woman of the South. Xenia, OH: Aldine Press, 1892.

Le Pèlerinage de Charlemagne. Introduction by Félix Klein. Paris, France: Lahure Press, 1925.

Doctoral thesis: *L'Attitude de la France à l'égard de l'esclavage pendant la Révolution.* Paris, France: impr. de la cour d'appel, L. Maretheux, 1925.

The Third Step. (memoir)--n.p., n.d. Lemert and Bhan estimate it was published in 1945 (346).

Ed., *The Life and Writings of the Grimké Family* and *Personal Recollections of the Grimké Family.* 2-volume set. Washington, D.C.: Privately printed, 1951.

Other Publications

"The Higher Education of Women." *The Southland* (April, 1891): 186–202.

"Miss Florence M. Hunt: First Colored Female to be Appointed to the Surgeon General's Office." *Washington Bee* 18 (August 26, 1899). Reprinted from *The Southern Workman.* Available in the *Negro History Bulletin* (Jan-Sept, 1996): 35–36.

"Colored Women as Wage Earners." *Washington Bee* 18 (August 26, 1899). Reprinted from *The Southern Workman.* Brief excerpt available in the *Negro History Bulletin* (Jan-Sept 1996): 33-4. Full article available online at Howard University's Moorland-Spingarn Archives: <http://www.huarchivesnet.howard.edu/9908huarnet/cooper1.htm>

"The Social Settlement: What It Is, and What It Does." First published in the
Oberlin Journal. Reissued as a pamphlet. Washington, D.C.: Murray
Bros. Press, 1913. Reprinted in Lemert and Bhan.

"Do Two and Two Make Four?" The New York *Independent* (a reformist
newspaper). n.d. Referred to by Kaplan (x).

"Simon of Cyrene." Poem. Privately printed: n.d. (available in Hutchinson
180).

Lyrics, "Alma Mater." Dunbar High School, 1916. Musical arrangement by
Mary Europe (in Hutchinson 147).

"Aunt Charlotte." Commemorative poem marking the death of Charlotte
Forten Grimké (1914). Privately printed (in Hutchinson 185).

"The Humor of Teaching." *Crisis* magazine (Nov. 1930): 387 (available in
Lemert and Bhan).

"Angry Saxons and Negro Education." *The Crisis* magazine (May, 1938):
148 (available in Lemert and Bhan).

"College Extension for Working People." *Journal of the Alumnae Club*
(Oberlin), n.d. (referred to in Chateauvert 271).

"Christmas Bells: A One Act Play for Children." Privately printed: probably 1930s, as it was written and performed to raise funds for Frelinghuysen (referred to in Hutchinson 184).

"My Ten Years' Stewardship." *Decennial Catalogue for Frelinghuysen Uni-
versity*. Washington, D.C.: Murray Bros., probably 1940–1941, when
Cooper retired from the Frelinghuysen presidency (referred to in
Who's Who in Colored America 1941–44, 133).

"Ethiopia's Paean of Exaltation" (lyrics), 1942. Musical arrangement by
Harry T. Burleigh (Hutchinson 186).

"Hitler and the Negro." Privately printed around 1942 (in Lemert and
Bhan).

"Legislative Measures Concerning Slavery in the United States: 1787–1850."
Originally written in French in 1925 for her dissertation defense, but
translated by Cooper and privately published around 1942 for Frelinghuysen students (in Lemert and Bhan).

"Equality of Races and the Democratic Movement." Originally written in
French in 1925 for her dissertation defense, but translated by Cooper
and privately published around 1942 for Frelinghuysen students (in
Lemert and Bhan).

Unpublished Writings

"The Tie That Used to Bind." Short story (referred to in Hutchinson 136).
Based on the experiences of Cooper's brother Andrew, a veteran of
the Spanish-American War denied his military benefits.

"Sketches from a Teacher's Notebook: Loss of Speech through Isolation." The essay, probably written around 1923, analyzes the impact of lynching on an isolated black family in West Virginia (in Lemert and Bhan).

"From Servitude to Service." School curriculum/pageant about key figures in Black history (referred to by Baker-Fletcher, 39). Probably written in the 1930s.

"The Negro's Dialect." A linguistic and cultural studies analysis of stereotypes of "Black Speech" in popular media, probably 1930s (in Lemert and Bhan).

"On Education." Essay calls for Black educators to move away from authoritative pedagogical styles and drill-based assessments, probably 1930s (in Lemert and Bhan).

Speeches

"Womanhood: A Vital Element in the Regeneration and Progress of a Race." Washington, D.C., 1886.

Address, American Conference of Educators: Washington, D.C., 1890.

"The Needs and the Status of Black Women." Congress of Representative Women: Chicago World Columbian Exposition, 1893 (in Lemert and Bhan, see "Intellectual").

Address, Second Hampton Negro Conference: Hampton, Virginia, 1894.

Address, First National Conference of Colored Women: Boston, 1895.

Address, American Negro Academy: Washington, D.C., 1897.

"The Negro Problem in America." Pan-African Congress: London, 1900.

"The Ethics of the Negro Question." Biennial Session of Friends' General Conference: Asbury Park, New Jersey, September 5, 1902 (in Lemert and Bhan).

"Ideals and Reals or What do You Want?" Guthrie, Oklahoma, 1909 (Hutchinson 82).

Memberships and Organizations

Established St. Augustine's college outreach program for African Americans in Raleigh (1886).

Member, North Carolina Teacher's Association (the organization demanded equal education for whites and blacks in North Carolina).

Editor, "Women's Department," *The Southland* magazine (founded 1890). Cooper described *The Southland* as "the first Negro magazine in the United States" (Hutchinson 89).

Member, Hampton Folklore Society.

Charter member (1892) of the Colored Women's League of Washington, D.C. (incorporated 1894). The League offered kindergarten and day-care, vocational education, and fought urban poverty, housing discrimination, and employment discrimination.

Interim editor and supervisor of the "Ethnology and Folkore" column for *The Southern Workman* (mid-1890s), a publication of the Hampton Institute.

Co-founder, secretary, and member of the Washington Negro Folklore Society.

Chair, NACW (National Association of Colored Women) Committee to study Georgia convict system (peonage/forced labor) and Florida state school laws (1895).

Member, 1900 Pan-African Congress delegation from the United States and elected officer of the Congress's Executive Committee.

Member, Bethel Literary and Historical Association, one of the most active cultural and political organizations in Washington, D.C.

Member, Book Lovers' Club, a literary association and political organization. The BLC helped found the first YWCA in 1905 in Washington, D.C., the Phyllis Wheatley Y, which was also the area's first and only independent black YWCA. The BLC also founded Frelinghuysen University.

Lifetime member, Phyllis Wheatley YWCA.

Member, Wheatley YWCA Board of Directors.

Chair, YWCA girls' programs, and supervisor, Camp Fire Girls.

Co-founder (1902) and supervisor (1906), Colored Settlement House, Washington, D.C. 1906. Independently run, the CSH was the first social service agency in Washington, D.C. for African Americans. It offered after-school programs, nursery school and daycare, savings accounts, boys and girls clubs and summer camps, and more.

Supervisor (1911–1915) and Chief Guardian of the Washington, D.C. Camp Fire Girls.

Member, Alpha Kappa Alpha Sorority, Xi Omega Chapter.

Founder (1930), Hannah Stanley Opportunity School .

Member, NAACP.

Member, National Association of Educators.

Member, National Association of College Women.

Member, Classical Association of the Atlantic States.

Member, World Fellowship of Religions.

Member, National Council of Christians and Jews.

Member, Southeast Sociological Association.

Member and President, Societé des Amis de la Langue Française

Employment

Peer educator and tutor, St. Augustine's, North Carolina (1868–1881)

Tutor of Algebra, Oberlin College (1881–1884)

1884: Chair, Department of Languages and Science, Wilberforce University, Ohio; taught mathematics, languages, and literature.

1885: Professor of Mathematics, Latin, Greek, and German, St. Augustine's, Raleigh, North Carolina.

1887: Teacher of Mathematics and Science, M Street High School, Washington, D.C.

1901–1906: Principal of the M Street High School.

1906–1911: Professor of Languages, Lincoln University, Missouri.

1910–1930: Teacher of Latin, M Street/Dunbar High School, Washington, D.C.

1930–1941: President of Frelinghuysen University, Washington, D.C.

1941–1943: Professor at Frelinghuysen.

1940s–early 1950s: Registrar of Frelinghuysen.

Summer Employment

1885: Secretary to Bishop Benjamin W. Arnett.

Taught summer school or engaged in summer "War Work" in Cottage City, Massachusetts; Wilberforce, Ohio; Raleigh, North Carolina; State Teachers Association, Hampton, Virginia; Jefferson City, Missouri; Indianapolis, Indiana (1919); Wheeling, West Virginia (1920).

CHAPTER 1

"A little more than ordinary interest in the underprivileged"[1]

Cooper's Lifelong Commitment to Liberation

Born into slavery in Raleigh, North Carolina in 1858,[2] Anna Julia Cooper lived to be 105; she died just a few months before the signing of the Civil Rights Act of 1964. Throughout her lifetime, Cooper saw reflective thought as having a specific purpose: to develop a critical consciousness informed by an intersectional politic of freedom. Unquestionably, the idea that theory and practice must be linked was axiomatic. Because her astute philosophy of liberation was shaped by and connected to the particulars of her lived experience, piecing together the available details of her life story, including information about her childhood, her education, her relationships with family and friends, and the politics she negotiated as an educator, activist, and writer, can deepen our understanding of her scholarly work.

Yet the purpose behind attending to the lived conditions out of which Cooper's work emerged is not merely a contextual one. Rather, the objective in reassessing her life story is better to comprehend Cooper as an historical agent who sought actively to "shape the historical conditions" she lived within through writing, teaching, and community work (Carby, *Reconstructing* 95). Like other African American women writers and activists in her time, Cooper sought to create "intellectual constituencies" (96) and to "court" newly imagined communities (Glass 23) so as to "bring into being the new world order [she] envisioned" (Foster 179). In her various roles as a black feminist, Cooper engaged in critical analysis of the politics of race, gender, class, and nation in order to help transform the world around her.

Consistently, she pushed her readers, her students, and her colleagues to question everyday reality and to transform, rather than assimilate to, a world shaped by violence, inequality, poverty, and oppression.

"Linguist, educator, humanitarian, idealist"[3]: A Biographical Overview

Cooper began her life as Anna (Annie) Julia Haywood in 1858, the daughter of Hannah Stanley (Haywood) (1817–1899), who was enslaved; though she never identified him, it seems that Cooper's "father" in name only was Dr. Fabius J. Haywood, her mother's master.[4] Cooper grew up with her mother, who worked as a domestic and a nurse during slavery. Cooper also had two older brothers. The eldest, Rufus Haywood, was born around 1836 (d. 1892); a carpenter and a musician, he married a woman named Nancy. Andrew Haywood, born in 1848 (d. 1918), was also a musician; he worked as a bricklayer and fought in the Spanish American War. He married Jane Henderson, who worked as a cook (Hutchinson 26, 136). Later in life, Cooper would adopt Andrew and Jane's five grandchildren, who were orphaned in December 1915, and take in her then elderly sister-in-law Jane Haywood. Cooper helped Andrew and Jane fight for Andrew's long-denied military disability benefits and pension, which were finally awarded in 1918 after nearly twenty years of petitioning the government (136–37).[5]

After emancipation in 1863,[6] Hannah Stanley (Haywood) worked as a domestic in Raleigh until she was too elderly to continue doing so. Cooper and her mother would remain close, and in the 1890s, Cooper helped her mother retire and move near her in Washington, D.C. Many years later, in answering a 1932 survey of Black college graduates, Cooper wrote that while some may choose to remember her for her doctorate as her most exemplary achievement, she would prefer to be remembered for creating, in 1930, the Hannah Stanley Opportunity School, "dedicated in the name of my slave Mother to the education of colored working people" (in Hutchinson 155).

Cooper implies that her mother's relations with Haywood were forced, not consensual. Thus, right from infancy, as Cooper recalls, her worldview was shaped by an awareness of the mutually reinforcing politics of race and gender oppression, both from her family and from other, older slaves around her (Hutchinson 4). This critical race-gender consciousness would be further cultivated after emancipation, when African Americans in Raleigh were active in both community and statewide organizing for civil rights (19–24). In addition, the newly formed St. Augustine's Normal School and Collegiate Institute (founded in 1867), in which Cooper enrolled when it opened its doors in January 1868, was a hub of intellectual activity. Created under the auspices of the Freedmen's Bureau and the Episcopal Church, St. Augustine's offered a liberal arts education. As David W. H. Pellow documents, these early years at St. Augustine's were formative in shaping Cooper's comparative, Black Atlantic view of race politics and history. For example, the Black nationalist bishop of Haiti, James Theodore Holly, not only guest-lectured there but also enrolled his own sons as well other children from Haiti at the school (Pellow 63).

Cooper entered St. Augustine's as a scholarship student, along with another girl from Raleigh, Jane Thomas, with whom Cooper would retain a lifelong friendship. Despite her mother's many sacrifices so that Cooper might attend school,[7] there was not much money at home. In fact, Cooper occasionally alludes to her mother's hardships in her speeches and writings, emphasizing the privation experienced by "that patient, untrumpeted heroine, the slave-mother," who, after emancipation, still was not "released from self-sacrifice, and many an unbuttered crust was eaten in silent content that she might eke out enough from her poverty to send her young folks off to school" ("Intellectual" 203). Hannah Stanley earned a meager living as a domestic, and Cooper's older brothers were already married with growing families of their own to support.

Eager to learn and stay at St. Augustine's, Cooper began her lifetime of work as an educator around the age of ten as a gifted peer teacher to supplement her tuition scholarship. In fact, she and Jane Thomas were the first female students employed as teachers at St. Augustine's (Hutchinson 26). However, all was not perfectly smooth at school, particularly with regard to gender politics under the second principal, the Reverend Dr. Smedes. Later, in *A Voice from the South*, Cooper would refer to this period at St. Augustine's. When it comes to education, she wrote, girls tend to be thought of merely as a "*tertium quid*"[8] whose development may be promoted if they can pay their way and fall in with the plans mapped out for the training of the other sex" (*Voice* 44). In other words, at the same time that Cooper's education at St. Augustine's introduced her to the political philosophy of a Black diaspora, it also introduced her to sexism.

These early experiences with forward-thinking race advocacy combined with simultaneous sex discrimination affected Cooper's political worldview: for the rest of her life she would advocate both race and gender liberation without ranking one form of freedom over the other. Although she wanted access to the full curriculum at St. Augustine's, the administration attempted to deny Cooper the right to take courses in Greek and Latin (offered exclusively to boys studying to become ministers since, as Cooper recounts it, the principal presumed that the girls were only at school to find a husband) (*Voice* 77). Cooper persisted and successfully petitioned the St. Augustine's administration to be allowed entry to all courses. She completed her high school diploma in 1877 and continued in her studies and teaching at St. Augustine's until 1881. Cooper would remain fond of St. Augustine's, despite the hurdles, and later wrote, "That school was my world during the formative period, the most critical in any girl's life. Its nurture & admonition gave ... shelter and protection from the many pitfalls that beset the unwary" (Hutchinson, facsimile of Cooper's account, 20).

In 1877, she married George A. C. Cooper, a St. Augustine's Greek teacher and theology student who had come to Raleigh from his home in Nassau, British West Indies (now the Bahamas) to prepare for the ministry. In June 1879 he became the second Black male ordained in the Episcopal Church in North Carolina; however, he died unexpectedly a few months later. Anna Cooper never remarried and seems to have kept him close to her heart. For instance, nearly twenty years after his death, she visited his home in the Caribbean (Hutchinson 131). Over fifty years after his death, in 1931, Cooper commissioned a stained glass window from an African American artist, Frank J. Dillon,[9] in George Cooper's memory for the chapel at St. Augustine's; it depicts Simon of Cyrene carrying Jesus' cross.[10] She also chose to be buried next to him in the former "colored section" of the City Cemetery of Raleigh, on East Hargett Street.

Of course, George Cooper's passing meant certain hindrances for Anna Cooper. For instance, she had to be financially independent: she was never to be well off and was in fact "constantly at economic risk" (Lemert 20). Certainly, taking in seven children — two foster children (Emma Lula Love and John Love), orphans of her friends, John Lorenzo and Sallie (Constance Jordan) Love[11] from Asheville, North Carolina in the 1890s, and five adopted grandnieces and grandnephews, plus her sister-in-law, in 1916 — was not an easy feat on her teaching salary, particularly as the D. C. Board of Education would deny Cooper some of her rightful promotions up until her retirement in 1930, even suggesting, while refusing to produce any evidence, that she did not adequately pass basic teacher assessment tests in the 1920s.[12] Interestingly, in the early 1890s, perhaps not quite realizing the degree to which her insights would be relevant to her own life, Cooper outlined the gender- and race-specific economic burdens facing African American women, many of whom were single heads of households ("Wage Earners").

Yet despite these and many other obstacles, her husband's passing also offered Cooper the freedom to pursue her education further and, later, to work as an educator and scholar at a time when, once married, women were not allowed to work in most public schools (although widows could do so). After his death, Cooper continued to study beyond her high school diploma and to teach at St. Augustine's, but she was clearly longing for more. Yearning for a college degree and seeking a progressive, coeducational, racially inclusive liberal arts education, Cooper entered Oberlin in the fall of 1881 with a tuition scholarship, advanced placement for her extensive studies at St. Augustine's, on-campus employment because she was self-supporting, and a place to live off campus (in the home of a white family, the Churchills, with whom she enjoyed a lifelong correspondence and friendship).[13] As at St. Augustine's, Cooper enrolled in the "Gentleman's Course" at Oberlin to earn a classical education on par with men (K. Johnson 15). Cooper was among the first cohort of African American women to graduate from Oberlin.[14] The first, Mary Jane Patterson, was in the class of 1862; she too took the "Gentleman's Course" and, after graduation, went on to become the first African American female principal at the prestigious "M Street" High School in Washington, D.C., where Cooper would also later become principal. The next three African American women to graduate, Mary Eliza Church (Terrell), Ida A. Gibbs (Hunt), and Anna Julia Cooper, were in the class of 1884 (see Figure 1.1).

As many have noted (Gabel 20–21, Hutchinson 36–38, Lemert 21), Cooper had neither the time nor the money to participate in all that college had to offer. Unlike her younger classmates Church and Gibbs, who lived on campus and were active in extracurricular activities, and whose tuition was paid for by their relatively well-to-do parents, Cooper lived off campus and worked throughout college.[15] Nevertheless, despite struggling against

Figure 1.1 Group portrait (left to right) of Anna Julia Cooper, Ida Gibbs Hunt, and Mary Church Terrell taken in Cooper's T Street home to mark the 1952 reunion of the three African American women graduates of Oberlin College, Class of 1884.

racist, sexist, and economic "discouragements to ... higher education" (Cooper, *Voice* 77), Cooper earned her B.A. in mathematics at Oberlin in 1884. She recalls delivering her graduation address, "Strongholds of Reason," rather "mannishly." Cooper wrote that she was not interested in "pretending to read an 'essay' as a lady properly should," much to the chagrin of some of Oberlin's women administrators (Cooper, 1941 letter to Alfred Churchill, in Shilton).

Following graduation, Cooper became chair of languages and science at Wilberforce University in Ohio, where she taught courses in math, languages, and literature. In 1885, after working during the summer as secretary to the African American bishop, Benjamin W. Arnett, Cooper returned to Raleigh, where most of her extended family still lived, to take a position as a professor at her alma mater, St. Augustine's. There she taught math, Latin, Greek, and German. As when Cooper had been a student, St. Augustine's continued to foster an international approach to Black history and culture in terms of its curriculum, its student body, and its faculty. For example, other St. Augustine's faculty from this period included Cooper's former St. Augustine's classmate, Henry Beard Delaney,[16] who would become the first elected African American Episcopal bishop in North Carolina, and the Reverend Mason H. Joseph, an Antiguan who would later move to London and become president of the African Association (later the Pan-African Association) (Pellow 67).

During this period, Cooper also engaged in activism and community service. For instance, she helped establish a college outreach program for African Americans in the city of Raleigh and was an active member of the politically engaged North Carolina Teachers' Association, which protested to the state legislature about educational disparities across the state for Black and white students (see Hutchinson 43). On the basis of her college teaching at Wilberforce and St. Augustine's, Oberlin awarded Cooper an M.A. in mathematics in 1887 (Figure 1.2 is a later portrait of Cooper in her M.A. regalia). That same year, Cooper was recruited to teach math and science at the only high school for African Americans in Washington, D.C., the highly regarded Washington (Colored) Preparatory High School, known customarily as the M Street High School because of its address, and later renamed Dunbar High (see Figure 1.3). Founded in 1870, the prestigious M Street High was the largest public high school for African Americans in the nation; it offered a rigorous education in a politically engaged learning environment. Other renowned M Street/Dunbar faculty included Mary Burrill, Eva B. Dykes, Jessie Redmon Fauset, Ernest E. Just, Angelina Weld Grimké, Euphemia L. Haynes, Kelly Miller, Georgiana Simpson, Mary Church Terrell, Robert Terrell, and Carter G. Woodson.

Figure 1.2 Anna Julia Cooper, portrait in her M.A. regalia. Courtesy of the Scurlock Studios Records, Archives Center, National Museum of American History, Smithsonian Institution.

Working at M Street would become a major part of Cooper's life, not only because it was her job for more than 35 years, but also because she saw teaching as her calling. In fact, Karen Baker-Fletcher contends that Cooper "placed teaching on an equal par with preaching" (42). And yet, it is also true that throughout her life Cooper's role as an educator went beyond the parameters of one institution or school. By no means do I seek to downplay Cooper's role as a teacher: it was absolutely central to her life's work — in fact, she taught well into the 1940s at Frelinghuysen. Rather than diminish the meaning of teaching in her life, what I want to suggest

Figure 1.3 Dunbar High School. Courtesy of the Scurlock Studios Records, Archives Center, National Museum of American History, Smithsonian Institution.

is that she was a public intellectual in the fullest sense. Cooper was a pedagogical force not only in the classroom but also as an outspoken public speaker, a highly regarded author, and a dedicated community advocate for civil rights and sex equity. Thus, over and above her rising prominence at M Street, Cooper's work as an increasingly visible orator, public intellectual, and community activist also blossomed at this time.

For example, her well-known volume *A Voice from the South by a Black Woman of the South*, the "first book-length feminist analysis of the condition of African Americans" (Guy-Sheftall, "Evolution" 8), was published in 1892. The 1890s constituted a period of "ferment of black female intellectual activity" (Carby, *Reconstructing* 96), in terms of both publishing and public advocacy or activism. In fact, Frances Smith Foster (179) names 1892 "the midwife to modern American literature," the year not only of the publication of Cooper's *A Voice from the South*, but also of Lucy A. Delaney's *From the Darkness Cometh the Light; or, Struggles for Freedom*, Ida B. Wells's *Southern Horrors: Lynch Law in All Its Phases*, and Frances Ellen Watkins Harper's *Iola Leroy; or, Shadows Uplifted*.

A Voice from the South was acclaimed nationwide. From Iowa to Boston, New York to Chicago, Philadelphia to Detroit, in both the black and white press, Cooper received praise for her examination of race relations and for her feminist analysis (see Hutchinson 104). *A Voice* was also known and admired by scholars and activists abroad. For instance, her friend and colleague, the "eminent West African statesman, Edward W. Blyden," wrote from Sierra Leone to his friend, the Reverend Francis Grimké, about Cooper's work. Blyden remarked, "'I can never forget Anna J. Cooper, brilliant, thoughtful'" (in Kaplan x). Over a century later, *A Voice* is still in print and widely available, and Cooper continues to be appreciated for her contributions to Black feminist theory, particularly for her insightful analysis of the interlocking nature of race and sex politics and identities. For instance, Mary Helen Washington describes *A Voice* as "the most precise, forceful, well-argued statement of black feminist thought to come out of the nineteenth century" (xxvii).

As a speaker, Cooper was invited to address a wide range of audiences. For example, she spoke about institutionalized discrimination in the church and called for equitable education in terms of both race and gender before the national convention of African American Episcopal clergymen in 1886. In 1890 Cooper addressed the National Association of Educators' convention, emphasizing the need for women to pursue higher education, particularly African American women. At the Congress of Representative Women at the Chicago Columbian Exposition in 1893, Cooper was one of six African American women[17] asked to speak, after much protest against the exclusion of African Americans from the Exposition. Not content to merely discuss Black women's "progress" in isolation, Cooper pressed white feminists to become more progressive by abandoning their exclusionary, racist practices and narrow vision of women's rights for a wider platform of liberation politics. Cooper also addressed the first national conference of the NACW (National Association of Colored Women) in 1895, the Second Hampton Negro Conference in 1894, the first Pan-African Congress in 1900, and the biennial national conference of the Association of Friends (Quakers) in 1902.[18]

Interestingly, Cooper was the only woman invited to speak before the all-male American Negro Academy, founded in 1897; however, she was not asked to be a member.[19] Cooper was also among the few women invited to attend the first meeting of the predominantly male Niagara Movement (Chateauvert 262). The fact that the ANA and the Niagara Movement both organized around "the race" but excluded Black women from membership and full participation signals the increasingly masculinist gender politics shaping operative definitions of the "race" and the "race problem" at the turn of the twentieth century. As Jonathan Scott Holloway argues, an "abiding historical amnesia" means that today we tend to overlook the fact that Cooper's arguments in *A Voice from the South* and in her first decade of public speeches pre-date those made later, and to more acclaim, by male ANA members (such as W. E. B. Du Bois or Kelly Miller). Generally speaking, it is primarily the "race men" who continue to be recognized as contributors to "what many historians consider the central black political and intellectual debate of the twentieth century," and not women such as Cooper (J. Holloway 27). This "amnesia" is exacerbated by the fact that, in her own time, Cooper's male colleagues did not always fully acknowledge her ideas, or those put forward by other African American women (Washington xl). Some, like Du Bois, despite his relatively pro-feminist outlook, even used Cooper's ideas, but without attribution (xlii).

In addition to her work as an author and orator in the 1890s, Cooper engaged in other scholarly work focused more specifically on labor and economic issues as well as on questions of culture, particularly the preservation of African American folklore. For example, she served as the "Women's Department" editor for the first African American magazine in the nation, *The Southland* (founded 1890). She also worked as an interim editor and supervisor of the "Folklore and Ethnology" column for *The Southern Workman*, published by the Hampton Institute. A few of the essays she published in *The Southern Workman* remain readily accessible today, including her "Colored Women as Wage Earners," in which Cooper makes a case for unpaid domestic labor as productive wage labor and calls for an end to misogynist-racist analyses of Black women's paid labor as surplus labor.

Furthermore, during this period Cooper co-founded and served as secretary to the Washington Negro Folklore Society. The Society sought to collect and document African American folklore before it disappeared from cultural and familial memory (Moody 2–4). This was a time of increased violence toward African Americans and of intensified denigration of African American culture (consider the rise of both lynching and minstrelsy, for example). It was also a reactive moment in some branches of African American education to suppress folk language and culture lest they be seen as signs of "backwardness" — an assimilationist model Cooper did not support. Cooper did not just advocate for the significance of folk culture in her organizational endeavors. In *A Voice*, for example, Cooper emphasizes the importance of African American folklore and music and suggests that they should become the building blocks of a distinctive African American literary and artistic movement. She writes, "A race that has produced for America the only folk-lore and folk song of native growth, a race which has grown the most original and unique assemblage of fable and myth to be found on the continent ... has as yet found no mouthpiece of its own to unify and perpetuate its wondrous whisperings." Reiterating the value both of the spoken word and of speaking for oneself, Cooper draws an analogy to Chaucer to suggest that the same kind of loving justification of African American linguistic and aesthetic traditions needs to be undertaken by African American writers (*Voice* 224).

Clearly, Cooper's reputation in the United States was on the rise in the 1890s, but she was also known internationally for her Black feminist scholarship. For example, in 1900 Cooper was one of only a few African American female representatives to participate in and address the first Pan-African Congress in London (see Walters 253–62). In addition to serving as a delegate, Cooper was one of two Black women invited to present a paper. Cooper discussed "The Negro Problem in America," while her long-time friend and colleague Anna H. Jones, a black educator, club activist, and linguist who lived in Kansas City, Missouri, presented "The Preservation of Race Individuality" (Hutchinson 110–11). Cooper's colleague and friend Ella D. Barrier, who taught at M Street and served as secretary to the Washington, D.C. Colored Women's League, and her sister Fannie Barrier Williams, who worked in Chicago as an activist and writer, also attended (Pellow 67). In addition to serving as both a delegate and plenary speaker, Cooper was among a small group of elected officers of the Pan-African Congress Executive Committee. This committee drafted a series of policy statements, sent to heads of state around the world, about the right of all people to self-rule and full citizenship. They also urged Queen Victoria to end colonial rule throughout the British Empire and to end the Boer War in South Africa (Walters 260).

Finally, in addition to her roles as teacher, orator, and international human rights advocate, Cooper was active in the Black women's club movement. At the national level, Cooper served as chair of an 1895 NACW Committee to study Georgia's exploitative system of convict peonage and Florida's inequitable state school laws (Hutchinson 96). She also spoke at the first convention of the NACW in Boston, urging Black women to organize at the national level (94). Locally, in Washington, D.C., Cooper was a charter member of the Colored Women's League (founded 1892, incorporated 1894). The League organized to offer milk for babies, daycare and kindergarten classes, and industrial education courses for adults, and it fought urban poverty, housing discrimination, and employment discrimination (Harley, "Anna" 91).

Always passionate about local issues, Cooper served as chair of the League's "Alley Sanitation Committee and was that organization's corresponding secretary for a number of years" (Hutchinson 93). Although today the Alley Sanitation Committee may not sound like a particularly outspoken political group, it was: the committee protested the utter lack of housing for poor African Americans in Jim Crow Washington, D.C. As members of this committee and other organizations would argue, rather than being the outcome of any "inherent" biological "flaw," being forced to live in the city's alleys in inhuman conditions of abject poverty led to psychological isolation, illiteracy, unemployment, malnutrition, and high morbidity and mortality rates (see Borchert 45–47). Over a decade later, the committee worked in coalition with black ministers such as Francis Grimké, with whom Cooper was very close, to create the Alley Improvement Association in 1908, because Washington's poorest Black citizens, still denied access to adequate housing, continued to live in shacks in the back alleys of the nation's capital. Issues of poverty and lack of basic housing for many of the District's African American residents would continue to be pressing concerns for decades to come.

In the midst of her extensive work as an activist and intellectual, in January 1901 Cooper was promoted to the position of principal of the M Street High School, following former principal Robert H. Terrell's stepping down upon his judicial appointment. Yet Cooper's promotion did not slow her down as an activist. Not only did she use her leadership position to fight for educational equity across the lines of race, as I will discuss shortly; she continued to be heavily involved in public service to Washington's African American community in other ways. For instance, Cooper was co-founder (1902) and supervisor (1906) of the Colored Settlement House, the capital's first social service agency for African Americans. The Settlement House was financially autonomous and governed by a community board. Intentionally independent of federal monetary support and also of white social service "expertise," it offered after-school programs, nursery school and daycare, savings accounts, food for infants, sports programs for girls, boys' and girls' clubs, summer camps, and more.

Meanwhile, during her tenure as principal Cooper sought and received accreditation for M Street from elite universities in the Northeast (such as Harvard), which meant that graduates would no longer have to take entrance examinations to attend university; their M Street education was considered sufficiently rigorous to meet the most stringent entry standards. Cooper also refused to use the "racially derogatory textbooks" mandated by the school district (Chateauvert 262); independently, she revised the curriculum and ordered new books. Under her leadership, M Street students continued to score, on average, higher than white students in district-wide tests, debunking increasingly popular eugenic theories of race and intelligence. In addition, many graduates continued to break the color line by gaining entrance and scholarships to Ivy League schools such as Brown, Cornell, and Harvard, while others pursued higher education at prestigious historically Black colleges and universities, including Howard, Fisk, and Atlanta. Graduates also went on to found important Black educational institutions, including Nannie Helen Burroughs's National Training School for Women and Girls.[20]

However, Cooper's vision of Black education as being naturally on par with the full range of educational opportunities offered to white students was at odds with the powerful Booker T. Washington "Tuskegee Machine," particularly his narrow, conciliatory emphasis on a separate, unequal, and exclusively industrial educational paradigm. Rather than toe the line and concede to the wishes of Congress, the D.C. Board of Education, and Booker T. Washington's behind-the-scenes influence, Cooper held firm to M Street's legacy of offering full college preparatory as well as industrial and vocational curricula. Cooper did not believe these "different" curricula to be incompatible: she thought that every person deserved a well-rounded education grounded in the liberal arts. Her radical resolve led to a drawn-out public battle, covered at length in the Washington *Post*, to discredit her professionally as an educator and public leader, but also personally as an African American woman (see Hutchinson 66–83). Unfortunately, these months of excruciating and aggressive conjecture about Cooper's public and private life (chiefly based on racist and misogynist stereotypes, not solid facts) have guaranteed that a century later, we have little in-depth information available to us about her personal life which she seems to have guarded closely after this acutely painful and prolonged episode of public harassment.

In many ways, though, it should come as no surprise that insidious racism and sexism helped ensure the loss of her leadership position. Cooper was portrayed as an "ineffectual" principal whose students were supposedly out of control (drinking and smoking in school), coddled and supported excessively in order to "keep up" with an education ostensibly beyond their grasp, or even romantically involved with Cooper herself.[21] According to a January 5, 1907 article in the Washington *Post,* Cooper was also denied her pay, despite a petition for her salary ("Not Entitled"). Hutchinson asserts that "From the beginning, Anna Cooper's tenure as principal of the M Street High School was marked by turmoil and controversy, for she had refused to compromise her convictions and principles in exchange for expediency and the approval of her superiors" (81).

The reality is that Cooper was *too* effective as a teacher, principal, and public intellectual. As William T. Menard, an African American resident of Washington, writes in his September 1, 1905 letter to the editor of the *Post*, Cooper "has done more for the advancement of colored youth than the combined efforts of her predecessors. ... The colored people of this city ... heartily indorse her administration and hope to see her continued. ... [T]he [white] defamers of the M Street High School must submit their proof and not unsupported allegations if they desire to supplant the efficient principal, Mrs. A. J. Cooper, with a candidate of their selfish selection." Unfortunately, rather than any firm or real evidence of Cooper's supposed incompetence, unsupported allegations turned out to be enough to oust her: "Cooper lost out because she represented a substantial force against the view of what Negroes should be" (Paul Phillips Cooke in K. Johnson 83). Rather than her being guilty of the stereotypically feminine failings (soft, weak, coddling, and romantic), with which she was charged, her actual offense was daring to take on ostensibly incontrovertible truths about "natural" human hierarchies of gendered and raced capacity, intellect, and public role.

In the eyes of powerful white Washingtonians seeking to reinforce Jim Crow supremacy, it was bad enough that the M Street school had been accredited by the Ivy League, that Cooper, its principal, chose a curriculum and textbooks not authorized for use by the district, that M Street students scored, on average, the highest marks in the district on standardized tests (contradicting the rationales repeatedly presented by the board of education to justify eradicating the liberal arts curriculum), and that, upon graduating, they gained entrance and scholarships to elite universities. But then, international attention came to the M Street High School and to Cooper's leadership. After touring Washington's public schools at the invitation of President Theodore Roosevelt, the French scholar and priest l'Abbé Félix Klein wrote in his book-length study of American education that Cooper was head of one of the most illustrious schools he had come across in the nation. Moreover, he expressed deep admiration for her teaching skills and described her scholarly expertise as superlative (Klein in Hutchinson 58–59; see also Klein, *Pays* 286–90).

As Baker-Fletcher contends, "Such an estimation of a colored high school — especially directed by a single Black woman — was unheard of" (53–4). Cooper, in her typically dry manner, likewise remarked that Klein's praise "caused a general raising of eyebrows in the United States and a few red faces in Washington" ("Third Step" 321). When writing about the incident to Oberlin alumni, she concluded that the "dominant forces of our country are not yet tolerant of the higher steps for colored youth" ("Class Letter" in Hutchinson 83). Cooper might well have added that these same forces were not yet ready for her, either — and were, in fact, prepared to go to great lengths to shove her off these "higher steps."

After all other attempts to overthrow M Street's liberal arts curriculum proved futile, white citizens and members of the board of education revealed the depths of their bigoted mindset; they invoked the specter of the immoral and wanton Black woman. Cooper was accused, unjustifiably,[22] of having an affair with John Love, an M Street student who was also her foster child (she had taken in John and Lula Emma Love after the death of their parents). Cooper was forced to find men of influence, both Black and white, to write letters on her behalf attesting to her character, her abilities, and her intellect (see, for example, Hutchinson 73–75). Hoping to take advantage of political conditions of increased racist antagonism and sexist backlash in Washington and across the nation, the board sought to silence Cooper and her supporters by using deception, delay, and bureaucratic loopholes. For example, witnesses there to support Cooper were required to wait outside "private" sessions of the board for hours, late into the night, to provide testimony that she was an upright and respectable member of society, only to be given a few minutes to present their case because of the midnight hour.

Many have speculated about the seeming absence of public support for Cooper on the part of her female colleagues and friends during this period. However, when one considers the aggressive racist-sexist climate emerging around the M Street debate, their apparent silence is not all that surprising. For example, would the antagonistic board of education have considered Black women's testimony or support? Even those eminent men, Black and white, who advocated for Cooper before the board have remained practically invisible in the historical record. Certainly their testimony, both written and oral, was barely attended to or accorded much weight. Thus, women's silence in the public record does not necessarily indicate lack of solidarity with or complete absence of support for Cooper. Actually, the fact that Cooper continued in her highly visible public roles at the Wheatley YWCA, in the Bethel Literary Society, and at the Settlement House could be understood as a show of solidarity and support by her Black female colleagues and allies.

Fortunately, following months of intense debate and underhanded meetings, even these last-ditch efforts to eliminate the M Street curriculum were unsuccessful: the liberal arts offerings stayed in place. Since they had failed to dismantle M Street's legacy and had likewise failed to discredit Cooper, the board of education's final and essentially retaliatory decision was simply to not hire her back, as teacher or as principal, for the fall of 1906. Consequently, from 1906 to 1910, Cooper left Washington to become professor of languages at Lincoln University in Kansas City, Missouri, where her friend, the linguist, educator, suffragist, Pan-African Congress delegate, and active NACW leader Anna H. Jones, lived. Although little is known about this period of Cooper's life, a facsimile of a flyer advertising a speech by Cooper in Guthrie, Oklahoma in 1909 ("Ideals and Reals or What do You Want?" Hutchinson 82), suggests that she remained active on the lecture circuit while a professor at Lincoln. Cooper also retained close ties with Washington while working in Missouri. Eventually, in the summer of 1910, after a change in the leadership on the D.C. board of education, Cooper was invited to return to teach Latin at M Street, where she remained until 1930.

There is no question that these concerted efforts at public humiliation negatively affected Cooper, as they would anyone. However, Lemert finds the M Street High School controversy to have been the cause of an increased "isolation" for the "single, widowed" Cooper. Repeatedly, he emphasizes that Cooper was a "solitary" figure (5, 12–14, 17, 20), even suggesting that her philosophical outlook was itself also "isolating" (14). Yet there is plenty of evidence that Cooper continued to lead a full and active intellectual, political, and social life, as she had prior to this awful debate. For instance, as I have already documented, Cooper maintained lifelong friendships with Jane Thomas, the Churchill family in Oberlin, John and Sallie Love in Asheville (whose children she later took in), and many others from her days in North Carolina and Ohio. Upon moving to Washington, Cooper quickly developed new circles of friends.

As with relationships developed earlier in life, the neighbors and colleagues with whom she fostered tight-knit relationships were politically engaged in fighting inequality locally, nationally, and internationally. During her first year of teaching at M Street, Cooper had lived in the home of the outspoken Reverend Alexander Crummell and his wife; she remained close with the Crummells for years to come. Cooper also developed a strong, sisterly friendship with the civil rights advocate and educator Charlotte ("Lottie") Forten Grimké (Figure 1.4); Cooper would later write a memoir about her and edit a collection of her writings. In addition, Cooper was close to Forten Grimké's husband, the Reverend Francis Grimké, an advocate of racial equality and social change. He and Cooper would correspond regularly in the twenty years following Charlotte's death, and upon his own death he would leave to Cooper all of Charlotte's writings, diaries, letters, and journals. Moreover, Cooper was quite close to Ella D. Barrier, a colleague at M Street and a club movement activist. Barrier and Cooper traveled to Toronto in 1891 in a teacher exchange and later to London in 1900 to participate in the first Pan-African Conference along with another of their friends, Anna H. Jones.

Cooper and the Grimkés hosted weekly salons in their homes: Friday evenings at the Grimkés' focused on art and literature, and Sunday evenings at Cooper's centered on music. These gatherings were attended by local and international Black and white educators, artists, politicians, writers, and musicians, including Edward Blyden, Mary Churchill (who published under the name David Churchill), Samuel Coleridge-Taylor, Helen Pitts Douglass, and Richard T. Greener (Cooper, *Personal* 8–9). In many ways, the Grimkés' and Cooper's turn-of-the-century salons prefigure the better-known "Black Renaissance" salons held by poet and playwright Georgia Douglas Johnson in the 1920s at her S Street home; there, Alain Locke, Anne Spenser, Langston Hughes, Jessie Redmon Fauset, Marita

Figure 1.4 Group portrait (left to right) of Anna Julia Cooper and Charlotte Forten Grimké (seated), Ella D. Barrier, Rev. Francis J. Grimké, and Fannie Shippen Smythe (standing). Courtesy of the Association for the Study of African American Life and History.

Bonner, Angelina Grimké, Jean Toomer, and others met to discuss Black culture, politics, and history.

In no way, then, would I characterize Cooper's life as lonely, solitary, or bereft of intimate friendship. To a degree, Lemert acknowledges Cooper's active intellectual and social life in her early years in Washington, and he concedes that although Cooper was solitary, she was not "alone" (14).

However, the continual emphasis on her solitude obscures the many friendships and relationships Cooper cultivated throughout her lifetime. Though Cooper may not have had close personal ties with her high-profile (and far more privileged) Oberlin and later M Street colleagues, Mary Church Terrell and Ida Gibbs Hunt (an observation that seems to crop up in almost every introduction to Cooper's work), there is no indication of outright animosity or evidence of a poor working relationship with them.[23] Moreover, by speculating about why certain of Cooper's relationships did not go beyond the level of professional collegiality, we risk diminishing, even erasing, both the activism and the importance of the many other "race women" with whom she *was* close.

In addition, a portrait of Cooper's life as centered on her home life above all else, combined with an almost pitiful, spinsterish solitude epitomized by prim and "classically Southern" domestic "virtues" (Lemert 4), such that "Everything she did seemed always to issue from or return to her homes" (7), does not correspond to the Cooper I have come to know over the past fourteen years: an outspoken, witty, passionate Black feminist intellectual and activist who traveled widely, who had friends across the country and abroad, and who had a rich and close-knit albeit nontraditional family life. Of course, Cooper's pattern of relationships does not necessarily follow those of other women. We should be careful not to gauge Cooper's many friendships as inconsequential or her complex family life as lesser simply because they do not conform to conventional models of intimacy and kin — models that not only uphold marriage as the utmost human bond and blood offspring as the normative ideal, but also perpetuate a rather narrow, dualist distinction between public and private intimate relationships.

Perhaps, then, Cooper is interpreted as solitary because, in Washington, D.C., her active social life was interwoven with her extensive work as an educator, public intellectual, and activist: many of her relationships existed within a threshold space between public and private realms and were focused on simultaneous collective and individual self-realization. In other words, just as the community organizations Cooper belonged to and supported did not draw strict lines of division between intellectual pursuits and political advocacy, Cooper did not designate separate "spheres" in her own life for her scholarly, community, and social activities or relationships. For example, Cooper was an active member of the Bethel Literary and Historical Association, the "pre-eminent debating society and forum for racial issues in Washington, D. C. at the turn of the twentieth century." Its activities "were reported widely in the black press, both locally and nationally," and "from its inception, meetings addressed clearly racial topics, emphasizing African heritage and the progress of blacks in the United States" (Moore 93–4). The association also "sponsored lectures on numerous topics, such as the Egyptians, the Zulus, and various aspects of African culture, in addition to contemporary issues affecting African Americans" (R. Harris 15). In the interest of developing cross-cultural understandings of Black identity and fostering alliances with other communities of African descent in the Americas, the Bethel Literary and Historical Association facilitated an international exchange of black teachers in 1891 with Canada. Cooper was among three teachers to go to Toronto; the others were her friends and colleagues Parker Bailey and Ella D. Barrier (Hutchinson 107). This trip, organized for the purposes of political action and cultural exchange, was also personally transformative for Cooper. She refers to it in *A Voice from the South* as a crucial if brief experience of bodily freedom as a Black woman in the public sphere (88–89). Here we see the personal and political overlapping, both in terms of the friends Cooper traveled with for professional purposes and in terms of the philosophical insights gained from her embodied, "private" experiences.

Another organization Cooper belonged to was the rather innocuous-sounding Book Lovers' Club, also quite a radical community organization. For example, members of the Book Lovers' Club were pivotal in the 1906 creation of a group of schools that would, in 1917, become Frelinghuysen University (closed around 1960), a college for working black adults "designed for the non-elite population" with satellite campuses, night classes, and affordable tuition (Chateauvert 265). Lula Love, Cooper's foster child, was an integral part of both the Book Lovers' Club and, later, of Frelinghuysen. In fact, when Cooper served as president of the university from 1930 to 1941, Lula Love Lawson would serve as vice president. Here again we see a perfect example of the public and private, intimate and professional, familial and educational, and the personal and political interwoven in Cooper's life.

In 1905 the Book Lovers' Club helped to found the first YWCA in Washington, D.C., the Phyllis Wheatley Y, which was from its start organizationally autonomous and financially independent from the (predominantly white) national Y movement.[24] It was the first and only Black YWCA in the capital and very politically active. For example, the organization protested death-penalty hangings to President Taft, addressed Congress about pervasive harassment and violent beatings of African Americans in Washington (particularly during the violent "Red Summer" of demonstrations and riots in 1919), urged Congress to resolve wage disparities and poor working conditions for African Americans, offered food, housing, and employment to counteract Jim Crow discrimination, and, with the NAACP, helped the mothers of the Scottsboro Boys (who had been falsely accused of raping a white woman) fight their case all the way to the Supreme Court.[25] Cooper was a lifetime member of the YWCA, served on its board of directors, and was supervisor of girls' programming and co-founder and "Guardian" of the Camp Fire Girls.

At the Y, Cooper made many close friends; in fact, from 1910 to 1915, after returning from her teaching position at Lincoln University in Missouri to teach again at M Street, Cooper would live with her longtime friend, Emma Merritt. Merritt was an M Street graduate who was a highly regarded teacher and principal at the Garnet School in Washington, a dedicated board member of the YWCA and of the Southwest Settlement House, and a president of the Washington, D.C. branch of the NAACP. Also a scholar of French, mathematics, and psychology, Merritt studied at Howard University and at the Columbian University (now George Washington University). She was an innovator of experiential education and, by the 1920s, would become a sought-after national consultant on Black education.[26]

While living with Merritt, serving as a leader at the YWCA and for the Camp Fire Girls, and working full time as a teacher at M Street, Cooper also studied French literature, history, and phonetics at the Guilde Internationale in Paris in the summers of 1911, 1912, and 1913. Then, in the summer of 1914, Cooper enrolled as a doctoral student in the Department of Romance Languages at Columbia University, where she began her annotated translation from medieval to modern French of the epic poetry cycle *Le Pèlerinage de Charlemagne*. Cooper would pursue her doctoral studies at Columbia from the summer of 1914 through the summer of 1917, studying under three linguists: professors Alexander, John Lawrence Gerig, and H. F. Muller (Cooper, "Foreword" 231).

Being self-sufficient and not married allowed Cooper to lead an unconventional life not concerned with marital or parental obligations — that is, until she adopted her brother's five grandchildren in December 1915. In January 1916, Cooper moved out of Merritt's home and bought her own house, on credit, in the LeDroit Park neighborhood of Washington, near Howard University, not far from the YWCA and the Social Settlement house where Cooper was actively involved, and also near Dunbar High School (the new name for M Street, chosen by Cooper to honor the poet Paul Laurence Dunbar). Even taking in five young children when she was nearly sixty did not slow Cooper down. Although Cooper supported them well into their adulthood, she also sent them to boarding schools in order to be able to continue her full-time teaching, her community advocacy, her pursuit of a Ph.D., and her summer employment, including War Service work during World War I.

Cooper finished her translation of *Le Pèlerinage de Charlemagne* around 1917. It was to serve as her doctoral thesis at Columbia, for an annotated and updated version of the text in French (based on the sought-after but rare Koshwitz German edition, which Cooper had used as the basis for her translation) was much needed. Yet to complete her Columbia University degree Cooper would have had to fulfill a one-year residency requirement in New York, an impossibility given her financial responsibilities to her adoptive children, since it might have meant sacrificing her job at M Street; and the advent of World War I also made long-term planning difficult. However, Cooper remained determined.

Eventually, with the help of her longtime friend in France, Félix Klein, Cooper was able to transfer her Columbia credits to the Sorbonne, University of Paris, where she enrolled as a doctoral student in the summer of 1924 and lived in the home of a Mme. Léger, with whom Cooper held "a friendship unlimited by color, creed or nationality" (Cooper in Gabel 68). At this time Cooper was awarded a fellowship for international research by Alpha Kappa Alpha, the first Black sorority in the United States, of which she was a member.[27] However, the Sorbonne required an entirely new dissertation for the Ph.D., based on a committee-approved research topic; the years of painstaking translation of *Le Pèlerinage* only counted toward Cooper's general degree credits, but not her thesis. She therefore began her newly approved area of research, French attitudes toward slavery during the Revolution.

After facing much sacrifice, a bout of bad health, and overt opposition from her school district supervisors (who threatened to terminate her contract because she traveled to Paris to do archival research while on sick leave), as well as implicit resistance from her Sorbonne examiners, including the renowned sociologist Célestin Bouglé,[28] Cooper completed and defended her Sorbonne doctoral dissertation in the spring of 1925 at the age of sixty-six. Cooper was the fourth African American woman to earn a Ph.D. in the United States (the third to do so while working at Dunbar High) and the first Black woman to earn a doctorate at the Sorbonne. Cooper's degree ceremony in the United States took place at Howard University in December 1925. Alpha Kappa Alpha organized the proceedings and Alain Locke, the well-known African American philosopher, gave the keynote address. Cooper's dissertation, *L'Attitude de la France à l'égard de l'esclavage pendant la Révolution* (France's Attitudes toward Slavery during the Revolution),[29] offers an insightful analysis of how the politics of race and issues of slavery affected revolutionary uprisings and shaped eventual outcomes both in France and in Haiti.[30] Though rarely placed in this context, Cooper's dissertation should be considered an important intellectual and political contribution to Black modernism, to the Harlem Renaissance, and to the development of a comparative anticolonial methodology.

The year 1925 marks the emergence of many important works in African American literature, culture, and history: Marita Bonner's feminist essay

"On Being Young — A Woman — and Colored," in *The Crisis* magazine; Thomas William Burton's *History of the Underground Railroad: American Mysteries and Daughters of Jerusalem*; Countee Cullen's poetry collection *Color*; Zora Neale Hurston's play *Color Struck*; Georgia Douglas Johnson's lynching drama *A Sunday Morning in the South*[31]; James Weldon Johnson's edited *Book of American Negro Spirituals*; Alain LeRoy Locke's edited collection *The New Negro: An Interpretation*; Lena Beatrice Morton's *Negro Poetry in America*; and three publications by Carter G. Woodson — *Free Negro Heads of Families in the United States in 1830, A Brief Treatment of the Free Negro*, and *Negro Orators and Their Orations*.

In 1925 Cooper published *Le Pèlerinage de Charlemagne* in Paris; her translation is still in use in Europe today. Unfortunately, Cooper was never able to secure distribution in the United States for *Le Pèlerinage*, although portions of it were reprinted with Cooper's permission in an American anthology of medieval literature (see Shilton). Cooper's dissertation met the same fate, despite the efforts of her friend Alfred Churchill (whose family she had lived with while at Oberlin), by this time a professor at Smith College (Gabel 69). Churchill tried to help Cooper find a willing publisher, but to no avail. This trend of rejection would remain an obstacle to Cooper's efforts to continue to have a public voice. For example, in the late 1920s and early 1930s, Cooper applied both to the Brookings Institution for a fellowship and to the American University to research and write a history of African Americans in Washington, D.C.; however, she writes, both "raised the color bar," and without funding she could not pursue that project (Cooper in Gabel 82). Mary Helen Washington hypothesizes "that a life of professional uncertainty and of financial insecurity made it difficult for [Cooper] to continue her writing" (xxxix). It is clear that systemic discrimination was an underlying cause of Cooper's ongoing professional and monetary uncertainties and of her diminished visibility as a public intellectual. An increasingly hostile racist climate in the 1920s and 1930s, combined with ever-present sexism, made it difficult if not nearly impossible for the more mature Cooper to publish or distribute her later major works in the United States, or even to pursue other research projects in new areas.

In 1930 Cooper retired from her teaching position at Dunbar High School and became president of Frelinghuysen University (later renamed the Frelinghuysen Group of Schools after a biased accreditation movement in the 1930s led to the eventual demise of many Black educational institutions, including Frelinghuysen).[32] As she had always done, Cooper juggled her work as an educator with her scholarly and community work in the 1930s. For example, in correspondence with Francis Grimké she discusses her continued stewardship and financial management of the Colored Settlement House (see Hutchinson 123). And although she had neither the time nor the resources to produce any book-length manuscripts while working at Frelinghuysen, Cooper did publish occasional short essays in the *Oberlin Alumnae Club Journal* and in the NAACP's *The Crisis* magazine in the 1930s, including "The Humor of Teaching," in which she advocates a culturally relevant, constructivist model of Black education, and "Angry Saxons and Negro Education," where Cooper takes on Booker T. Washington and accommodationist ideology. There is also reference to Cooper's writing a children's play, "Christmas Bells," as part of a fundraising campaign for Frelinghuysen (Hutchinson 184). Regrettably, there seem to be as many unpublished essays by Cooper in the 1930s as published ones; for instance, Lemert and Bhan have located (and now published) two important essays, "On Education" and "The Negro's Dialect," while Baker-Fletcher refers to a Black history curriculum and pageant from a time period entitled "From Servitude to Service" (39).

Frelinghuysen's mission was to serve adult, working African Americans in Washington, D.C. who, for financial and other reasons, were unable to attend Howard University, the only other option for post-secondary education in the district. As Leona C. Gabel explains, "Frelinghuysen was an effort to fill a serious need. ... [I]n the thirties, Anna Cooper drew attention to the shrinking of educational opportunities [for African Americans]. ... Out of seven full-time universities in Washington there was but one [Black] institution; and in a list of eighty-eight part-time colleges and special schools, not one would admit [an African American]" (71). Frelinghuysen operated small, satellite neighborhood campuses around Washington, offered classes at night and on weekends, and granted both undergraduate and graduate professional degrees (in social work, nursing, pharmacy, and law) and degrees in traditional liberal arts subjects such as history, theology, and fine arts, as well as high school equivalency courses and business courses. Cooper set up innovative internships in the professions for Frelinghuysen students and also collaborated with a few Howard University professors, including Carter G. Woodson, who supervised some students studying history, and Sterling Brown, who donated his entire personal library to Frelinghuysen (Chateauvert 269). The Hannah Stanley Opportunity School, named after Cooper's mother, was financially independent from Frelinghuysen (Hutchinson 166); it was the only school in the District of Columbia to offer instruction to adults with cognitive disabilities (Frelinghuysen Flyer). Like many of its students, Frelinghuysen struggled financially, particularly after the D.C. Board of Education, adversaries of Cooper's for over three decades since the M Street battle, refused it the right to grant baccalaureate degrees (168–69). Cooper eventually tried to secure federal funds through the WPA Education Division but was unsuc-

Figure 1.5 Frelinghuysen class meeting in Cooper's T Street Home. Courtesy of the Scurlock Studios Records, Archives Center, National Museum of American History, Smithsonian Institution.

cessful, and she donated much of her home on T Street for administrative and teaching purposes (Figure 1.5). She retired from the position of president in 1940 but continued teaching there into the mid-1940s and worked as registrar until around 1950.

In the 1940s, well into her eighties, Cooper turned her attention to writing a book about the life of Charlotte Forten Grimké, with a particular focus on Forten Grimké's experiences teaching freed slaves in the Sea Islands off South Carolina after emancipation, as well as a thorough documentation of Forten's life and background as a free African American, a longtime goal of Cooper's. Her two-volume *The Life and Writings of the Grimké Family* and *Personal Recollections of the Grimké Family* was privately published in 1951. Cooper also wrote a short memoir about her own life, *The Third Step*, privately published around 1945, and the lyrics to "Ethiopia's Paean of Exaltation," which was musically arranged and performed by Harry T. Burleigh[33] in New York in 1942 (see Hutchinson 186). Later, during the 1950s, Cooper also asked the historian Ray Allen Billington to edit Forten Grimké's teaching journals (Kaplan xi–xii), which were published in 1953 as *The Journal of Charlotte Forten: A Free Negro in the Slave Era*. Although Cooper lived for many more years, there is little information available about the last decade of her life. She died February 27, 1964, at the age of 105, in Washington, DC.

Questioning the Biographical Imperative

When it comes to interest in African American women's ideas, the descriptive attention given to the details of their lives frequently takes precedence over serious assessment of and engagement with their theoretical claims. The biographical can, ironically, function as a strategy of delegitimation. As Bob Corbett writes in his online review of Frances Richardson Keller's 1988 translation of Cooper's doctoral thesis, "Keller's focus on the author, rather than her provocative book ... [is] somewhat demeaning. Certainly Cooper achieved extraordinary things. ... But [her dissertation] stands as a scholarly achievement independent of any biographical data of the author." Thus, although it can be tempting to celebrate Cooper's life and work as exceptional, for she was an intensely driven and insightful person, this impulse to honor her can also result in a reductive form of tokenism. I have therefore long debated whether to write this biographical overview.

The paradox I am trying to name, and also to avoid, is akin to the trend in contemporary film toward "documentary looking" at African American lives described by Valerie Smith. She writes that despite "good intent," documentary representation more often than not is still a form of "spectacularization of the bodies of people of color," a twist on the persistent "voyeurism" that has long shaped representations of "the other" (V. Smith, *Not Just* 119). Similarly, Coco Fusco warns that "the desire to look upon predictable forms of Otherness from a safe distance persists" (50). Consequently, not only might focusing on Cooper's life story diminish her intellectual contributions: it could also reinforce a reductive and violating way of seeing.

One could go further with Fusco's and Smith's lines of reasoning and argue that, when it comes to African American women's ideas and lives, a pernicious, racialized sexual gaze transforms their bodies and biographies into spectacles of flesh. That is, the particular form of the "spectacularization" process Smith describes could be characterized as *specularization*, or specular interpretive methods, especially since countless slave women's bodies were the objects of involuntary medical experimentation (without anesthesia) by the "father" of American gynecology, J. Marion Sims, who invented the speculum for use in the cruel surgical "experiments" he performed in his back yard (see Kapsalis). Thus, concerns about the biographical are not merely about abstract intellectual issues; rather, the worry is that, even when rooted in good intentions, the biographical impulse can unwittingly reenact histories of physical brutality and epistemological violation.

To clarify, in no way am I suggesting that Cooper's experiences do not merit notice, or that her life story is not of any interest; in fact, they are politically and epistemologically relevant to her work. As I argue at the beginning of this chapter, there is much to learn by attending to the historical, political, and interpersonal contexts of Cooper's ideas. Fleshing out the particulars of her life adds dimensionality and nuance to our understanding of her theoretical premises, sociopolitical analyses, and community activism. In addition, it helps us better appreciate how Cooper and other Black women writers and educators of the period sought to be change agents through the acts of writing, teaching, and public speaking as well as through community service and advocacy. Nevertheless, the danger is that admiration can simultaneously be a form of distancing, of putting someone in her "place," curbing her impact and silencing her voice even as she comes to be perceived as an exemplary figure. In seeking a more fine-tuned taxonomy of emotions with regard to interracial dynamics, Dionne Brand distinguishes "veneration" from the sentimentality often thrown at famous Black cultural figures. While sentimentality is a form of adulation that turns a person into a commodity, a distant object "suspended in time, out of context," Brand argues that according someone veneration entails a culturally aware form of respect in which a figure such as Cooper would be understood as speaking "a kind of historical speech in a continuum, a language sent and understood in action" (150). Veneration therefore requires attentive cultural and historical contextualization alongside refusal of an exceptionalist interpretive lens.

Yet even with Brand's distinction in mind, I remain wary: a primary objective of this book is to undermine, rather than reinforce, the very real problem of biographical or bodily hypervisibility that tends, particularly for theorists and writers who are women of color, to be paired with theoretical or philosophical obscurity. For instance, I have found, anecdotally, that when colleagues or students know something about Cooper, they often focus on a few details about her life but show scant interest in her ideas (although this bifurcation is rarely conscious). Drawn most to the various "firsts" in Cooper's life (e.g., that she was among the first Black women to graduate from Oberlin, or to earn a Ph.D.), people marvel that Cooper was born into slavery and rose to such heights of achievement. Becoming all body, no mind, Cooper's life story gets transformed into a wellspring of "amazing" experiences and "unique" qualities, while her thoughtful analyses and insightful philosophical premises fall to the side as secondary or disappear from view entirely. This, too, is dangerous: as Cooper tells us (*Voice* 230), adulation is the flip side of denigration — they are deeply intertwined.

Moreover, despite Cooper's efforts to craft narrative and political space for Black feminist ideas and voices to be heard, with her voice one among many — *a* voice, not *the* voice of Black feminism (Foster 187), there is still the worry that she will be read simply as an "iconic figure" (Springer, "Black"), a much-admired member of the hall of fame with Sojourner Truth, Ida B. Wells, and others, up on a distant pedestal. One of the key problems here is that "cultural icons become devoid of history and content" and therefore "wordless" (Wallace, *Dark* 175). In a paradoxical twist of fate, Cooper, as icon, becomes a voiceless *Voice from the South*, and her interdisciplinary analyses, border-crossing methods, philosophical insights about oppression, and intersectional theories of liberation are pushed aside or ignored.

Of course, this dynamic is not unique to Cooper; it fits a well-established pattern of "undertheorizing" African American women's ideas while engaging in a (not necessarily conscious, but nevertheless problematic) preoccupation with the bodily or biographical. As Hazel Carby argues, nearly a century after Cooper published *A Voice from the South*, "Black feminist criticism has frequently been reduced to an experiential relationship" (*Reconstructing* 16). This is why, for instance, Rachel Lee questions the "nominalistic figuration" of women-of-color theorists in women's studies: she protests the ongoing failure "to take seriously the bodies of knowledge" produced by women of color, even as their lived bodies are upheld as sites rich in experiential knowing and as they are celebrated for their capacity to "reinvigorate" feminist scholarship (83–85). A "life story" approach is *not* atypical in analyses of theorists such as Cooper; to the contrary, it is practically obligatory.

However, the biographical imperative does not beleaguer equally the interpretation of all theorists or philosophers. A critical discussion of the major contributions of, for example, a well-known white male theorist does not *necessarily* begin with a lengthy reflection about his origins, his educational experiences and family life, and his life struggles. Questions of how or whether his race, class, or gender affected perception of his life work or presented obstacles (or, perhaps, conduits) to success are not expected, nor is speculation about his friendships or life relationships — whether he was sufficiently close to his intellectual peers, or whether interpersonal tensions in his life loom so large that we should focus on them instead of his philosophical premises. However, these are the types of questions that have preoccupied much of the discussion about Cooper.

The point is not that biographical and historical introductions contextualizing the life and ideas of major thinkers of any ilk could not exist; they can and do. Rather, the key issue here is that a thorough summary of biographical information, combined with speculative fascination about the meaning of these details, is, by and large, not requisite, except in the case of those whose bodies or identities are marked as "different" in some way from the normative. On the whole, we seem to like to think of "universal" thinkers as living the "life of the mind" separate from the "life of the body"; in contrast, for those who are always already perceived as more "embodied," the operative "rules" of analytic assessment are different (Gordon, *Existentia* 22).

Hannah Arendt argues that this mind/body dualism in political philosophy is a "false distinction between *vita activa* and *vita contemplativa*" (Bogues, *Heretics* 9). Similarly, Lorraine Hansberry complains with regard to critical discussion of Simone de Beauvoir's *The Second Sex*, "We have had to endure ... the exhaustive, casual, ill-informed, and thoroughly irrelevant commentary ... on [Beauvoir's] personal life." Slyly, Hansberry emphasizes the overlooked irony here: "the fact of such gossip about ... the leading woman intellectual of our time is in itself something of a tribute to the accuracy of [her] thesis" ("Simone" 128). Nevertheless, mind/body and thought/action dualisms continue to hold sway. Therefore, in scholarly studies of a theorist's premises, we do not generally expect (and may even shy away from) a focus on the messiness of lived identities, of national and cultural politics, and of the exigencies of economic need and the crushing reality of oppression. However, when it comes to "minority" theorists — implicitly or overtly marked by their gender, race/ethnicity, sexuality, disability, citizenship, or class — there seems to be a penchant for their life stories yet perfunctory interest in or attention to their ideas.

This is not to suggest that the story of a person's life is merely descriptive or summative; biographical essays, too, always offer an interpretation, and sometimes reveal surprising assumptions, even condescending attitudes. For instance, Lemert opens his biographical essay by focusing on Cooper's mixed-race beauty — "a beauty so commanding that she has become a virtual emblem of the 'Black Woman of America'" — before discussing anything about her life or about her ideas (1). Further compounding the problem of beginning with remarks about Cooper's beauty (which is troubling enough), he implicitly traces Cooper's unusual good looks, "the classic figure of a cameo," to her white "slaveholding father" (2), even though Cooper suggests that Haywood most likely *raped* her mother, given her mother's lifelong silence on the matter (Cooper in Hutchinson 4). Also problematic, though differently so, is Gabel's suggestion that experiences of slavery were not so severe in North Carolina. Although the Haywoods owned 271 slaves in Raleigh when Cooper was born and had slaveholding interests in other states, including Tennessee, Alabama, and Texas (Hutchinson 14), indicative of a setup both sizable and lucrative, Gabel suggests that slavery in North Carolina was "never as profitable nor as extensive as elsewhere in the South" and adds that it "was perhaps the most liberal in its attitude toward blacks," at least until the 1830s (9). Gabel indirectly supports a comparative calculus of suffering that ultimately trivializes oppression.

Undoubtedly, such readings of Cooper need to be challenged. But rather than read these two examples as anomalous, we need to understand them as inherently part of a larger set of issues raised by the biographical imperative itself. Lewis R. Gordon describes this overall dynamic as the "problem of biography in Africana thought" — the "ongoing practice of locking black intellectuals and their productions in the biographical moment" (*Existentia* 22, 26). Gordon maintains that this practice entails more than an obligatory biographical summary; it involves an analytic wrinkle in which the biography itself becomes the "text for political interpretation" rather than the ideas and theories at hand (27). He concludes that the "implication — insidious, patronizing, and yet so familiar and presumed — has achieved the force of an axiom: *White intellectuals provide theory; black intellectuals provide experience*" (29, italics original). Toni Morrison's critique of the ad hominem method of interpreting African American literature, which delimits its contributions to the realms of passion, realism, nature, or sociological relevance, but not to universal aesthetic pleasure or intellectual production ("Unspeakable" 31–32), comes to mind here as well.

Furthermore, even when "minority" thinkers are recognized for in fact producing "theory," the acknowledgment can be misleading, a kind of misrecognition. The attention accorded philosophers, writers, or theorists from the "margins" is often fleeting, and their ideas frequently remain "undertheorized." Moreover, "only a portion" of their writings is likely to be read or referred to with any substance (Alcoff, "Unassimilated" 255–56). Certainly, one could argue that this has been the case for Cooper. For example, most critical discussions of Cooper attend only to *A Voice from the South*, or even just a sampling of the essays therein. There is little analysis of her dissertation, her later essays are generally overlooked, and there are still too few book-length studies exploring Cooper's intellectual contributions. It is true that Cooper is being taught more frequently and cited more often, and that most of her works are once again in print and easily accessible. However, as Linda Martín Alcoff argues in the case of Gloria Anzaldúa's work, just because someone's ideas are "often cited" does not necessarily translate into adequate, serious, or enduring critical attention. Anzaldúa, contends Alcoff, "remains undertheorized" and "her effect remains to be developed" ("Unassimilated" 256); I maintain that an undertheorization of both philosophical effect and political impact also holds true for Cooper.

At the same time, I remain rather suspicious of too disembodied a tale — the "mind" floating above reality, mysteriously disentangled from the life of its body, somehow positionless and "pure." A reactive response in which any aspect of the biographical would become "off limits" would not really address the greater issues here, either. We should not force Cooper into a narrow set of preconceptions about how a "major thinker" should be represented or approached. Here I have in mind Emma Amos's 1994 painting *Work Suit*,[34] in which Amos portrays herself, as a black female artist, painting a white female nude while wearing a body suit of a white male, the representative or normative "artist" body (though made less "authoritative" in that his "suit" is also nude — his birthday suit). For once the nude black female body is *not* represented, it is not available for viewing: Amos is in charge of her self-presentation, although her agency is clearly embedded in a larger matrix of race and gender politics. Even if Amos may not be able to break entirely free of these systemic forces, she can still leverage space within them. Amos can be interpreted as using her body, and its encasement in the white male "work suit," to critique the race and gender politics of art, of artistic authority, and of artistic representation.

Similarly, Cooper references her own embodiment in her work, both as a means to theorize from lived experience and to craft "an unprecedented self" (Alexander 338), a new black female subjectivity that is neither fixed, essentialist, nor singular. Thus, in seeking to be accountable to the problems raised by the biographical imperative, the solution does not lie in simply portraying Cooper in ways that adhere to normative conventions of disembodied, universal philosophical discourse, of "proper" ways to think about theorists and their ideas. Surely it is also important to refuse to emulate the politics of authority and the epistemic models we seek to undo. There must be a way to break the mold and approach theory and theorists differently, via a contextual and historically grounded methodology.

Finally, there remains the very real issue that many people know very little, if anything at all, about Cooper — not her writings, her speeches, her community activism, or her work as an educator. Moreover, the two main biographical texts about Cooper (Louise Daniel Hutchinson's 1981 *Anna J. Cooper, A Voice from the South* and Leona C. Gabel's 1982 *From Slavery to the Sorbonne and Beyond: The Life & Writings of Anna J. Cooper*) are out of print. In contradistinction to the problems of tokenism, delegitimation, and erasure raised by the biographical imperative, there are equally grave dangers in having little or no substantive biographical material available. Such an absence implies both that a life such as Cooper's is not really worth documenting and that her life's work as a Black feminist intellectual does not hold lasting historical and political value. The lack of readily available information can have other repercussions as well, including the potential for the circulation of considerable inaccuracies about Cooper's life. For example, at a recent auction of African American historical materials, in which a first edition of *A Voice from the South* sold for nearly $4,000, the biographical data presented by the auction house was unintentionally incorrect. For example, it stated that Cooper's mother was free, not enslaved; that her father was a slave rather than a white slave owner; and that her Ph.D. was from Howard University rather than the Sorbonne. Although Cooper's "value" as a (literal) commodity rose beyond market expectations at the sale, the basic facts about her life were completely inaccurate.[35]

So, methodologically and ethically, I have been torn. To begin with the biographical is, I fear, to invite exactly the kind of objectifying mindset Cooper challenged as a scholar, educator, and activist. On the other hand, to exclude her life story or to reduce it to a chronological list of details presents other problems, including erasing how "black women speak from a multiple and complex social, historical, and cultural positionality" (Henderson 119). In fact, Cooper argues passionately for the political, ethical, and philosophic value of speaking from multiple locations, and she outlines a reflexive and situated phenomenology. Consistently, she upholds the validity of theorizing from lived, embodied experience. Moreover, Cooper contends that *all* knowledge is located, partial, and particular; this partiality is not the undoing of knowing "proper," but rather embodies the promise behind coalitional approaches to understanding grounded in self–other recognition and mutuality (May 78–80).

Therefore, the only conclusion I could come to was this: given that Cooper makes a strong case for a socially located, embodied, and historicized model of knowing, to have no account of her life would do her ideas and analyses an injustice. In other words, to avoid discussing sociopolitical contexts, to silence questions of identity and historical location, and to forgo a sense of how they shaped the direction of her life and her work would create an untenable and undesirable disjuncture between form and content. Cooper's commitment to a vision of liberation was grounded in her particular historical contexts and lived experiences. Because she called for theorizing from the specifics of our lives, I have offered the best portrait of Anna Julia Cooper's life that I could piece together from the limited materials available.

CHAPTER 2

"Life must be something more than dilettante speculation"[1]

Cooper's Multidimensional Praxis[2]

Anna Julia Cooper did more than theorize change in the abstract: she was dedicated to linking dissident thought with transformative practice. Her outspoken scholarship, community service, and efforts to secure equal rights are actions characteristic of a "freedom fighter" (Baker-Fletcher 159); rather than accept given reality, she sought to transform it. Yet Cooper's role as an activist has yet to be fully recognized in the literature, despite the fact that much of her work as a public intellectual, radical teacher, and community leader can be considered instances of "direct action" that both fostered and contributed to a wide-ranging Black feminist "culture of resistance" (Collins, *Black Feminist* 12). Such oversight may be due to a rather narrow conceptualization of "direct action" or activism. For instance, many recognize the work of Sojourner Truth, Harriet Tubman, Ida B. Wells, Ella Baker, or Fannie Lou Hamer as definitively "activist," whereas the work of an educator or intellectual like Cooper is often pushed aside as less radical or dismissed as accommodationist and apolitical. However, this implicit dualism between "thinking" and "doing," or the "political" and the "intellectual," is false and must be rejected in order to understand Cooper's work in particular, as well as Black feminist activism, or "culture of resistance," in general.

Cooper's perseverance is clear in her lifelong quest for educational equity. In the case of the M Street High School battle, Cooper fought the proposed substandard curriculum for African Americans, which she sarcastically describes as "'a course of study commensurate with their alleged inferior abilities'" (Cooper in Harley, "Anna" 92). After a heated twelve-month struggle, the board of education forced Cooper to step down as principal (Hutchinson 66–83, Foster 186), but in a larger sense she succeeded, for M Street maintained its full curriculum. Cooper's steadfast public resistance and palpable outrage, her willingness to lose her only means of support and put her career and character on the line, her refusal to accommodate racist and sexist ideologies about her "appropriate" role as a Black woman, and her rejection of an inferior curriculum for African American students all illustrate an intense devotion to realizing social change, rather than simply theorizing about principles of equality in the abstract.

Less well known (perhaps because Frelinghuysen students represented far more disenfranchised members of Washington's African American community than did M Street students) are Cooper's efforts to save Frelinghuysen. In what must have been yet another blow (both personally and politically), Frelinghuysen lost its university status in the 1930s under her tenure as president. To keep the institution viable, Cooper donated her home to house classes, the admissions office, and the library, and worked without salary as president, professor, and registrar (see Figure 2.1) for well over a decade. Unfortunately, the racist politics of accreditation impacting Frelinghuysen, like many other African American educational institutions at the time, did not seem to be considered an essential cause or top priority, locally or nationally, among leading (male) civil rights advocates, as some of Cooper's correspondence reveals. For example, her impassioned pleas for help, for signatures on a petition to save Frelinghuysen, would be ignored by the NAACP education campaign in the decades building up to *Brown v. Board of Education*, as well as by influential leaders in Washington.[3]

To understand adequately Cooper's (and many of her contemporaries') modes of activism, we must counter reductive ideas about what activism looks like or where it can be located. As Kimberly Springer asserts, "Our areas of activism are, historically, wide-ranging" (*Still Lifting* 1). Guy-Sheftall maintains that overall, "the history of African American women's activism ... has been grossly ignored or distorted" ("Preface" xix). In addition to the distorting impact of racism and sexism, another factor underlying the misrepresentation of Black women's activism is a normative "methodology of public protest" for studying social movements and political protest (Sowards and Renegar 57). Aaronette M. White argues that by focusing primarily "on the role of formal social movement organizations," social movements researchers have "privileged white, middle-class, male-dominated organizations and emphasized structural factors as explanations for periodic shifts in social movement activity." Thus they obscure "micromobilization factors" as well as more "informal social movement

Figure 2.1 Cooper standing by a bust of Frederick Douglass at Frelinghuysen's registrar's desk in the parlor of Cooper's T Street home. Courtesy of the Scurlock Studios Records, Archives Center, National Museum of American History, Smithsonian Institution.

communities" ("Talking" 190–91) even though micromobilization efforts, such as creating autonomous organizations and networks of resistance, are key to successful collective organizing (G. Tate 147–58).

Moreover, in accounts of contemporary civil rights activism, a gendered division of labor often emerges in people's perceptions or accounts of movement participation: women are more likely to be perceived as "organizers," whereas men tend to be readily characterized as "leaders" (Payne). Certainly this bias has also affected perceptions of African American women's activism in the 1890s and early 1900s. Additionally, much social movement theory has overlooked how women of color have developed "a different way of conceptualizing ... oppositional activity" and how they have long recognized that an "ethical commitment to egalitarian social relations [can] be enacted in the everyday," not just in sites familiar to the dominant social order (Sandoval 42, 62).

Delineating the history of Black women's political action, Springer points to African American women's varied forms of resistance during slavery, their roles in abolition and suffrage, the national impact of the grass-roots Black women's club movement, the use of the church as a site of activism, their civil rights organizing, and their activist contributions as public intellectuals (*Still Lifting* 1). Refusing narrow definitions, she includes an array of activities as activist, such as "the provision of social services," organizing, pubic protest, unionization, "writing as resistance, political education, consciousness-raising, autobiography as 'political witnessing,' public statements in major U.S. newspapers, and filing lawsuits" (3). By building on Springer's working definition of "direct action" in the contemporary period, we can better appreciate Cooper's range of advocacy, in her texts and in her community, as both activist and oppositional in orientation.

Patricia Hill Collins argues that a foundational premise of Black feminist ideologies of liberation is the idea that "teaching people how to be self-reliant fosters more empowerment than teaching them how to follow" (*Black Feminist* 157). In accordance with this principle of self-reliance as an essential aspect of empowerment, Cooper consistently called for African Americans' collective autonomy. This ethic of (collective) self-determination is evident, for example, in many of the organizations and associations Cooper belonged to and helped to create that were grounded in the fundamental precept of independence from the "help" and assistance of white philanthropists. But she also fought within the African American community for the ideal of self-determination for *all* African Americans, no matter their class or economic status; she rejected the notion of intra-racial class condescension, not just to white paternalism (and/or maternalism) from the outside. Thus, in a letter to Walter White, Cooper asked for the NAACP's *political* support for Frelinghuysen University and its poor, working-class adult constituency, but not monetary support or any form of paternalistic benevolence. Cooper wrote, "I trust your habit of concentrating on the 'war' against open violence will not render you and the Association for which you stand, less sensitive to the deeper movement toward a broader and a self-determined development from within. We are asking neither doles nor appropriations ... we are sure it is nobler to stand on our own feet" (NAACP Papers).

In addition to an ethic of self-definition, self-reliance, and collective autonomy, Cooper consistently promoted coalitional political models as essential to achieving long-term change. In contrast to single-issue activist platforms, Cooper, like many other Black feminists, advocated an intersectional methodology of liberation. Across her lifetime, Cooper challenged the interlocking dynamics of race, gender, nation, and empire. As a public intellectual and community advocate, she addressed a diverse range of audiences, at home and abroad. Cooper also worked within a variety of political organizations, from her work as column editor for the *Southern Worker* and *The Southland*, to her role on the board of the Phyllis Wheatley YWCA and organizer of girls' programs for the Camp Fire Girls, to her contributions as a member of the Pan-African Congress Executive Committee and the Bethel Literary Society. Cooper's capacity to focus on several political issues simultaneously and her acute ability to employ many different methods, sources, and rhetorical tactics in her scholarship are part of what makes her compelling, but her adeptness at multiplicity has also meant that her life's work lends itself to a wide spectrum of interpretations, often conflicting.

While many find Cooper to be a forward-thinking public intellectual, her philosophy, analytic methods, narrative voice, and community work are sometimes seen as less than radical, in terms of both approach and ramification. Over the past three decades a spirited interpretive debate over Cooper has emerged, with most of the discussion focused primarily on *A Voice from the South*. Little scholarship has taken into account Cooper's full range of writings, much less her community activism or work as a radical educator. Critics have focused on how Cooper borrows from eugenics discourse, alludes to True Womanhood ideology,[4] employs Eurocentric or erudite modes of writing, stereotypes other ethnic groups, or draws a distinction between her life and the everyday lives of most black women. Some characterize Cooper as elitist both in her scholarship and in her activism. Others find her to have been held back by too deep an investment in the very ideas and practices she sought to transform.

Across these critical debates, the underlying concern is to question whether it is viable, politically and ethically, to engage with, borrow from, signify upon, or even mock the "Master's Tools" (Lorde, *Sister* 110), or whether doing so is too complicit, inherently compromising, and politically untenable. Such issues are essential to explore as we reexamine past liberatory thought paradigms. But I would also argue that, too frequently, the ambiguity built into many of Cooper's arguments is seen as an unsound dimension of her theorizing in terms of both politics and methodology. In addition, the types of direct action that Cooper engaged in are rarely recognized as activist or political in nature.

It is patronizing, however, to diminish Cooper's various forms of community advocacy as outside the parameters of activism "proper." In her scholarship as in her career, Cooper was not interested in merely fitting in to the status quo. Instead, she sought to transform the polity and eradicate all institutionalized abuses of power, in domestic and international policy, as her work at the 1900 Pan-African Congress in London illustrates. There, concerns about the "conditions under which Africans and people of African descent were forced to live" were discussed. Moreover, Eurocentric approaches to African history and culture were reevaluated and reframed away from a deficit model toward a more diasporic evaluation of the significant (but usually overlooked or suppressed) contributions of Ethiopian and Egyptian cultures. Finally, a third focus of concern was to examine "the plight of southern Africa," to object to the rise of empire, and to oppose the Boer War (Pellow 67–68).

In addition to her work as an outspoken author and public speaker who participated in the formation of a transnational Black feminist public sphere and to her community leadership as a controversial teacher and principal who refused all forms of inequality in education, there are numerous other examples of Cooper's participating in "direct action." She helped to create autonomous community organizations that provided space for housing, employment, education, and protest action (e.g., the Wheatley YWCA), to found social service agencies outside the purview of white social science "experts" and white-controlled government funds (e.g., the Settlement House), and to create an independent network of schools for working poor adults and for adults with disabilities (e.g., Frelinghuysen).

Thus, while I agree that Cooper's multivocal methods and range of community causes can make it seem, at times, that definitive statements about her ideas and her voice are nearly impossible, it is also problematic to equate her adroit and agile use of plurality with confusion, uncertainty, or vagueness. Cooper's life was dedicated to ensuring that those without a public voice should be listened to and respected, granted legal equality, and accorded their rightful place in the nation's history and collective memory. Perhaps, then, the challenge lies in developing flexible interpretive strategies able to attend to Cooper's different vocal registers or resonances without silencing them, and more expansive notions of political action or of counter-publics able to recognize a broader range of activities as, in fact, activist.

In tandem with constrained definitions of activism, the contested debates about Cooper's theorizing also often suffer from an (unconscious) assumption equating theoretical astuteness with forms of reason grounded in univocal rhetorical styles and monological methodologies. Many of Cooper's forms of activism, whether textual or organizational, do not fit "public protest and confrontation" models of rhetoric (Sowards and Renegar 58). Likewise, her analytical premises do not always match up to traditional notions of theoretical "coherence." Moreover, when assessing Cooper many critics look to *A Voice from the South* in isolation and put aside her later writings as well as her tireless community advocacy. Rather than focus on her work as a philosopher, educator, and activist atomistically, taking into account all the dimensions of her work in a holistic way reveals the degree to which Cooper believed in a "decolonizing pedagogy." This critical method starts from three key premises: that the internal and external world can be changed through praxis, that social reality is malleable, and that all humans have the potential to be agents of change (Tejeda et al. 16).

Given that "some of the most compelling ... black feminist writing treads the boundary" between supposedly distinct genres or forms of criticism (V. Smith, "Black Feminist" 685), too narrow an approach to Cooper suppresses the complexity of her practice and oversimplifies the nature of her analyses. To reveal more of the decolonizing dimensions of Cooper's ideas and actions, it is essential to account for the contested political contexts in which she lived and to attend to the full range of her work as a scholar and activist. This calls for approaching her double-voiced, sometimes ambiguous analyses as grounded in "interstitial politics," or politics enacted "in the cracks" among and between multiple political terrains (Springer, "Interstitial" 155). Moreover, if we begin with the assumption that Cooper is trying to teach us something with her multiplicity and multivocality, we take up her invitation to participate actively in making meaning from the constant movement and transgression in her texts. By delving into (rather than cementing over) the "fissures" — by seeing the apparent cracks in her arguments as unexpected sites of possible meaning rather than as intrinsic flaws — we can bring a more complex portrait of Cooper's words and work to the fore.

In other words, we should not be so swift to decry Cooper's having created rhetorical, theoretical, and organizational spaces characterized by their built-in capacity for plural readings or meanings, even if they seem contradictory. Why presume that such tensions are (solely) problematic — must ambiguity and multiplicity only be interpreted as irrevocably uncertain or essentially indecipherable in terms of meaning? It is far more fruitful and interesting to approach Cooper's diverse forms of political work, from the textual to the organizational, with the assumption that there is something else there to be teased out. Why not presuppose, for instance, Cooper's rhetorical tactics to be instances of rhetorical activism?

Instead of confusion, Cooper's textual dissonance could signal a particular use of "language at a formative threshold," an intentional use of polyphony that challenges us as knowers (K. Holloway 618). Just as "truants" or runaway slaves "challenged the regulations dictating bondspeoples' location, regulations that were designed to affirm slave holders' dominion over the movement of the enslaved" (Camp 1), Cooper's textual transgressions, particularly her use of multiplicity and ambiguity, can be understood to contest and undermine any presumed authority over her ideas by her audience(s). While navigating her theoretical and rhetorical ambiguities, we are all too aware that, even if we so desired, we could have no dominion over Cooper. Whether textually or pedagogically, locally or internationally, in the classroom or in the community, Cooper persistently defied containment and resisted control. Just as truant slaves "created [an alternative] mapping of Southern space that would play an important role in the exodus from slavery during the civil war" (Camp 15), Cooper crafted an alternative mapping of both cognitive space and political terrain in her texts, laying the groundwork for a journey into the realm of the possible, rather than the constrained and oppressive spaces of the already-known.

Eugenicist or Existentialist?

In examining Cooper's efforts to counteract white supremacist discourse (e.g., "What Are We Worth?" in *A Voice from the South*), Stephanie Athey contends that Cooper's reliance on eugenic language and ideology perpetuates problematic notions of national belonging, of racialized gender autonomy, and of biological foundations to culture. In particular, Athey finds Cooper's attempt to counter Richard Louis Dugdale's influential 1877 study about the "costs" to society of "degeneracy" (entitled *'The Jukes': A Study in Crime, Pauperism, Disease, and Heredity*) to be complicit with Social Darwinism (40–59). This is not the sole instance in which Cooper alludes to eugenic discourse. For example, in 1902, she uses phrases such as "fitness to survive" and "stronger, truer, purer racial character" to discuss "The Ethics of the Negro Question" (208, 214). Seeking to emphasize the undeniable "Americanness" of African Americans, whose "citizenship is beyond question," Cooper implies that those who become citizens via "adoption or naturalization" perhaps have "other allegiance[s]" and even hold some "secret treachery" (215).

Yet elsewhere, Cooper so thoroughly decries Social Darwinism and xenophobic attitudes toward immigrants that it is hard to believe she advocates these premises. For example, in her 1913 pamphlet "The Social Settlement: What It Is, and What It Does," Cooper mocks both the notion of innate superiority and religious justifications for dominance. She writes: "Let a man convince himself that natural selection and survival of the fittest in some way involve responsibility for the uplift of his entire group, and if he is mean anyhow, it will not be hard for him to conclude that he is doing God's service by excluding hated groups or races from all enjoyments and advantages sought for his own" (219). Cooper emphasizes that eugenic ideology is an entirely unscientific means to justify unearned privileges, boost arrogant selfishness, and impose "unnatural" social hierarchies among humans.

Nevertheless, Athey concludes that Cooper ultimately defuses her own critiques and undermines her vision of coalition across the lines of race, class, and gender. Athey is not alone in her concerns. Baker-Fletcher has reservations about "elements of a liberal social evolutionary theory evident in Cooper's thinking" (68), while West questions Cooper's "progressive theory of humankind" and faith in the Enlightenment idea of perfectibility (96). Certainly, I do not want to rationalize bigotry or bias on Cooper's part, nor do I want to suggest that playing upon people's fears of immigrant "masses" or of subsequent "degeneracy" is tenable. However, the context for Cooper's statements about immigrants and their "secret treachery" is also relevant. Her remarks are embedded in the midst of a larger, multifaceted analysis of the politics of national belonging. Much as Du Bois would later argue, Cooper advances the premise that rather than existing "in opposition to the ideals of an American republic," African Americans "embody them" (Carby, Race 28). Granted, Cooper celebrates the idea of "progress" and maintains that African Americans personify democratic ideals, but by contending that they are exemplars of what is most quintessentially American, she also pushes the bounds of the discourse and redefines what it means to be American.

While reworking normative conceptions of democracy and progress, Cooper simultaneously makes visible their underside. To equate economic profit with liberty is, she argues, unethical: this conflation has been manipulated to justify slavery, labor exploitation, imperialist expansion, and the uses of violence as a means of social control, including rape, lynching, and war. Cooper does not simply celebrate American democracy, in its past or present incarnation, nor does she meekly adhere to traditional notions of progress. Instead, she aims to disrupt our faith in these ideals in order to redefine them by highlighting the role of exploitation and violence, at home and abroad, in the formation and maintenance of the U.S. nation-state.

In contrast to this less than "progressive" history, Cooper wants to delineate an "ethical sense of the nation" ("Ethics" 207). However, she finds there are two major obstacles to doing so: a desire to evade structural racism, in terms of both domestic and international policy, and a drive to maximize profits at any cost. She describes a pervasive exhaustion with questions of race, such that "The American conscience would like a rest from the black man's ghost," particularly in these times of "commercial omnipotence and military glorification." Such glorification of power and dominance is linked to another major hindrance to real liberation: a voracious economic imperative. Although an expanding economy is usually touted as the sine qua non of American democracy, particularly now that "Northern capital is newly wed to Southern industry and the honeymoon must not be disturbed" (209), Cooper suggests that both "progress" and "ethics" will be hindered if the market continues to take precedence over all other demands, including the need to invest in "social capital" for every citizen as well as the rights of all people to wage equity, equal education, and adequate housing ("Wage Earners").

Thus, while Cooper takes on a rather nativist tone in "The Ethics of the Negro Question," she does so in an attempt to get at the heart of a moral dilemma: whether the nature of community and the foundational premises of citizenship should be supremacist. It is within this context that Cooper points to the subtle ways that immigrants take part in and benefit from American racist taxonomies and cultural practices. Immigrants' "secret treachery" turns out to be their willingness to comply actively with and profit from white supremacy, not their immigrant status per se. Acquiescence to supremacy, suggests Cooper, is the *real* threat to the union, not the stereotyped specter of the dangerous black man, the fear-mongering myth of the black rapist (see "Ethics" 211).

This double tactic is similar to one Cooper had used ten years earlier in "Has America a Race Problem." There, she rejects race supremacy, xenophobia, and cultural intolerance (*Voice* 160–64), but propels her argument, in part, by ridiculing Anglo-Saxon superiority. Cooper borrows from a positivist, racialist theory of nation and literature developed by the French Comtean scholar Hippolyte Taine (a determinist approach I am fairly sure she thoroughly disagreed with, given her biting critiques of both positivism and biological determinism; see *Voice* 26, 125, and 292–93, for instance). Cooper quotes from Taine's description of "barbarians" who had "'Huge white bodies, cool-blooded, with fierce blue eyes, reddish flaxen hair; ravenous stomachs, filled with meat and cheese, heated by strong drinks'" (157). After duly mocking white triumphalist notions of Anglo-Saxon lineage, Cooper proceeds to object to immigrants' efforts to colonize, deport, or "amalgamate" black Americans elsewhere, thereby creating a "purer" (white) racial polity. She writes: "No power ... on this continent, least of all a self-constituted tribunal of 'recent arrivals,' possesses the right to begin figuring ... what it would require *to send* ten millions of citizens, whose ancestors have wrought here from the planting of the nation, to the same places at so much per head — at least till some one has consulted those heads" (172–73, italics original).

In "The Ethics of the Negro Question," Cooper builds on these earlier arguments to critique how immigrant groups learn to become white, how racism shapes union policy and collective labor identity, and how endemic racism and stereotyping affect Afican Americans on a daily basis. Discussing the inequities facing working Black men, she writes:

> The Negro workman receives neither sympathy nor recognition from his white fellow laborers. Scandinavians, Poles and Hungarians can tie up the entire country by a strike paralyzing not only industry but existence itself, when they are already getting a wage that sounds like affluence to the hungry black man. The union means war to the death against him and the worst of it is he can never be lost in the crowd and have his opprobrium forgotten. A foreigner can learn the language and out-American the American on his own soil. A white man can apply burnt cork and impute his meanness to the colored race as his appointed scape goat. But the Ethiopian cannot change his skin. On him is laid the iniquity of his whole race and his character is prejudged by formula. ("Ethics" 208)

Cooper is quite forward-looking in her analysis of the role of racism, especially the function of cultural stereotype and minstrelsy, in the self-concept of "white" male workers and in the collective identity formation of the working class. She anticipates ideas found in later, more widely recognized works, including W. E. B. Du Bois's 1935 book *Black Reconstruction in America*,[5] in which he puts forth the concept of whiteness as entailing a psychological "wage," if not a material one, as well as David Roediger's 1991 text, *The Wages of Whiteness: Race and the Making of the American Working Class.*

Athey also argues that Cooper is "enmeshed in the logics of eugenic feminisms" (41) in "What Are We Worth? " (*Voice* 228–85) and in "Womanhood: A Vital Element in the Regeneration and Progress of a Race" (9–47), particularly in how she accentuates the productivity of black women's labor, including reproduction. But here too, Cooper could be read quite differently. In fact, her focus on black women's productivity, in terms of paid, unpaid, and reproductive labor, can be seen as an early materialist Black feminist analysis. Cooper's examination of Black women's oppression under capitalism reveals that it is the working, reproducing Black female *body* that is a site of particular, not universal, forms of sexist and racist domination in the capitalist economy.

In pointing to the "value" or "worth" of Black women's reproductive labor, Cooper indirectly critiques how their bodies were used during slavery to "reproduce" wealth for the capitalist, slave-holding economy (e.g., "Ethics" 207). Moreover, in "Colored Women as Wage Earners," Cooper reminds us how "a large percentage of the productive labor of the world is done by women." Citing an Atlanta University study, Cooper adds that over 58 percent of "colored families" are "'supported wholly or in part by female heads'" while, at the same time, Black women's labor inside the home goes unrecognized as labor per se, which is wrong (n.p.). Repeatedly she underscores the materiality of exploitative work/embodiment and demonstrates how labor and productivity are concepts and measures that are raced and gendered, not "neutral." Moreover, Cooper's analysis of Black women as wage earners anticipates by a century the work of contemporary Black feminist social scientists such as Rose Brewer, who also documents how "Labor is not simply about waged work at the site of production. Within households, Black women perform a significant portion of the social reproductive labor" (24).

By offering other angles from which to read Cooper's discussion of reproduction and the role of womanhood in the "elevation of the race" (*Voice* 37) or her analysis of the "wages of whiteness" built into white supremacist ideologies of the nation, I am not suggesting that it is erroneous to fault Cooper's borrowing from or manipulation of racial categories or philosophies of gender roles intimately associated, directly or indirectly, with Social Darwinism. However, I want to emphasize that Cooper and her contemporaries were up against, among other things, a tenacious race-gender ideology that, "through the rubric of monstrously 'raced' Amerindian and African women, Europeans [and Euro-Americans] found a means to articulate shifting perceptions of themselves as religiously, culturally, and phenotypically superior to those Black or brown persons they sought to define" (Morgan 38). Cooper and her contemporaries had to negotiate such ideologies and perceptions daily; they were not working in a rhetorically or politically neutral situation, and their choices were highly constrained.

Taking these coercive dynamics and supremacist philosophies into account, Lewis Gordon interprets Cooper's essays quite differently. He reads her as delving into an existentialist inquiry about what it means to be defined as a "problem." Moreover, he sees Cooper as exploring how to find the impetus to keep on living in a world that degrades and denies one's personhood. Gordon argues that by approaching Cooper's work as an existentialist philosophical project, we can better see how she "addresses head-on the implications of demanding a race of people to justify their right to exist — in a word, their 'worth'" (*Existentia* 17). Further, he contends that the "ontological question of problematized existence and suffering" entails a twofold methodology: indicating questions of liberation while also critiquing "traditional, read 'European,' ontological claims" ("African-American" 34–35).

Gordon notes that in "What Are We Worth" (in *A Voice*) Cooper anticipates both Frantz Fanon and Jean-Paul Sartre by pointing out a core paradox embedded in the onus to prove one's subjectivity: that "there is no way a human being can justify why he or she exists" because his or her "existence is already subordinated in the very question" (Gordon, "Conversation" 105). However, Cooper does more than anticipate this impossible task; she actually names it herself in 1902 when she states, "a weak and despised people are called upon to vindicate their right to exist in the face of a race of hard, jealous, intolerant, all-subduing instincts" ("Ethics" 213). Cooper parodies the stereotype of the hard, cold Anglo-Saxon "race," and her reversal, ascribing degeneracy to those who dominate and exploit others, is spirited and daring. By approaching Cooper's political and ontological arguments as interstitial, we can see that at the same time that she partakes of the language, categories, and metaphors of dominant ideologies, in this case Social Darwinism, Cooper also undermines supremacist ideologies of citizenship and outlines a theory of problematized existence.

Elitist Writer and Educator, or Subversive Critical Theorist?

Cooper's narrative voice and her method of writing and speaking, particularly her tone and syntax, are also hotly debated. Cooper's "florid" prose style is sometimes read as both daunting and distancing; her formal, long, and complex sentences are interpreted as signs that she seeks to break away from the majority of the Black community and to ingratiate herself with primarily white and/or male, middle-class, literate audiences (Alexander 339, Baker-Fletcher 172, Washington xxx). Despite the fact that Cooper was born into slavery, grew up poor after emancipation, and dedicated her life to fighting institutionalized forms of oppression that perpetuate poverty (including child malnutrition, housing discrimination, unequal access to education, labor union bias, cultural intolerance and stereotypes, and limited employment options), Lemert finds that Cooper "did not very often employ the language of the poor" (34). Similarly, Baker-Fletcher asserts that Cooper "tended to emphasize what the formally educated could teach the less literate masses, rather than what the masses could teach the formally educated. She did not escape an attitude of condescension" (111–12). Baker-Fletcher concludes that although Cooper intended to speak "in solidarity" with other Black women, for the most part she spoke on *behalf* of, not with them (123).

However, speaking to or moving in elite circles should not necessarily be equated with complicity, although the comforts of privilege do pose a constant danger, a point Cooper herself makes in "The Gain from a Belief." Here she admonishes her (erudite male) readers not to be content to be "ensconced" in privilege: "Don't spend your time discussing the 'Negro Problem' amid the clouds of your fine havana, ensconced in your friend's well-cushioned arm-chair and with your patent-leather boot-tips elevated to the opposite mantel" (*Voice* 299–300). Likewise, clearly disagreeing with her audience of leading white feminists in her speech at the Columbian Exposition in 1893, Cooper reprimands them for their passivity in the face of social problems and for their narrow conceptualization of human rights. She advocates an active approach to social change and directs her audience to envision a radically inclusive democracy as their normative ideal. She asserts, "We want, then, as toilers for the universal triumph of justice and human rights, to go to our homes from this Congress, demanding an entrance not through a gateway for ourselves, our race, our sex, or our sect, but [through] a grand highway for humanity" ("Intellectual" 204–5).

Moreover, while Cooper's prose may at times be more ornate than plainspoken, her use of a scholarly style does not necessarily mean that she was addressing only one audience at a time. Negotiating political and psychological subordination can play out not only in terms of the questions asked, as Gordon suggests in his analysis of "worth" and existence (*Existentia* 17), but also in the act of writing as a way to fight against a culturally prescribed "relation of indenture" (Gates 43). It is therefore significant that Cooper modulates her voice quite a bit. I interpret her variations in narrative tone, from soothing to sarcastic, from cool to impassioned, or from center to margin, to signify an adept cross-cultural "code-switching." Her playful use of dominant discourses often undercuts the meanings they might ordinarily convey.

However, Cooper's skillful approach, akin to what Bakhtin identified as "double-voiced discourse" (Bakhtin 108), is often overlooked or interpreted to signify contradictory thinking on her part rather than strategic debunking.[6] In this way, her provocative humor, challenging sarcasm, and audacious irony go relatively unnoticed as innovative political tactics. For instance, would those in positions of privilege "get" Cooper's jokes and sarcastic jibes about them? Consider her mockery of "blue-blood legacies" in *A Voice from the South*: "If your own father was a pirate, a robber, a murderer, his hands are dyed in red blood, and you don't say very much about it. But if your great great great grandfather's grandfather stole and pillaged and slew, and you can prove it, your blood has become blue and you are at great pains to establish the relationship" (Cooper, *Voice* 103). She also finds that despite contemporary assertions about the magnificence of Anglo-Saxon and Nordic heritages, the "Goths and Huns, Vandals and Danes, Angles, Saxons, [and] Jutes" were a "clumsy horde of wild barbarians" who "pillaged and demolished" (156–57).

Later, she sarcastically apologizes for her different outlook on ethics, resulting from her lineage as an African American woman:

> I feel at times as if I have taken hold of the wrong ideal. But then, I suppose, it must be because I have not enough of the spirit that comes with the blood of those grand old *sea kings* (I believe you call them) who shot out in their trusty barks speeding over unknown seas and, like a death-dealing genius, with the piercing eye and bloodthirsty heart of hawk or vulture killed and harried, burned and caroused. This is doubtless all very glorious and noble, and the seed of it must be an excellent thing to have in one's blood. But I haven't it. I frankly admit my limitations. (196, italics original)

Cooper's so-called limitations, for which she appears rueful, lie in being connected to Simon of Cyrene and to Africa, "the fatherland of all the family," which had sheltered a "mysterious Stranger, when, a babe and persecuted ... He had to flee the land of his birth" (197). Cooper affirms her African heritage, showing it to be far more "noble" and "glorious" than that of the violent sea kings and aggressive blue-bloods. Moreover, throughout *A Voice* she draws analogies between Black women and that "mysterious Stranger," Jesus. Cooper uses literary techniques to draw parallel representations of Jesus and the Black woman of the South. Both are silenced, outcast, poor, suffering, and meek. More important, both have philosophies of freedom and liberation that, although censored, must be heard (Baker-Fletcher 69–70).

On the one hand, as Baker-Fletcher, Joy James, and Washington suggest, the majority of African Americans at this time did not have an education above the elementary level,[7] so Cooper's discourse was in some ways comparatively polished both in terms of tone and vocabulary. But on the other hand, most would also have been quite familiar with the church as a site of rhetorical flourishes, resistant discourse, literacy development, and community building. Therefore, it is simply not the case that only "elite" audiences would have found resonance or meaning in Cooper's positive references to Simon of Cyrene, or in her (potentially wrath-inducing, radical) analogies between Jesus and Black women, or in her liberationist readings of the parable of the rich man and Lazarus or of the Good Samaritan (in Luke 10:29–37 and Matthew 22: 37–39) (see Baker-Fletcher 47, 72–73).

Although steeped in Christian metaphor and history, so that today Cooper's Afrocentric affirmation of her heritage may go unnoticed (or cause discomfort for some readers), her revised genealogies, both Black and white, and particularly those outlined for Black women, are fairly defiant. Would intransigent "blue-bloods" find genealogies tracing them back to "bloodthirsty vipers" (158) as their forebears funny or, instead, utterly seditious? Embedded as they are inside apparently deferential apologies, for whom are these comic tales and amusingly revised lineages conceived? Given the fact that violent hate crimes against African Americans were, in Cooper's time, prevalent and overt tools of social control, it is also important to realize the risk she took in asserting such notions, even under the guise of a joke or under the irreproachable cover of theological reflection.

Cooper's use of word play suggests that she had in mind a wider audience: through sarcasm, allegory, allusion, and humor, she sought to speak to more than one group at a time. This is particularly clear in her liberationist readings of the Gospel and interpretations of biblical history. Cooper's overarching philosophy, which starts from the premise that each of us, given the chance, has full human potential, comes to light in her theological interpretations. For example, she saw the biblical figure Simon of Cyrene in a more radical way than did most of her contemporaries, even the Reverend Francis Grimké. She read St. Simon as "a volunteer and not just an accident of history" (Baker-Fletcher 51) — as agentially choosing to help carry Jesus' cross, not as a passive, stereotypical "accidental beast of burden happening at the moment to be caught in the denouement of the greatest Drama of the Universe" (Cooper, *Personal Recollections* 15).

In the stained glass window at St. Augustine's that Cooper commissioned in memory of her husband, her radical vision of St. Simon as an agent of history shines through. Most classical images of the fifth station of the Cross, including those at the Vatican, portray St. Simon as nearly white with a comportment expressing docility and subordination. In contrast, in Cooper's commissioned window, as in her poem "Simon of Cyrene," the dark-skinned African St. Simon expresses power and exudes agency. Placed visually above Jesus, Simon lifts the cross with all his might, muscles rippling. Looking each other in the eye, both Jesus and Simon see "A brother in the stranger": "These Two, a look revealing / Shot forth from heart to heart" (Cooper, *Personal Recollections* 15). The Reverend George A. Christopher Cooper Memorial Window combines an oppositional aesthetic pleasure ("Black is Beautiful") with a liberationist theological and historical message; this artistic commission can be seen as a form of activism through the arts.

Although Mary Helen Washington finds that "nothing in [Cooper's] essays suggests that [everyday Black men and women] existed in her imagination as audience or as peer" (xxx), and despite the fact that Baker-Fletcher concludes that Cooper's theological vision is hampered by her preference for a "Eurocentric model of worship" (46) that entails an "adulation of high, Anglican liturgy" (173) and "degrees of elitism" in general (111), I find definitive evaluations of Cooper's voice or theology as exclusionary or elitist to be relatively unsatisfactory because they obscure how her writing is tactically double-voiced in a Bakhtinian sense. In addition, there is an implicit cultural determinism or authenticity "test" embedded in trying to ascertain what genre of writing, what style or mode of discourse, "belongs" to whom.

Likewise, Foster disagrees with narrowly correlating the tone or shape of a sentence with an author's mindset. Refusing an essentialist notion of language or style, she asks that we refocus our attention to the historical circumstances and contexts of constraint and silence surrounding the history of African American writing. Foster sees Cooper's and other Black women's adoption of ostensibly Eurocentric models of discourse quite differently. She writes: "To assert that those who adopted forms and techniques of Western literature and addressed their remarks to an audience not confined to the African American community were really writing just to convince white people that they, too, could sing America is … an ingenuous and ignoble conclusion" (15). Questions of liberation, agency, and identity focusing on the "lived context of concern" (Gordon, *Existentia* 10) are not *inherently* "European" or "male," nor are they inherently questions that only "elite" people think about. Cooper suggests as much in her declaration that "The colored woman, then, should not be ignored because her bark is resting in the silent waters of the sheltered cove. She is watching the movements of the contestants none the less and is all the better qualified, perhaps, to weigh and judge and advise because not herself in the excitement of the race" (*Voice* 138).[8]

In analyzing the impact of European philosophy on African American thinkers such as Martin Delany, Maria Stewart, Anna Julia Cooper, and W. E. B. Du Bois, Gordon contends it is reductive to equate influence with either causality or imitation (as if Black and feminist thinkers can only be "given" ideas about freedom from others) (*Existentia* 9, see also "Introduction"). As Cooper declares, "imitation is the worst of suicides" (*Voice* 175). Moreover, in 1894, while overseeing the "Folklore and Ethnology" column of the *Southern Workman*, Cooper argued that what African Americans needed most was "deliverance" from normative whiteness. First, Cooper satirically states, "'to write as a white man, to sing as a white man, to swagger as a white man, to bully as a white man — this is achievement, this is success.'" A few pages later, Cooper adds her plea for liberation: "I heard recently of a certain great painter, who before taking his brush always knelt down and prayed to be delivered from his model and just here as it seems to me is the real need of deliverance for the American black man" (Cooper, *Southern Workman* 23.4, 131–33 in Moody, 2).

Like Cooper, by rejecting interpretive models that posit Africana thought as primarily mimetic, Gordon and other contemporary Black philosophers seek to debunk the notion of a "great chain of thought constructed around a hierarchical order" to match the Aristotelian "Great Chain of Being" model of civilization and human progress (Bogues, *Heretics* 2). As Mills highlights, this paradigm has led to an inherent paradox in much social contract theory, including the work of Kant, Hume, Voltaire, and Hegel. Despite assertions of universal personhood as a foundational concept, simultaneously there are "racial taxonomies" in which "blacks are almost always at the bottom, the last quasi-human link (or sometimes the missing link) in the Great Chain of Being before it descends unequivocally into the animal kingdom" (*Visible* 77). Rather than characterize Black/ feminist thought as if it were simply derivative, imitative, or "inherited" from those who dominate, or "lower" on the ladder of civilization, Gordon puts forth the less determinist and less patronizing notion of "opportunity" (*Existentia* 9).

Similarly, in her address to the Hampton Folklore Society, Cooper did not advocate thinking about Black folklore in ways that upheld Western notions of "civilization" or "progress." Rather, she "implored African Americans to free themselves from the Anglo Saxon standards by which their own traditions were judged primitive and lacking" (Moody 7). Moreover, in *A Voice from the South* Cooper admonishes her readers both to take advantage of "opportunities," such as education, and to be wary of internalized oppression and critical in their world outlook. She warns: "Don't let them argue as if there were no part to be played in life by black men and black women, and as if to become white were the sole specific and panacea for all the ills that flesh is heir to — the universal solvent for all America's irritations!" (172). One hundred years later, bell hooks recalls a similar admonition from her mother:

> Once mama said to me as I was about to go again to the predominantly white university, 'You can take what the white people have to offer, but you do not have to love them.' Now understanding her cultural codes, I know that she was not saying to me not to love people of other races. She was speaking about colonization and the reality of what it means to be taught in a culture of domination by those who dominate. She was insisting on my power to be able to separate useful knowledge ... from participation in ways of knowing that would lead to estrangement, alienation, and worse — assimilation and cooptation. (*Yearning* 150)

Like Gordon and hooks (and hooks's mother), Cooper distinguishes between learning and cooptation, the spark of critical consciousness and the passivity of rote imitation. She also points to the violence of internalized oppression.

In fact, Cooper's consistent loathing of the idea that African Americans should merely imitate whites (an idea she argued against in *A Voice from the South*, as a member of folklore societies, and in her later writings about education), adds another dimension to the matter of her supposed elitism. Although she is sometimes thought of simply as the "female Du Bois" who advocated a classical education to help advance the Talented Tenth,[9] the fact is that Cooper delineated a unique philosophy of education that does not fit the masculinist choice of deciding whether she follows most closely the outlook of either Booker T. Washington or W. E. B. Du Bois (K. Johnson 34; Keller, "Educational" 53). Cooper did not see industrial and classical models of education as exclusive choices, nor did she advocate that one model supersede the other. After all, Cooper's brothers Rufus and Andrew and her maternal grandfather were skilled carpenters and bricklayers. However, as opposed to narrowing the options or dividing them by social class or Talented Tenth, she wanted the full range of educational opportunities to be available to all people, equally. This outlook is evident across her years as an educator, but particularly in her work at Frelinghuysen, where, Cooper wrote, "Quite candidly we *dare* to be poor" (NAACP Papers, letter to the president of Howard University, emphasis added).

Cooper's alliance with and advocacy for some of the more disenfranchised populations in the nation's capital set her apart from both Du Bois and Washington. Early in her career, by refusing to choose between liberal arts and vocational education models, Cooper walked a difficult path while principal of M Street, ultimately losing her job. In the 1930s, when as president of Frelinghuysen she sought to keep the university's accreditation, Cooper found she still had to justify a "both/and" inclusive vision of education to the D.C. Board of Education. For example, in a letter to Dr. Learned on the board, Cooper defended Frelinghuysen: "We are poor, our constituency is poor," and "there is absolutely no [other] door open to the struggling colored man or woman, aspiring for the privileges of advanced education and not able to make the hours scheduled at Howard" (in Chateauvert 266). Consistent with her argument for universal and equal access to a liberal arts curriculum in the M Street struggle, thirty years later Cooper continued to fight for the premise that systemic oppression due to race, gender, poverty, adult status, or disability should not be exacerbated by lack of access to an excellent education.

Moreover, when discussing her "racial philosophy," Cooper makes it patently clear that she does not approve of any conciliatory, separatist "solid hand and separate fingers" ("Racial" 237) model of Black education, which Booker T. Washington had proposed in his 1895 Atlanta Compromise address — hence Cooper's "hand and fingers" reference. In a later article about Black education in the NAACP's *The Crisis* magazine, Cooper again dispenses with this "colored leader of white American thought" ("Angry Saxons" 259). His approach merely encourages "the domineering *thumb* to over ride and keep down every finger weak enough to give up the struggle" ("Racial" 237, italics original): it upholds inequality by fostering a two-tiered educational system in which an entire race of people is schooled for "servitude" and not "service." In her work as in her life, Cooper distinguished between collective accountability and an activist philosophy of service versus an acquiescent notion of servitude (Baker-Fletcher 38, 78).

As an educator and activist, Cooper held to her conviction that all forms of education, be they classical, professional, or vocational, full-time or part-time, should be sites of liberation. She understood educational settings as places where one learns to question rather than passively accept the world as it is, sites where one is encouraged to reject all forms of internalized oppression (see Cooper, "Humor" 234–35). In other words, Cooper sought to foster in her students and in her community what Paulo Freire would later describe as *concientización* — an overtly critical and political consciousness centered around the struggle for self-determination (Freire, *Letters* 181–83). Moreover, anticipating Freire's critique of "banking" models of education (*Pedagogy* 72–3), Cooper encouraged Black teachers to give up authoritative models of teaching that reduce knowledge to "cases" and teach passivity. Instead, she urged, take up a more "daring," interactive, and constructivist model of learning ("Humor" 235). She also deplored the "skill and drill" approaches to education that once again prevail in our assessment-driven times. Cooper asserted that educators should be free to address "the specific problems and needs of their pupils" rather than be "ridden with tests and measurements" (234). She believed that all forms of learning should make one "ready to serve the body politic" ("On Education" 251), rather than passively accept what is written as "true" in textbooks ("Humor" 234).

In addition to advocating critical pedagogy, Cooper identifies a wide range of impediments to equal education. For instance, she points to a prevalent indifference to endemic violence perpetrated against African Americans, specifically lynching, as a factor that must be addressed ("Sketches" 224–29). She also underscores the need for culturally relevant curricula and teaching styles to help African American students navigate, rather than be caught in, structures and "codes of power," anticipating the work of contemporary educators such as Lisa Delpit (293). Cooper concludes that "the wisest plan of education" will "note the forces against which [the students] must contend," including "the unrelenting struggle for survival." Further, she asserts that a "neglected people ... must be fitted to make headway in the face of prejudice and proscription the most bitter, the most intense, the most unrelenting the world has ever seen" ("On Education" 250–51).

Needless to say, Cooper also identifies sexism as another obstacle to equitable education. She criticizes the idea of an inferior "Ladies Course" (*Voice* 49), questions why a woman should be taught "that her value was purely a relative one ... to be estimated ... by the pleasure" she gives a man (65), and decries the idea of a woman's spending her whole life trying to figure out how to "nullify" herself for "some little man" (70). Instead, Cooper advocates the higher education of women and in particular of Black women (73–79). Moreover, in "Colored Women as Wage Earners," she recognizes that "It may be hard to do without your daughter's help while she studies a few more years in preparation for her labor, but the greater productiveness of that labor will more than repay your abstinence" (n.p.).

Cooper emphasizes that a comprehensive education will mean not only that a (Black) woman's "horizon is extended" (*Voice* 69), but also that her "thumping within" can begin to be "answered" by a "beckoning from without" (even though, as Cooper recalls, her own "thumping" was not encouraged or "beckoned" from without) (76). She adds that educated women will also be "less dependent on the marriage relation for physical support" (68) and more able to "tug at the great questions of the world" (75). Higher education will provide African American women with the means to become full citizens in their own right, not economically or emotionally dependent on men. Instead of being relationally defined, subjugated, and silenced, they will be self-defining, outspoken, and equal participants in the future of both the race and the nation.

Pawn or Skeptic of True Womanhood?

In other debates centered on issues of elitism and Cooper, some find that many of the clubs and organizations she was involved in, from the local Colored Women's League of Washington, of which she was a charter member (Harley, "Anna" 91), to the national NACW (National Association of Colored Women), were so invested in middle-class Victorian gender ideals that they unwittingly perpetuated class hierarchies among Black women. As Guy-Sheftall discusses, "a major objective of the black women's club movement was to persuade poor rural black women in the South to embrace the sexual morals of the Victorian middle-class" (*Daughters* 74). Harley ("Beyond" 259–60) and Washington (xxx–xlix) therefore find many of the clubwomen's tactics and programs to be patronizing in their outlook and attitude toward rural and working-class Black women. Alternatively, Giddings (*When* 85) and Nash (129) see in Cooper's work considerable evidence of coalitions across class lines more than stark divisions or condescending elitism.

As with other debates about Cooper's activism and scholarship, neatly bounded choices, such as trying to decide whether she was either "elitist" or "of the people," tend to oversimplify the nature of power, identity, and the historical context Cooper and her contemporaries had to negotiate. Because of her education, questions of class are quite complex in regard to Cooper: she had what we might now call "cultural capital" — or what Cooper named "social capital" ("Wage Earners"). But accruing social capital is not equivalent to perpetuating class elitism or to reinforcing (or even having) economic privilege. Cooper, for instance, never forgot where she came from (Baker-Fletcher 173, Hutchinson 60, Pellow 62) and reminded an interviewer in 1952 of her lifelong economic struggles ("Reunited Trio"). Cooper dedicated much of her life to addressing structural inequality and working with, not just on behalf of, poor African Americans.[10] She recognized how Black women's distinct gender roles were shaped by and rooted in legacies of work (Guy-Sheftall, *Daughters* 84–93; Jones), as had other Black feminists before her — including Maria Stewart, who in 1831 asked: "How long shall the fair daughters of Africa be compelled to bury their minds and talents beneath a load of iron pots and kettles?" ("Religion" 29). Like Stewart, who encouraged "independence," urging her audience to "sue for your rights and privileges," Cooper wanted African American women to be able to demand better working conditions and to fight for a better status and wage as laborers ("On Education" 255), and not be denigrated and abused, physically, emotionally, sexually, or economically. Rather than disparage Black women's employment in domestic service, the job Cooper's own mother held well into her old age, Cooper writes that she has "no word or thought averse to ... any honest toil" (255). Further clarifying her position on industrial education as a site for political struggle and not mere manual "training," she explains: "Enlightened industrialism does not mean that the body who plows cotton must study nothing but cotton and that he who would drive a mule successfully should have contact only with mules" (257).

Cooper knew from her own family's experiences that African Americans faced diverse forms of institutionalized discrimination and had little opportunity for employment other than menial work at low wages (Baker-Fletcher 133–34, Hutchinson 60). She identifies how "drudging toil" combined with widespread "poverty and destitution" (*Voice* 251–52), both in urban and rural areas, has many long-term effects on African Americans, including an inability to accumulate capital or to own property (trying to do so is "like gathering water in a sieve" 253), insufficient nourishment for mind and body, and much higher morbidity and mortality rates. About tenant farming Cooper writes: "I wonder how many know that there are throughout the Southland able bodied, hard working men, toiling year in and year out, from sunrise to dusk, for fifty cents a day ...! That they often have to take their wage in tickets convertible into meat, meal and molasses at the village grocery, owned by the same ubiquitous employer!" (252–53). As for African American women, Cooper remarks that "One often hears in the North an earnest plea from some lecturer for 'our working girls' (of course this means white working girls) .... But how many have ever given a thought to the pinched and down-trodden colored women bending over wash-tubs and ironing boards — with children to feed and house rent to pay, wood to buy, soap and starch to furnish — lugging home weekly great baskets of clothes for families who pay them for a month's laundry barely enough to purchase a substantial pair of shoes!" (254–55).

Nevertheless, many remain troubled by Cooper's allusions to True Womanhood because they seem to imply a classist outlook.[11] Washington finds that, in *A Voice from the South*, Cooper "does not imagine ordinary black working women as the basis of her feminist politics" and concludes that this is due, in part, to the fact that Cooper was "trapped in the ideological underbrush of true womanhood" (xlvi). Likewise, West critiques Cooper's "ideological wavering" and contends that her "repeated acquiescence to a discourse that ties womanhood to domesticity ironically ties her more firmly to the patriarchal ideals she attempts to overturn" (84–5). Claudia Tate asserts that this reliance on Victorian gender ideology is problematic (132, 156–7) but concludes that Cooper uses the rhetoric to argue for African Americans' access to education "as the most basic strategy for elevating themselves, their families, their communities, and ultimately their race" (160). Cooper's drawing on True Womanhood ideology is seen as perpetuating essentialist, complementary gender norms modeled on white middle-class values.

Although Guy-Sheftall agrees that many nineteenth-century women's education advocates were primarily interested in the "benefits that would accrue to society" by having more educated mothers and wives (such that the rationale for women's education was still tied to restrictive gender norms), she shows how Cooper advanced a different line of argument: "While [Cooper] agreed that such an education would make women better mothers and housekeepers, her primary concern was not education for True Womanhood. Cooper felt strongly that there were personal benefits to be gained from the pursuit of a liberal education" (*Daughters* 151). Rather than complementary feminine dependence, a relational identity and role circumscribed to the home, *self-actualization* and self-reliance are Cooper's primary concerns. Guy-Sheftall concludes, "For the first time, higher education for women is seen not simply as a means for them to help others but, as a vehicle for self-improvement, which is an end in itself" (152).

In place of advocating a "special" model of education on the basis of race, class, disability, or sex, "when it came to the question of why a person should be educated, Cooper's deepest answer seemed to be simply because they are a person" (Bailey 63). Though this has not been noted, Cooper clearly disparaged any form of segregated or "special" education; the Hannah Stanley Opportunity School, the Frelinghuysen school she founded in her mother's memory, provided "ungraded Instruction individual and elementary, to meet the needs of retarded learners" (Frelinghuysen flyer). Creating this inclusive educational space illustrates that she did not accept eugenic ideologies about race and disability. Cooper went to great lengths to fight for an education for those who were among the most subjugated within the educational system (and who continue to be unduly marginalized today; see Ferri and Connor, Losen and Orfield).[12]

Because of her unswerving liberationist inclination (Carby, *Reconstructing* 98; Baker-Fletcher 167), no matter the pedagogical milieu (school, text, public lecture, or church), Cooper's interpretive bent highlights the agential, active, and critical potential within each person. By focusing on societal structures and institutionalized limits, Cooper identifies the need to create a society in which that individual potential can be realized, not squashed. Moreover, as a reformer Cooper did not yield to gradualist paradigms, because she saw them as rationales for *resisting* rather than enacting change (Baker-Fletcher 75). This resolute refusal to uphold any notion of passivity in political life or individual consciousness is evident in her approach to women's virtues, for Cooper "proclaimed the purity and chastity — but most emphatically not the submission and domesticity — of black women" (duCille, *Coupling* 53).

Thus, in discussing "masculine" and "feminine" forms of thought (which would, at first glance, seem to fall in line with complementary True Womanhood gender ideals), Cooper insists that these qualities and outlooks are not biological per se and in fact must be learned and practiced by both sexes. Throughout her scholarship, Cooper repeatedly and vigorously argues against biological determinism. With regard to gender roles Cooper writes, "I do not ask you to admit that these benefactions and virtues are the exclusive possession of women, or even that women are their chief and only advocates. ... All I claim is that there is a feminine as well as a masculine side to truth. ... [B]oth are alike necessary in giving symmetry to the individual" (*Voice* 59–61). Cooper shows determinist gender roles and essentialist gender ideology to be inadequate social constructs, not ideal or natural essences (May 82): her gender categories are not biologically dependent (Carby, *Reconstructing* 101). Moreover, Cooper dismisses out of hand "ideologies of womanhood that had their source in codes of chivalry … as being elitist, applying only to an elect few" and as being complicit with race supremacy and domination (*Voice* 98).

Thus, Cooper's *manipulation* of concepts from True Womanhood discourse does not necessarily indicate her full *acceptance* of them, particularly when one considers that "in order to gain a public voice as orators or published writers, black women had to confront the dominant domestic ideologies and literary conventions of womanhood which excluded them from the definition 'woman'" (Carby, *Reconstructing* 6). For example, nineteenth- and twentieth-century visual representations of Black womanhood in both "low" popular iconography and "high" art have upheld this exclusionary notion of womanhood. As Lorraine O'Grady explains, "The female body in the West is not a unitary sign. Rather, like a coin, it has an obverse and a reverse: on the one side, it is white; on the other, non-white, or, prototypically, black" (14). To be precise, then, unlike Black women, who were "seen as immoral scourges" (Giddings, *When* 82), "White women had no need to vindicate their dignity in the midst of national cries that they were wanton, immoral, and socially inferior" (Terborg-Penn, "Discrimination" 21).

From this perspective, I maintain that Cooper's borrowing from True Womanhood discourse, even if in the contemporary period it seems "disappointing" (Washington xlvi), can still be read as a form of strategic redeployment. Clearly Cooper does at times seek to put her (differently) privileged audiences at ease, often by reassuring them of her confidence in their venerated beliefs — but usually just before she discredits them. Todd Vogel's analysis of Cooper's classical rhetorical techniques supports this reading. He sees Cooper as manipulating her audience via tactical references to complementary gender ideology in order to distract them from her adept use of "masculine" deductive logic. Rather than agree with True Womanhood ideology, Cooper uses it as a lure, only to dispose thoroughly of its premises.

Vogel writes, "Despite her use of deductive logic, Cooper appeared less threatening … by anchoring her reasoning in safe and familiar waters: women's claims to the domestic sphere. Once Cooper had pulled readers into that sphere and assured them of the ground rules, she could play with the audience's assumptions about women's role in society" and assert new definitions of womanhood, women's rights, and women's roles (95). Carby goes further than Vogel on this question — more than just redefining women's roles and rights, Carby sees a deep-seated critique of white women's role in white supremacy embedded in Cooper's use of True Womanhood discourse: "Cooper's conclusions were that racism was perpetuated and transmitted to future generations by women who instilled it in their children with their first food" (*Reconstructing* 104). Rather than accept the discourse, Cooper used it against itself and "exposed the historical and ideological framework within which white women defended their own class and racial interests" (102–3).

But surprisingly, Laura Behling claims that in her speech at the 1893 Columbian Exposition, Cooper plays the role of supplicant before white women. She contends that the primary reason Cooper and other Black women were invited to speak at all was that they were "safe" in that they were "least likely to challenge white standards" (180–81). She further argues that because they "subordinated their race in favor of their sex," Cooper, Coppin, and Williams "legitimized white women's social work in educating, both morally and intellectually, Black women" (176). Cooper's speech apparently shows her to be a "darker skinned replica of white women paying tribute to the humanitarianism of white society" (192). Failing to recognize Cooper's lifelong fight to dismantle white supremacy, sexism, and all forms of domination, Behling characterizes Cooper and her colleagues as duped and conciliatory. Worse, she suggests that Cooper's ideas are based in an imitation and adulation of white womanhood.

In contrast, I would argue that Cooper was no "pawn" of white women's bidding. As Carby's research illustrates, "the texts of black women from ex-slave Harriet Jacobs to educator Anna Julia Cooper are testaments to the racist practices of the suffrage and temperance movements and indictments of the ways in which white women allied themselves … with a racist patriarchal order" (*Reconstructing* 6). Cooper's rhetorical stance is not one of compliance: consider that Shirley Logan finds this very same speech remarkable not for Cooper's acquiescence, but instead because "it presents a feisty, no-nonsense Cooper, less willing ... to accommodate or to identify with the white women to whom she spoke" ('*We*' 113). In addition, Cooper emphasizes the particular struggle Black women had enacted to protect the sanctity of their own bodies and persons: "the painful, patient, and silent toil of mothers to gain a fee simple title to the bodies of their daughters, the despairing fight, as of an entrapped tigress, to keep hallowed their own persons, would furnish material for epics" ("Intellectual" 202). Pointing to legacies of resistance to sexual violence and abuse, Cooper breaks the polite veneer of silence stifling the truth about white men raping Black women as a tool of domination. Therefore, she clearly does *not* portray white society as either "humanitarian" or beneficent, nor does she rank her race as secondary to or separate from her gender. Instead, Cooper demonstrates how sexism and racism intertwine.

Moreover, Cooper's use of the phrase "*would* furnish material for epics" to end her sentence focuses attention on Black women's particular struggles (since an epic is a grand narrative of heroism and legendary battle) and simultaneously points to the exclusion of Black women's lives and stories from literary, historical, and philosophical canons. She underscores how these events have been relegated to the realm of the particular: they are not considered "universal" stories to live by and learn from. Cooper proceeds to reject categorically white women's objectifying benevolence. She shifts the focus of the "discussion from a [patronizing] question of what can be done to help black women to what must be done to help 'the cause of every man and of every woman who has writhed silently under a mighty wrong'" (S. Logan, '*We*' 114). Although it appears that Cooper's primary focus is on the domestic sphere[13] and Black women's claims to that space and role (already a somewhat radical move in that their morality, sexuality, and labor were consistently maligned through both stereotype and patently biased science), ultimately Cooper's larger argument centers on the need to foster Black women's agency and intellect so that they may fully actualize themselves, contribute to the public good, and take their rightful place as thoughtful, active citizens of the nation.

Wrestling with Domination: Decoding Cooper's Multivocality

Frances Smith Foster documents that the "extant literature from 1746 to 1892 ... proves that African American women, like African American men, deliberately chose to participate in the public discourse despite considerable Anglo-American resistance to their doing so. They appropriated the English literary tradition to reveal, to interpret, to challenge, and to change perceptions of themselves and the world in which they found themselves" (16). As contemporary readers, we must keep in mind this history of appropriation and "considerable resistance." Also relevant here is Bogues's insight that "black radical intellectual production engages in a double operation" of engagement and critique (*Heretics* 13). Thus, what if we attend at least as much to the figurative, allegorical, and ambiguous in Cooper's writings as to the literal, declarative, and factual? I contend that we could begin to see different registers of meaning in her words if we did not try to straighten out Cooper's bending of voice, if we stopped desiring singularity out of her "mingling of languages" (K. Holloway 620).

As a writer, teacher, and activist, Cooper refused to succumb to the pressure of the iron thumb of domination: she was nobody's fool. Yet she wrote, fought, and lived in a world that sought to suppress alternative viewpoints through legislation, through the social imagination, and even through state-sanctioned violence in the form of lynching and rape. Of course, she points to this in her mockery of the panic over Black "domination" that, since the time of slavery, "cowers in the white man's heart" despite the fact that whites "outnumber [Blacks] five to one, with every advantage in civilization, wealth, culture, with absolute control of every civil and military nerve center" ("Ethics" 214). Cooper suggests that whites' constant effort to regulate and reinforce a hierarchical social order reveals it to be constructed, not "natural" — an important distinction and insight on her part.

But this does not mean that Cooper was naively optimistic about social change. Here is a fear of otherness and racial difference so great that whites seek to reinforce their ostensibly "natural" supremacy via violent material, philosophical, and institutional means. As Bogues documents, the "defeat of Reconstruction ... marked the reorganization of America as a racial state of white supremacy. The character of this reorganization was bolstered by the development and popularity of a set of ideas about human evolution, biology, and the manifest destiny of the Anglo-Saxons" (*Heretics* 52). Cooper therefore insists on renaming this historical period to expose what was really going on. She writes that Reconstruction "would be more properly termed the period of white sullenness and desertion of duty" (*Voice* 192). Later, she describes the "progressive" era that followed as "the most trying period of all [colored people's] trying history in this land of their trial and bondage" ("Ethics" 207–8): it was a time when "colorphobia" and "prejudice" (208) reigned supreme, alongside rampant materialism and an "Accursed hunger for gold" (207).

To the supposed threat of Black domination Cooper sardonically retorts: "Negro domination! Think of it! The great American eagle, soaring majestically sunward, eyes ablaze with conscious power, suddenly screaming and shivering in fear of a little mouse colored starling, which he may crush with the smallest finger of his great claw" (214). Cooper's contemporary Ida B. Wells also debunked the "invented" pretense of "Negro domination," the "alleged menace" of "wild beasts" endangering white females whose individual "honor" must be defended as an inherent part of the national "honor." Wells argues that the "wholesale murder of human beings" was thereby rationalized as a justifiable deterrence strategy, even though it was merely invented to "palliate" the crime of lynching and had no basis in fact ("Lynch Law").

As is readily apparent in Cooper's own wording, the "trying period" in which she wrote and worked was an era of overt abuse of "conscious power." It "represented a high point for the native-born white and the nadir for blacks, as historian Rayford Logan observed" (Guy-Sheftall, *Daughters* 159).[14] The period was also marked by particular kinds of gendered racism, or racist sexism, for Black women: as Cooper's contemporary Lawson A. Scruggs (a fellow North Carolinian and an ally of African American activist women) commented in 1892, "When an Afro-American woman does arrive at any eminence, it is well known that she has *fought* a *fierce* and *bloody battle* almost *every step of her way*" (207, italics original).

Cooper therefore had the onus of writing, teaching, and speaking out against the predominant "supremacist metaphysics" (Watson 477) of her time, including theories of dominance and inferiority centered on innate hierarchies of race, sex, disability, and class as well as xenophobic and evolutionary notions of nation/civilization. This was true not only in the 1890s, at the beginning of her writing career, but throughout her lifetime. For instance, in 1925, her chief doctoral examiner at the Sorbonne, the Durkheimian sociologist Célestin Bouglé, believed in an evolutionary hierarchy of world civilizations, with the "Nordic" ones being more "naturally" suited to democracy (Lemert and Bhan 270). His highly influential *Les idées égalitaires: une étude sociologique*, which Cooper had been assigned for her oral *soutenance* or dissertation defense, was in its third printing in 1925. Although Bouglé had the power to decide whether Cooper would receive her Ph.D., she refuted his ideas both in her dissertation and in her doctoral exams.[15] In the meantime, while facing her Sorbonne examiners, Cooper almost lost her job at Dunbar back home; district administrators fought her every step of the way in her decade-long battle to earn her doctorate (Hutchinson 131–53).

Moreover, many of Cooper's contemporaries, who might be considered her allies and colleagues more than (outright or obvious) adversaries, including black male activists and white feminists, also internalized these hierarchies of personhood. For instance, at the 1925 meeting of the International Council of Women in Washington, D.C., "Because Afro-Americans would be in attendance, the Daughters of the American Revolution refused to allow the ICW to use the auditorium of Memorial Continental Hall. When it was agreed among the whites that Afro-Americans would not have open seating but would be required to sit in a segregated gallery, the members of the [black] NACW walked out" (Neverdon-Morton 201). This kind of action on the part of white feminist organizations was not new. For example, in 1903 the NAWSA (National American Woman Suffrage Association) board "endorsed the organization's state's rights position, which was tantamount to an endorsement of white supremacy in most states." In addition, "Despite endorsement of black suffrage, Anna Howard Shaw [(president of NAWSA from 1901 to 1915)] had been accused of refusing to allow a black female delegate at the Louisville suffrage convention in 1911 to make an antidiscrimination resolution" (Terborg-Penn, "Discrimination" 24).

Furthermore, Cooper openly rebuked Shaw in 1892 for her exclusionary politics and myopic thinking. Shaw posed the problem of women's rights as that of "Woman versus the Indian," so that women end up "plaintiffs" in a ridiculous lawsuit Cooper aptly names "Eye vs. Foot." In contrast, Cooper advocated a politics of solidarity so that all marginalized and oppressed groups might gain their rights together. She asked, "Why should woman become plaintiff in a suit versus the Indian, or the Negro or any other race or class who have been crushed under the iron heel of Anglo-Saxon power and selfishness?" (*Voice* 123). Cooper clarified that the truly "philosophic mind" — that is, Cooper's and her black feminist colleagues' — "sees that its own 'rights' are the rights of humanity." In contrast, "All prejudices, whether of race, sect, or sex, class pride and caste distinctions are the belittling inheritance and badge of snobs and prigs" (that is, Anna Shaw and her NAWSA compatriots) (118).

This inability on the part of white feminists to imagine a multifaceted definition of womanhood and actively to pursue meaningful coalition politics was not new. Unfortunately, neither was the willingness of white women to engage in behind-the-scenes "agreements" across regional and national bounds, nor their diehard attachment to Jim Crow white supremacy — or "chivalry," as Cooper wryly called it — as an inherent part of what it meant to be female and feminist. These tenacious ties to a white middle-class concept of nation and of womanhood were, and in many ways continue to be, poisonous to relations among feminists across the lines of race and class.

Certainly, racism on the part of white feminists is only one example of the obstacles someone like Cooper faced. As Guy-Sheftall observes, "That black and white men had similar conceptions of womanhood is indicative of the extent to which members of a given culture, despite their ethnic identity, accept, at least to some degree, the sex-role stereotypes foisted upon them by virtually every institution. This means that black women must confront the sexist attitudes of black and white men alike" (*Daughters* 159). There is ample evidence of prominent black men spouting sexist platitudes and proclaiming masculinist definitions of "the race." For example, the influential scholar, civil rights leader, and lawyer Kelly Miller, who would become dean of Howard University (and whose views on women were not anomalous), wrote to the NAACP magazine *The Crisis* in 1915 about "The Risk of Woman Suffrage." Miller proclaimed, "Woman is physically weaker than man and is incapable of competing with him in the stern and strenuous activities of public ... life" (in Guy-Sheftall, *Daughters* 72). Arguing that no women actually "needed" the vote, including Black women, Miller added, "The Negro [male] cannot get justice or fair treatment without the suffrage. Woman can make no such claim, for man accords her not only every privilege which he himself enjoys but the additional privilege of protection" (in Cuthbert 78, fn. 13).

Such attitudes were a constant in the lives of Black feminists. For instance, twenty-three years prior to Miller's 1915 public assertion of women's weaknesses, Cooper had already protested that "the colored woman too often finds herself hampered and shamed by a less liberal sentiment and a more conservative attitude on the part of those for whose opinion she cares most. ... [T]he average man of our race is less frequently ready to admit the actual need among the sturdier forces of the world for woman's help or influence" (*Voice* 134–35). Almost forty years later, in outlining her "Racial Philosophy," Cooper suggests that this kind of thinking had not diminished. She writes, "We women are generally left to do our race battling alone except for empty compliments now and then" ("Racial" 236). Here she privately disparages the powerful Miller's lack of understanding of institutionalized oppression, evident in what she sarcastically refers to as his "one time suggestion of self-effacement" as a viable strategy to deal with the realities of racism (237). Yet Cooper did not succumb to the masculinism found, explicitly or implicitly, in a wide array of Black activist and educational organizations, including the American Negro Academy, the Niagara Movement, and even the M Street School. Neither did she give in to the tenacious white supremacy within feminist organizations.[16]

Thus, even if we stand by the standard criteria of "leadership" in the social movement literature, Cooper's life work clearly fits these measures. In her varied roles, Cooper helped to "provide an ideology justifying action," to educate both "followers and leaders," to attain public support as well as express the concerns and needs of her community, and to delineate goals and suggest solutions (Barnett 167). Moreover, if we move beyond a gendered division of activist labor ("leading" versus "organizing") in the history of civil rights and feminist political action, we can better recognize Black women's advocacy of participatory democracy, creation of autonomous community spaces and networks, and uses of rhetorical and classroom spaces to teach critical consciousness as effective forms of radical action. As Gayle Tate argues, we must not measure the worth or courage of social change agents only by singular, public events (such as rebellions or revolutions): less obvious forms of resistance are also powerful in effecting change. She identifies more covert forms of political action, including the "creation of psychic shelter," the use of folktales to pass on oppositional knowledge, creative and tenacious forms of survival, "socialization in subversion," and the teaching of affirmation or self-love (35–57).

Certainly, Cooper's activism, whether textual or organizational in form, and whether overt or covert in nature, has not been fully appreciated. In looking back on her work, it is important to think about what it means to persevere under circumstances of constraint and to recognize in her words and actions a refusal to be defeated by deliberate obstacles, unkind feeling, and malicious prejudice. As an educator and public intellectual interested in social transformation, Cooper did not merely refuse supremacist philosophies on an individual level: she sought collective change. In addressing the wider public, though, Cooper had to navigate long-standing and deep forms of resistance to Black women's "talking back" (hooks, *Talking* 5). Moreover, she had to develop narrative strategies by which her voice could be heard, with which she could begin to navigate the likely "fetishization" of what she, as a Black woman, had to say (Shohat 9). The trouble lies in the fact that although "multiple publics exist ... in a stratified society these multiple publics have unequal access to the dissemination of ideas" (Kelly 126).

As Cooper points out, "White America has created a *terra incognita* in its midst, a strange dark unexplored waste of human souls from which if one essay to speak out an intelligible utterance, so well known is the place of preferment accorded to the mirroring of preconceived notions that instead of being the revelation of personality and the voice of a truth, the speaker becomes a phonograph and merely talks back what is talked into him" ("Ethics" 209). Attending to these hostile sites of "preferment" and contentious contexts pushes us, as contemporary readers, to realize the extent to which Cooper was radical and outspoken in her time, even if today her words may not seem resistant because much of her critique is indirect, underground, or double-voiced. As Trinh T. Minh-ha explains, "Just because we who are marginalized *adapt* our positions to our circumstances does not mean we *submit* to them!" (*Cinema* 191, italics original).

Cooper emphatically tells us that she does *not* want to be listened to as if she were merely a "phonograph," nor does she plan to stay in her "place" — a place that is, in any case, no place, a terrain of absence and of the unimaginable, *terra incognita*. She utterly rejects being used as a mirror to reflect what the dominant "world" already knows. As Marlon Riggs would ask nearly a century later, "My mouth moves, but you hear your own words. What nature of ventriloquism is this?" ("Unleash" 103). Therefore, coming to voice or daring is not Cooper's only challenge. As Baker-Fletcher suggests, when Cooper uses the metaphor of "muteness" in *A Voice from the South*, it

> is not simply a referent to Black women's silence. It refers to their *subjugation*. It is a signifier for the multiplicity of oppressive acts employed to silence them. The muffled strain of the Negro, startling to Euro-American ears with its cry for liberty, justice, and equality, the assertion of the innate freedom of each voice, is a jarring sound to those whose will for power is based in selfish greed and a desire for domination. (136, italics original)

To be precise, then, the reversals, opacities, and layers in Cooper's writing signal a desire to enact change alongside a recognition of the fact that the fabric of language is shot through with power. María Lugones describes how, although such ambiguity may *seem* paradoxical, a sign of illogical uncertainty or analytic haziness, it can be a form of "survival-rich" ambiguity that is inherently a sign neither of surrender nor of accommodation. This type of ambiguity, she argues, illustrates a refusal to succumb or adapt fully to the dominator's world and, at the same time, highlights the limitations and exclusions of that world ("Playfulness" 395–98). It is essential, therefore, to attend not just to what Cooper says in a literal sense, but also to trace the spirit of her words and ideas as they unfold by noticing allusions, hearing sarcasm, and unpacking allegories.

I do not want to brush aside questioning of Cooper's tone or syntax, or entirely to disregard her manipulation of problematic discourses. However, it is crucial to heed bell hooks's reminder that "when the radical voice speaks about domination we are speaking to those who dominate. Their presence changes the nature and direction of our words. Language is also a place of struggle" (*Yearning* 146). She concludes that "While [a counter-language] may resemble the colonizer's tongue, it has undergone a transformation" (149). Consequently, just to be *heard*, and not wanting to be confined to that *terra incognita* she was expected to occupy, Cooper had to develop methodological strategies that would invite potentially obdurate audiences to rethink established ontological and epistemological assumptions and to abandon hallowed theological, philosophical, historical, and ethical presuppositions. As a teacher, activist, and scholar, Cooper had to conjure an audience for a Black feminist politics of resistance.

To understand the world from her standpoint, Cooper's audience must be willing to participate in a major epistemic shift, to change taken-for-granted ideas about self, other, and everyday reality. Cooper, ever the teacher, devises a textual method or "pedagogy" to invite this decentering, to create space for an altered, other-oriented imagination to take shape. And yet, as Gloria Anzaldúa reminds us, the "path to *conocimiento*" — to transforming consciousness — is neither linear nor easy ("Now" 540–43): like Cooper's philosophical method and textual voice, this path is varied, curved, and multilayered because it starts from "the overlapping space between different perceptions and belief systems" (541). As the next chapter explores, Cooper's painstaking methodology and calculated narrative voice embody her struggle against those who would prefer to twist her analyses into a comfortable, reassuring mirroring of the self-same. Refusing readerly control, she contests those who would curb her oppositional voice into a kind of compliant, predictable background music to be played for soothing entertainment on the "phonograph."[17]

CHAPTER **3**

"If you object to imaginary lines — don't draw them!"[1]

Cooper's Border-Crossing Methods

A key reason that Cooper's method and voice can be difficult to characterize has to do with the ways in which political struggle, cognitive resistance,
and corporeal revaluation affect her arguments and shape her sentences.
Because language can be riddled with ideologies that conflict with one's
own values and basic assumptions and that stigmatize one's body, even der-
ogate one's person, the act of writing entails working within and simultaneously resisting "prevailing mode[s] of being" (Anzaldúa, "Haciendo" xxii).
Cooper had to devise a way to write against the grain and still be understood, to fight epistemic erasure and oppressive modes of thinking yet meet
her audiences where they were, to acknowledge and name the destructive
effects of sexual violence and degrading stereotypes without internalizing
or reinforcing them. It is this constant navigation of treacherous waters
that can be uncovered in Cooper's winding, multidirectional sentences, her
double-voiced strategies, and her nonlinear forms of argumentation.

There is plenty of evidence in Cooper's work to indicate that she knew
she was writing against the grain, battling dehumanizing assumptions,
even as she extolled the wonders of liberty and democracy.[2] Although
Cooper states with confidence that she will surely receive a "fair trial" and
will be "heard" by her impartial audience (*Voice* ii), she also anticipates
that she will be seen as a representative of "a people who are habitually
reasoned about *en masse* as separate, distinct, and peculiar" (Cooper, "On
Education" 250). She therefore spends ample time establishing her author-

ity as a knower. To those who might doubt a woman's capacity to reason or to speak publicly, Cooper recalls the precedent set by "Sappho, the bright, sweet singer of Lesbos," Aspasia, author "of one of the most noted speeches ever delivered by Pericles" (*Voice* 62–3), the Native American rights activist Helen Hunt Jackson, the Quaker abolitionist and feminist Lucretia Mott, and Dorothea Dix, a social advocate for the mentally ill (128). In case her audience specifically rejects Black women's rationality, creative capacity, and political authority, Cooper points to the contributions of the author Frances Watkins Harper, "who could sing with prophetic exaltation," the orator and activist Sojourner Truth, "that unique and rugged genius," the educator Hallie Quinn Brown, "effective lecturer and devoted worker," Fannie Jackson Coppin, "teacher and organizer, pre-eminent among women of whatever country or race" (140–2), the sculptor Edmonia Lewis (276), and the poet Phillis Wheatley, who "paid her debts *in song*" (275, italics original).[3]

By acknowledging her contemporaries and identifying her predecessors, Cooper emphasizes that she is not a lone voice: she stands on the shoulders of others and directs her audience not to tokenize her as if she were "exceptional."[4] She also stresses that adulation and denigration are twin sides of the same problematic form of perception: objectification. Cooper writes:

> There are sections of this country in which the very name of the Negro ... stirs up such a storm of [negative] feeling that men fairly grow wild and are unfit to discuss the simplest principles of life and conduct where the colored man is concerned. ... [T]here are a few nooks and crannies, on the other hand ... in which that name embodies an idealized theory and a benevolent sentiment; and the black man (the blacker the better) is the petted nursling, the haloed idea, the foregone conclusion. (*Voice* 230)

Cooper instructs her readers that she wants neither to be put on a pedestal nor disparaged: she wants to be recognized as an equal giving testimony "at the bar" and suggests that her audience approach her as such (ii).

"Frankly, I think my color will be a barrier"[5]: Navigating Disjointed Realities

Thus, at the same time that Cooper asserts the promise of democratic meritocracy and professes her faith in an equal rhetorical field, her myriad efforts to establish her authority suggest that she knows there are holes in the premises she declares she has faith in. Later, Cooper expresses her skepticism more overtly. In a 1930 essay, "The Humor of Teaching," she warns Black teachers not to internalize racism and not to be overly enamored with white-mandated education standards, school curricula, or textbooks, but instead to believe in their own authority and that of their students. Cooper writes, "A white man doesn't always mean all he says in a book, and hardly ever does all he suggests in a speech. A lecturer must sell his books. ... He must get out a new edition of an old thought. ... By and by another 'authority' comes along with another brand new wrinkle; ridicules all you've been told ... and proceeds to give you the latest, the only true and accepted" theories ("Humor" 234).

Charles W. Mills explains that marginalized people frequently "know that what is in the books ... [was] never intended to be applicable to them in the first place, but that within the structure of power relations, as part of the routine, one has to pretend that it does" (*Visible* 4). Of course, today we cannot conclude definitively that Cooper pretends to believe in the ideologies she seems to admire, but Mills's insights suggest that what may look to contemporary readers to be merely Cooper's flattery of her audience, apparent veneration of universal reason, or trust in humanism may in fact signal how, "as part of the routine," she might have had to assert her belief in these ideals to be rhetorically and politically persuasive, even if she knew (and went on to prove in her own research) that they were not considered applicable to oppressed groups or were not conceived with them in mind. In this regard, bell hooks would later remark, "There may be no ready audience for my words" (*Yearning* 24–25).

Cooper's textual efforts to be understood do not stem only from abstract, theoretical concerns about tokenism, methodology, or narrative authority: they also reflect the considerable, tangible difficulties she faced trying to get her work published. For example, realizing at the age of one hundred that nobody else would be likely to publish her analytic essay about ethics, race, and national identity, "The Ethics of the Negro Question" (1902), or her linguistic and cultural studies essay, "The Negro's Dialect" (1930s?), Cooper deposited $279.65 in an account to ensure their publication.[6] Repeatedly, she had asked W. E. B. Du Bois to publish her biography of the Grimkés, but to no avail.[7] And although not a lot is known about the circumstances surrounding the publication and distribution of her other writings, we do know that Cooper met with outright prejudice in her attempts to distribute and copyright, in the United States, her highly regarded translation from medieval French into modern French of the eleventh-century epic, *The Pilgrimage of Charlemagne* (a text, incidentally, known for its subtle uses of parody, a literary technique also effectively used by Cooper in her own work).

After a few summers at La Guilde Internationale in Paris, Cooper began doctoral coursework in 1914 at Columbia University and started her glos-

sary and translation of *The Pilgrimage*. Completed in 1917, the translation counted toward her doctoral requirements at Columbia. Unable to
fulfill Columbia's residency requirement, she later published *Le Pèlerinage
de Charlemagne* in 1925 in Paris, where it was well received.[8] But in the
United States, despite demand for her Paris edition (e.g., it was used in
courses at Harvard [Shilton] and portions were reprinted in an anthology of medieval French literature[9]), Cooper could not secure an American
distributor because of racism. In fact, she could not even *donate* her 500
bound copies of the text to her "beloved Alma Mater," Oberlin College, for
their fundraising campaign (Shilton). Correspondence from the Oberlin
archives demonstrates the accuracy of Cooper's fear that her "personality"
(i.e., her race, and to a lesser degree her gender) would impede publication
of her work in the United States (Shilton).[10]

Cooper's need to assure us of her "right" to speak and be heard, alongside
her well-founded fear that prejudice would negatively affect her everyday
life as a scholar, educator, and activist and would bring about the belittle-
ment, if not total refusal, of her ideas, suggests that she was trying to negotiate at least two worlds at once in her texts and in her life: an ideal world
in which her personhood would not be questioned and, simultaneously,
lived reality in which she had to contest daily the weight of being perceived
and treated as "other." Regularly, Cooper had to keep alive her dream of
a transformed, equitable world and insist upon her inherent metaphysical
value while at the same time deflecting what she describes as countless
"studied attempts at persecution and humiliation"[11] that arose because of
her ongoing refusal as a scholar, teacher, and activist to comply with the
terms and expectations of the status quo.

Given this bifurcated reality, Mills argues that marginalized people's "fight
for their personhood" is only sometimes "overt; at other times, circumstances
will make it necessary for resistance to be clandestine, coded" (*Visible* 112).
If we are careful to notice it, Cooper suggests as much in her allusion to the
biblical parable of Lazarus (*Voice* 24). Baker-Fletcher explains:

> Through a play on words, Cooper recalled the biblical story of the
> rich man and Lazarus, the poor man who begged for crumbs outside
> the rich man's doors (Luke 16:19–31). Like the rich man who went to
> hell when he died and yearned to come up from the dead to warn his
> relatives about the imminence of death and the threat of hell, Cooper
> 'came up from the South' to plead deliverance from socio-economic
> inequality for Black women. Just as Abraham told the rich man that
> 'though one came up from the dead' none would hear him, Cooper
> questioned her audience's ability to hear what she had to say. (47)

Cooper suspects that her words may not be heeded, and so, through analogy, calls her audience out on its bias while placing herself in the role of Abraham. Obliquely, she asserts the visionary nature of her ideas. Although Cooper claims to build on the prophecy of the "king" or "Moses" known as the Reverend Alexander Crummell (*Voice* 24), she implicitly *surpasses* him in authority as "she is the very subject of which he speaks — she is a black woman from the South, not a distant observer." By means of association, Cooper intimates that *she*, in fact, may be more than (or as much as) Crummell the "embodiment of Moses and the prophets" (West 85).

Cooper's many modes of address, including her uses of parable, analogy, derision, and humor, suggest she is speaking with a "forked tongue" (Anzaldúa, *Borderlands* 55). Anzaldúa emphasizes that "code-switching" is not simply about tonal modulation or language variation: it is a weapon employed to contend with the violent suppression of voice and difference (80) and to fight against disparities in rhetorical, cultural, epistemological, and material power. Similarly, Cooper's use of code-switching (suddenly changing from flattery to sarcastic critique, for instance) often provides her with a way out of what she calls "the perplexing *cul de sac* of the nation" to which she has been relegated (*Voice* i). Rejecting her role as a silenced "skeleton in the closet" (i), Cooper uses her voice to debunk coercive modes of reasoning, to defy ontological subjugation, and to refuse stifling historical interpretations, for the "God of history," she wryly concludes, "often chooses the weak things of earth to confound the mighty" (299).[12]

Though Cooper is clearly determined to defeat her detractors and triumph over her oppressors, here, through humor, she also indicates the inherently incommensurable rather than equal rhetorical and ontological position from which she, a "weak thing," is trying to speak to, and conquer, "the mighty." Recently Ofelia Schutte has described similar dynamics of "incommensurability" as they play out in the predicament she names the "problem of the culturally successful Latina." To claim her "position as a cultural agent in terms recognized by the dominant cultural group," Schutte explains how she needs "to be knowledgeable in the language and epistemic maneuvers of the dominant culture." Yet no matter how knowledgeable she becomes in that language and episteme, she still confronts a conundrum because these are the very same linguistic and philosophical practices that "mark" her as "other" in the first place (53). Like Cooper, Schutte is expected to "discursively perform the speaking position ... of the dominant culture" so that she can be "recognized as a real agent in the real world," even if this modality of speaking "exists in tension" with, and to some degree "shuts out," even erases, what she knows differently and seeks to express (54). It is in this context that we can characterize Cooper's efforts to be heard as a form of "verbal warfare for human dignity" (S. Logan, 'We' 1).

Though just a common, black-winged bird — a "starling" — Cooper aims to disrupt the dominant reality and oppressive power of the "eagle" (Cooper, "Ethics" 214). Nevertheless, the predicament of contending with an incommensurability of speaking position, cultural power, and epistemic authority does bear on Cooper's scholarship. As Bogues explains, for the "black radical intellectual there is a profound disjuncture between the lived experiences of being a racial/colonial subject and the account of this lived experience by his or her learned discursive system. This disjuncture … is the source of acute tension in the political discourses of many radical black thinkers" (*Heretics* 14). Bogues's astute observations offer insight as to why, generally speaking, the "ambiguities and tensions in [Cooper's] writing defy easy explanation" (Bailey 59): she reveals an "intimacy with the discourse of the Other" and, like many other Black women writers to follow, incorporates "into [her] work competing and complementary discourses" (Henderson 124). By using this methodological dialectic of appropriation and subversion,[13] Cooper's analyses contest the historical, material, political and epistemological conditions under which she wrote and, at the same time, are also affected by them.

Accordingly, rather than signs of incoherence or illogical analysis, some of the apparent inconsistencies in Cooper's work[14] can be understood to reflect underlying "acute" tensions about the meanings of race, gender, and nation in the polity at large. Again, at the most basic level, Cooper has the onus of proving her humanity, her intellectual capacity, and her right to speak. Moreover, supremacist theories of humanity have played out in particularly excruciating ways upon Black women's bodies: there are specific racist-sexist tools of dehumanization that Cooper had to navigate, which must be acknowledged. Perhaps the most pervasive and pernicious of these strategies has been "the repeated refrain in white racist political discourse among men and women … [about] the immorality and promiscuity of Black women" (Cole and Guy-Sheftall 77).

For example, as Guy-Sheftall points out, the influential Georges Leopold Cuvier's ostensibly neutral and purely anatomical examination of Saartjie Baartman focused primarily on her genitalia and her skull to emphasize her innate difference, even different species status. Cuvier concluded "that he had 'never seen a human head more resembling a monkey's than hers'" (in Guy-Sheftall, "Body" 18). However, in contrast to analyses like Cuvier's, which reveal a presumption of an inherent "partitioned social ontology" (Mills, *Racial* 16), Cooper appropriates this subjugation and marginality — her having *not* been thought either rational or a full person — and suggests that they provide her with a distinctive outsider-within understanding that makes her a "touchstone" of ethics, objectivity, and rationality (*Voice* ii–iii, 93, 138–9). Cooper refutes, and asks her audience to rethink, widely accepted notions of rationality — what its characteristics are and who "has" it.

For instance, Cooper exposes illogic and blatant sexism in Auguste Comte's influential positivism, a "philosophy of *natural science*, originating in and proved by pure observation and investigation of physical phenomena" (*Voice* 293). Dryly, Cooper points out that Comte posited non-universal "man" as the observer, with the "*loving sex*" — "one's wife, mother, and daughter" — as the observed, or "the ones to be worshipped; though he does not set forth who were to be the objects of woman's" thought (292, italics original). Comte's sexist bias is clearly *not* "pure": it is his foregone conclusion that women are irrational and emotional or, at best, mere objects of "worship," while the supposedly neutral knower is definitively male, and therefore not universal. In her mockery of venerated tenets of positivism, agnosticism, and skepticism, and pointing to the implicit exclusion built into debates about "man" and "reason," Cooper also quotes Robert Green Ingersoll[15]: "'The average man,' says Mr. Ingersoll, 'does not reason — he feels.'" Cooper adds, "surely 'twere presumption for an average woman to attempt more. For my part I am content to 'feel.' The brave Switzer who sees the awful avalanche stealing down the mountain side threatening death and destruction to all he holds dear, hardly needs any very correct ratiocination on the mechanical and chemical properties of ice" (294–95).

Here Cooper discredits some cherished (and normalized) philosophical binaries: reason versus emotion, man versus woman, white versus black. Moreover, in ridiculing what she calls "theoretical symmetry and impregnable logic" (283), and deriding philosophies founded on supposedly "universally" replicable observations of phenomena to be "paraded pretty much in the spirit of the college sophomore who affects gold-bowed spectacles … — it is scholarly, you know" (296), Cooper pushes for a more holistic epistemology in which feelings and thoughts together are recognized as epistemologically significant. Thus she rejects the fact/value distinction — the idea that natural facts are inanimate, simply there to be observed or discovered, whereas value belongs to the realm of human sentiment and partiality, such that "good" or reliable knowledge practices must entail abstraction or protection from the bias that value would introduce to the knowing process. Cooper exposes how value, situation, and context all affect the knowing process, even in the cases of illustrious agnostics (Ingersoll) and positivists (Comte) who practice "pure" observation.

Rather than universally replicable observations of "physical phenomena" and "paradable" propositions, Cooper advocates situational knowing grounded in the particulars of lived experience. To create space in the polity for her body and her ideas (her ontological presence and epistemological expertise), she endeavors to revise, from her standpoint as a Black woman, the nation's history and self-concept, particularly the origins of capitalist democracy, and invites her audience to shift its point of view and modify its historical memory as well. Therefore, rather than glorify the founding fathers and first settlers, Cooper takes them down off their pedestal to outline how "these jugglers with reason and conscience" simultaneously declared "a religion of sublime altruism" while engaging in the slave trade, "forcing [slaves] with lash and gun to unrequited toil, making it a penal offense to teach them to read the Word of God," and raped black women while "pocketing the guilty increase, the price of their own blood in unholy dollars and cents" ("Ethics" 207). Given this history of human exploitation used to gain wealth and power for some at the expense of others, Cooper calls for reparations in the form of subsidizing Black education, stating that other people's full "coffers" and "our present poverty [are] due to ... two hundred and fifty years [of our] digging trenches, building roads, tunneling mountains, clearing away forests, cultivating the soil in the cotton fields and rice swamps till fingers dropped off, toes were frozen, knees twisted" (*Voice* 193).

Cooper also reminds her readers that African Americans have been at the core, not the margins, of American political and cultural life: "Homogeneous or not, the national web is incomplete without the African thread that glints and ripples thro it from the beginning" ("Ethics" 213; see also *Voice* 224–5). By characterizing this thread in the fabric of the nation as glinting, Cooper affirms both her African roots and her American belonging: she makes clear that there is no contradiction in so doing. In addition, she asserts that African Americans have been here as long as anyone, save for Native Americans, who have "the best right to call themselves 'Americans' by law of primogeniture" (*Voice* 163) and who have endured the violent "occupancy" of their land and nation by refusing to partake in this so-called civilization (194).

In crafting her arguments, Cooper has to walk a tightrope: she has to establish her personhood and, simultaneously, controvert her "subpersonhood" in the *operative* "differential and hierarchical social ontology" of the nation, as opposed to the *idealized* democratic ontology of human equality and universal rights (Mills, *Racial* 101). Mills defines "subpersonhood" as an essential component of the racial contract (white supremacy) that masquerades as the seemingly neutral social contract of liberal political theory. Although social contract theory insists on the universality of all persons in the polity, at the same time it also delineates another "subset of humans," supposedly closer to (or still in) a "state of nature." Mills explains that such persons have "a different and inferior moral status, subpersons, so that they have a subordinate civil standing in the white or white-ruled polities" (*Racial* 11). For example, Collins's analysis of representations of Black sexuality illustrates a particular manifestation of the racial contract outlined by Mills. She writes: "Whether depicted as 'freaks' of nature or as being the essence of nature itself, savage, untamed sexuality characterizes Western representations of women and men of African descent" (*Black Sexual* 27).

Occasionally, rather than confront these premises head on, Cooper ostensibly obliges proponents of "state of nature" theories and agrees that yes, perhaps African Americans can be thought parallel to nature — that is, if you have the exceptionally beautiful, distinctively American, and awe-inspiring grandeur of Yosemite in mind (*Voice* 178). Yet at other times, Cooper directly challenges theories of subpersonhood and the political and philosophical binaries distinguishing the "state of nature" from "civilization." Pointing to the kinds of odious queries that stem from ontological hierarchies, Cooper shows contempt for those who ask her questions about "her people's" suitability for full membership in the polity. Sardonically, she writes, "Is it not a mistake to suppose that the same old human laws apply to *these people?* Is there not after all something within that dark skin not yet dreamt of in *our* philosophy? Can we *seriously* take the Negro as a man 'endowed by [his] Creator with certain unalienable rights' such as 'Life, Liberty, pursuit of Happiness' and the right to grow up, to develop, to reason and to live his life?" ("Ethics" 212, emphasis added).

Of course, the "subpersonhood" Cooper fights/writes against is multiply "othered." Consequently, she seeks to find a means to assert her humanity and "claim the moral status of personhood" (Mills, *Racial* 118) in a way that does not subsume one "subperson" identity category to another via a "hierarchy of oppressions" framework (Combahee 275, B. Smith xxviii). Cooper wants to prove her womanhood and yet reject white middle-class notions of what being a woman means (e.g., *Voice* 80–126). Simultaneously, she wishes to affirm her blackness but refuse a masculinist definition of race and racial belonging (e.g., *Voice* 31, 75–78). In addition, Cooper seeks to demonstrate how, as a Black woman, she is a model "American," and yet to decry the nation's building itself up via genocide of Native Americans and violent dependence upon and perpetuation of African slavery (e.g., 163–74). Moreover, Cooper critiques xenophobia, as in her provocative mockery of "America for Americans!" chauvinism. Cooper writes, "America for Americans! This is the white man's country! The Chinese must go. ... Exclude the Italians! Colonize the blacks in Mexico or deport them to Africa" (*Voice* 163). Rather than resort to the default "American" violent solution to cultural differences, to "Lynch, suppress, drive out, kill out!" (163), Cooper calls for her readers to understand how global and local politics and concerns interconnect so that exclusionary, intolerant models of "freedom" or of "nation" are insufficient and small-minded.

Acknowledging the range of conceptual structures, power inequities, and ontological imbalances (P. Williams 45) affecting Cooper's narrative structure and speaking position, and understanding the many ways in which there is no inherently "free" space from which to write, is essential to deciphering her flexible, multifaceted methodology. Cheryl Wall uses the musical metaphor of a "worried line" to help describe the ways in which "contemporary black women writers revise and subvert the conventions of the genres they appropriate, whether the essay, the lyric, the memoir, or the novel. ... [T]hey rewrite canonical texts in order to give voice to stories those texts did not imagine" (*Worrying* 13). Wall's insights about contemporary Black women's literature help to highlight how, over a century ago, Cooper reworked and subverted many of the philosophical, theological, scientific, literary, and pedagogical conventions of her time.

Yet, at the same time, given incommensurability in speaking positions, power, and discourse, we must also acknowledge that not everything *can* be told, not every story given voice. Calling attention to the unspeakable, Cooper names (but does not elaborate on) the "Black Woman's ... unnamable burden inside" (*Voice* 90). Cooper also frequently uses ellipses in her writing. These ellipses signify Cooper's performance of silence as a mode of speaking: simultaneously, they make visible what Margo Perkins has characterized as the deployment of "textual withholding" (17). Thus Cooper suggests that we must attend not only to the nameable, or spoken, but also to the fact that there are silences that "teach" or reveal to us something about what cannot really be spoken, particularly as it relates to trauma and suffering (Ellsworth 22).

In fact, some of the politics of the inexpressible are evident in the ways that Cooper refused her whole life to discuss her biological father, who owned both Cooper and her mother, Hannah Stanley (Haywood). Cooper wrote, "Presumably my father was her master, if so I owe him not a sou & she was always too modest & shamefaced ever to mention him" (in Hutchinson 4). Later, in founding the Hannah Stanley Opportunity School at Frelinghuysen, Cooper would drop "Haywood" from her mother's name entirely, as she had in her own name (although biographical sources occasionally refer to her as "Anna Julia Haywood Cooper," Cooper did not use the Haywood name). Although Cooper never again publicly discussed her mother's "shame" or her own rejection of the Haywood "lineage," her silence on the matter is not meaningless: to the contrary, it speaks volumes.

Carole Boyce Davies summarizes some significant aspects of the politics of Black women's speech and writing as they confront inexpressibility with a phrase borrowed from her own mother: "'It's not everything you can talk ... but ...'" (339). Davies argues that the first part of the phrase, before the "but," "locates the ways in which speech for the dispossessed is received" and, simultaneously, "identifies its opposite: it's not everything people will hear" (339). However, the "full version" of the phrase, with the conjunction "but" and the ellipses at the close, signals resistance to silence/silencing and resolve to be heard. Davies therefore identifies a "tension between ... the limitations of spoken language and the possibility of expression, between the space for certain forms of talk, and lack of space for Black women's speech" (340), a tension that leads to the textual strategy of "multiple ways of voicing" (including reversal, interruption, and subversion — all tactics used by Cooper) in order to effect a "repositioning" of Black women in language (348).

In other words, if we look at Cooper as "worrying the line," while at the same time signaling to us that not everything can be articulated, then her apparently unsystematic methodology can be interpreted as indicating that she intends to tell us a different set of stories than are usually told *and* that some things are beyond the frame of tellability or are stifled by the circumstances of hostility in which she lives and works. Rather than presume that Cooper took up language uncritically, accepting its silences and exclusions passively and without question, we must recognize the numerous ways in which she was fundamentally "at odds with language" (Trinh, "Commitment" 245) to better appreciate her epistemological and political significance.

Contending with Epistemologies of Ignorance

To comprehend more fully how Cooper's relationship to writing and speaking is inherently both fraught and freeing, it is vital to understand that she had to develop a particular set of political, rhetorical, and philosophical techniques to negotiate her different audiences' investment(s) in what Mills and others characterize as "epistemologies of ignorance" (Mills, *Racial* 18–19, 96–98; Sullivan and Tuana; Tuana and Sullivan). In order to maintain "conferred dominance" and to uphold the predominant and powerful "myth of meritocracy" (McIntosh 100–1) in the United States, Mills underscores how beneficiaries of an "epistemology of ignorance" have "structured opacities" built into their knowledge practices, such that "evasion and self-deception" about privilege, power, and inequity become the de facto epistemic norms, even as truth, objectivity, and transparency are the *declared* epistemic norms (Mills, *Racial* 1–40). Or, as Anzaldúa asserts, "We are collectively conditioned not to know that every comfort of our lives is acquired with the blood of conquered, subjugated, enslaved, or exterminated people" ("Now" 541). In fact, a key site of this collective, institutionalized "conditioning" or mandated ignorance Mills and Anzaldúa describe was, historically, education — Cooper's vocational calling. What were called "compulsory ignorance" laws, which made it illegal to educate African Americans, were an early influence on American education: the first of these laws was passed by South Carolina in 1740, with many other slave-holding states following suit (K. Johnson 15–16).

To draw attention to entrenched epistemologies of ignorance and their insidious workings, Cooper takes on the "objectivity" of the U.S. legal system, showing it to be patently biased and willfully opaque. Cooper writes about a white mob's lynching of a Black man that occurred "almost a stone's throw" away from President McKinley, on tour in the South. Alluding to the hoopla and fanfare following McKinley' presidential train tour, Cooper describes a parallel set of "Excursion trains with banners flying" for the "holiday festival" that was to follow the "hanging" with a "burning." There, a "Negro preacher who offered the last solace ... to the doomed man" was also killed and burned by the mob. Although a "shiver ran thro the nation at such demoniacal lawlessness," the attorney general, Cooper scathingly observes, stood apart from the fray to retain his objective detachment. His "cool analysis of the situation" led to the disingenuous "legal opinion that the case 'probably had no Federal aspects!'" ("Ethics" 210).

There are other instances in which Cooper focuses on specious practices of democracy. For example, in her doctoral exams, Cooper argues, as Mills does, that an epistemology of ignorance has been integral to the social contract (which has functioned as a racial contract) since the founding of the U.S. nation-state. Although Cooper argues that the "*Dred Scott* decision that the slave was a chattel (a 'thing,' not a person) was not from the beginning the conception of the fathers of the country" ("Legislative" 300), in this same essay she also critiques these apparently fair-minded founding fathers for their expedient evasion of and utilitarian compromise over slavery. Cooper writes, "In drawing up the Constitution ... the words 'Slave,' 'Slavery' and 'Slave Trade' were carefully avoided although evidently present in the conscious minds of all" (300). She adds that "*the fact of slavery as a skeleton at the feast* had already become an embarrassment ... requiring and exacting many compromises, much confusion in trying to reconcile the convenience of the moment with those principles elaborated in the Declaration of Independence" (301, italics original). Cooper's analysis here anticipates Mills's insight that while these prevalent forms of evasion will be thoroughly denied by the beneficiaries of ignorance, simultaneously they will be encouraged and rewarded because such epistemic opacities help to maintain and justify the status quo (*Racial* 18–19).

In other words, those who benefit from domination will be actively taught not to know the ways of exploitation even as they benefit from them. And, when they are confronted with the reality of their denial about the facts of domination, past and present, there will be a range of reactions, from angry repudiation to the "blushing and stammering confusion" Cooper sarcastically describes as arising when the "tardy conscience of the nation wakes up ... because convicted of dishonorable and unkind treatment of *the Indian*" (*Voice* 198, italics original). However, she emphasizes that in actuality, the nation's conscience has scarcely been awakened at all, for the only outcome is condescension, the guilt-ridden dispersal of "more blankets and ... a few primers for the '*wards*'" (198, italics original), not full citizenship. Here Cooper anticipates what Adrienne Rich characterizes as "white solipsism," which, though not always conscious, is nonetheless a form of "tunnel vision which simply does not see nonwhite experience or existence as precious or significant, unless in spasmodic, impotent guilt-reflexes" (306).

For its patent bias, Cooper critiques the Supreme Court, which is supposedly impartial, even consummately so. Cooper writes, "While in the eyes of the highest tribunal in America she was deemed no more than a chattel, an irresponsible thing, a dull block, to be drawn hither or thither at the volition of an owner, the Afro-American woman maintained ideals of womanhood unshamed by any ever conceived" ("Intellectual" 202). By upholding the legality of slavery and by ignoring, and thereby sanctioning, endemic sexual violence against Black women to maintain the "capital" of the slave economy, the Court endorsed not the rule of humanistic law but instead the normalization of human exploitation. Though this fact may not be obvious to those "highest" in the land, it is very clear to those who have been characterized as the "lowest." Moreover, although those who are most privileged only saw slave women as objects of property, Cooper underscores how African American women resisted extreme epistemic and bodily violence and retained their subjectivity.

Despite the fact that those in privileged social groups will be characterized as *exemplary* knowers (or epistemic agents) while those who are oppressed will be portrayed as faulty or deficient knowers, Cooper shows how, ironically, it is those "Communities systematically privileged by an unjust social order [who] will as a rule be less sensitive to its inequities, and this insensitivity will interfere with their 'attainment of knowledge'" (Mills, *Visible* 141). Methodologically and politically, Cooper penetrates this insensitivity to past crimes against humanity to have such wrongs acknowledged, engaged with, and addressed. Moreover, in breaking open the operative, taken-for-granted "logic" of domination, Cooper reveals the moral, political, and epistemological contradictions between professed (and celebrated) egalitarianism and practiced (though disavowed) exploitation (notably, she explores such incongruities at length in her dissertation).[16] In order to breach this "contractual" agreement to be silent about, ignorant of, or at the very least evasive about such realities and contradictions, Cooper often uses sarcasm or derision as a critical switchpoint to shift the analysis away from compliance with the dominant epistemic frame toward her own critical approach.

This tactic of reversal can be seen in Cooper's discussion of the "apparently sincere excuse" of the "Southern woman"[17] who not only complains that "'these people were once our slaves'" but who also whines, much like the influential Louis Agassiz,[18] that "'civility towards the Negroes will bring us on *social equality* with them'" (*Voice* 100–1, italics original). After calling attention to the illogical use of an "ambiguous middle" in the protests offered by the "Southern woman — I beg her pardon — the Southern *lady*" (108, italics original), such that civil liberties and political rights are falsely collapsed with social "association," Cooper redirects her audience's attention to the widely known but generally disavowed fact of white men's extensive and violent sexual exploitation of black women (111).

Cooper shows how privilege is clearly an impediment to knowing because communities steadily favored by inequality and discrimination "will have a vested interest in the system's perpetuation and thus be prone to evasion, bad faith, and self-deception about its true character. They will be more receptive to dominant social ideologies whose conceptual structure ignores, blurs over, or justifies the plight of the subordinated" (Mills, *Visible* 142). Cooper's astute observations about Southern ideologies as a particular form of "bad faith" illustrate Mills's point. She writes, "One of the most singular facts about the unwritten history of this country is the consummate ability with which Southern influence, Southern ideas and Southern ideals, have from the very beginning even up to the present day, dictated to and domineered over the brain and sinew of this nation" (*Voice* 101).

These dynamics of ignorance, evasion, and disingenuousness that Cooper faced have not, a century later, disappeared. They are tenacious practices of (not) knowing and (not) relating that are difficult to transform and that shape the choices one makes in speaking/writing from marginalized locations. Nonetheless, through her double-voiced tactics, Cooper demonstrates her learned command of established, predominant forms of knowledge and simultaneously pokes fun at elitism and decries supremacist thought. Cooper challenges the forms of language and discourse that have relegated her to the margins and that have been used against her to make her the object, not the subject, of speech. Rather than try to assess definitively whether she wrote and spoke with *either* a "free" *or* a "complicit" tongue, what if we interpret Cooper to be engaging in the "dissemblance" that those who are marginalized often find necessary (Hine, "Rape"; Mills, *Visible* 29)?

Foundational Differences: "No man can prophesy with another's parable"[19]

In fact, letting go of normative "either/or" frameworks in favor of a "both/and" model of analysis (Collins, *Black Feminist* 221) helps to reveal many of the nuances in Cooper's ideas. As Keller demonstrates, refusing an "either/or" approach to interpreting Cooper's ideas brings to light how her educational philosophy is unique: Cooper found a "resolution" between seemingly opposite and contradictory educational philosophies of her time ("Educational" 49). Moreover, Bailey finds "the non-dichotomous character (between the practical and the intellectual) of Cooper's vision" to be philosophically illuminating (60). By acknowledging that Cooper often bases her analyses in a set of assumptions different from those held by many of her contemporaries, we can better appreciate Cooper's prescience.

For example, given her fundamentally "non-dichotomous" outlook, like many contemporary Black feminists, Cooper consistently calls for a deeper connection between theory and practice. She suggests that because "purely theoretical or empirical" analyses are "devoid of soul" (*Voice* 37), "head, heart, and hand" (45) must be engaged together, for the most successful ideas, dreams, and political movements employ (and stem from) the whole person. Here, Cooper does not propose an overly idealistic notion of "non-dichotomous" engagement; rather, she suggests that critical consciousness requires facing up to what in contemporary terms would be called the simultaneity of privilege and oppression.[20]

Cooper shows how one can be *both* subjugated *and* unjustifiably privileged at the same time. She argues that refusing to acknowledge areas of overlap and complexity undermines efforts at social change because the operational "either/or" theories of oppression and privilege, or of atomized identities, are not only too narrow but also false. For instance, although white women suffer from sexism, they also tend to benefit unduly from their race and class positions; frequently this leads to limited concepts of who "women" are and what "women's issues" should be (*Voice* 54, 80–82, 87, 100–1, 108). Cooper contends that ignoring how gender, race, and class intertwine impedes political and social transformation because "no woman can possibly put herself or her sex outside any of the interests that affect humanity" (143).

Similarly, even though Black men are up against racism, even to the point of death via lynching, they also can profit unwarrantedly from the advantages accorded to masculinity (75–78, 134–35). Unfortunately,

Cooper dryly concludes, many of her Black male colleagues "do not seem sometimes to have outgrown ... the idea that women may stand on pedestals or live in doll houses, (if they happen to have them) but they must not furrow their brows with thought" (75). Cooper emphasizes that gender is raced, race is gendered, and both are shot through with questions of national identity, regional influence, class status, and more. For instance, warning against Western hubris in world politics, Cooper counsels Americans to think beyond the bounds of the nation-state and not "imagine we have exhausted the possibilities of humanity." She also cautions her readers not to think, "Verily, we are the people, and after us there is none other" (52–53).

Moreover, by telling a story about her train travels, Cooper astutely elucidates what Spelman characterizes as "the ampersand problem in feminist thought" (*Inessential* 114–32) — how conceiving of gender and race as neatly bound, discrete, comparable categories erases the experiences and ideas of Black women and obscures how all raced persons are gendered, and vice versa (May 87). To set up her philosophical analysis of the limits of binaries and exclusionary categories, Cooper recalls a waiting room in a Southern train station with "two dingy little rooms with 'FOR LADIES' swinging over one and 'FOR COLORED PEOPLE' over the other." Cooper then finds herself "wondering under which head I come" (*Voice* 96, capitalization in original). Brilliantly repudiating this impossible choice, Cooper refuses, like Nellie McKay a century later, to "take sides against the self" (McKay 277). This false choice is not merely an imagined or speculative scenario, for physical harassment was not an uncommon experience for Black women: Cooper's philosophical insight here is grounded in her own lived experience. Cooper's contemporary Lawson A. Scruggs in fact documents that, after publication of *A Voice from the South*, Cooper returned home to Raleigh in December 1892 to visit friends and family, only to be humiliated and evicted once more from a "Ladies" waiting room. He was outraged and insisted on documenting the incident in his book *Women of Distinction*. Scruggs wrote, "great negro women work hard and go through much that is far from ... pleasant after as well as before achieving greatness" (209).

By starting from the premise that all aspects of one's identity and lived situation interdepend, Cooper introduces and advocates for an intersectional and contextualized approach to ontology, rather than a hierarchical, particulate or "pop-bead metaphysics" (Spelman *Inessential* 15, 136) in which each "identity" seems isolable and, implicitly, rankable. Cooper shows how this erroneous isolation and separation of identities highlights one strand or facet of experience and pushes others to the rear, preventing an understanding of how oppressions form a matrix (Collins, *Black Femi-*

nist 225–27), how they are interlocking (Combahee 272) and simultaneous (B. Smith xxviii) in nature, not monistic (D. King 52). In other words, to best enact social change, we must begin by recognizing the intricate ways that seemingly different forms of domination interdepend, overlap, and reinforce one another — much in the way that an intersectional ontology focuses on the multidimensionality and complexity of the lived person.

Across her life, Cooper refused to "choose" one political goal at the expense of another; she insisted on thinking holistically and was continually frustrated by colleagues and allies who could not seem to see, as Cooper clearly could, that liberation would never be achieved via an either/or binary approach, but only through coalition politics.[21] For example, in her 1893 speech at the Columbian Exposition, Cooper insists that all women "take our stand on the solidarity of humanity, the oneness of life, and the unnaturalness and injustice of all special favoritisms, whether of sex, race, country, or condition" ("Intellectual" 204). Later, in a 1928 letter to the Oberlin Committee Campaign Fund of the Anti Saloon League of America, Cooper rejects placing her religious faith or advocacy of temperance (the 18th Amendment) in opposition to the fight for full citizenship and civil rights (the 14th and 15th Amendments). From her point of view, these various battles are interconnected and must be waged together, not at the expense of one another. Cooper writes:

> I am sorry I cannot enter wholeheartedly into the Campaign for downing [(i.e., endorsing)] Governor Alfred E. Smith. My own vote, it is true, *if I had one*, should go to Hoover. ... But, speaking personally, the 14th[22] and 15th[23] amendments to the Constitution are just as precious in my sight as the 18th and I am unable to warm very enthusiastically with religious fervor for Bible 'fundamentalists' who have nothing to say about lynching Negroes or reducing whole sections of them to a state of peonage worse than slavery. (Lemert and Bhan 336, italics added)

In addition to Cooper's perceptive "both/and" conceptual framework, her intersectional approach to metaphysics and her vision of a politics of coalition or solidarity, all of which are major theoretical contributions, her philosophical outlook is grounded in several other premises that are quite innovative and that diverge from many of the predominant assumptions of her time. Significantly, Cooper suggests that objectivity is an outcome of unequal power relations: objectivity, in its starkest (and most admired) "God's-eye" form, is a construct that serves the interests and needs of the powerful (*Voice* 185–6, 203–8, 216, 291–3). Moreover, "pure reason" tends to miss the "facts" that can be gleaned by paying attention to lived experience and to the particular nuances of different life circumstances ("Equality" 292).

Repeatedly, Cooper illustrates how perception is the end product of specific practices, values, and ideals: knowing is located, not disembodied, absolute, or universalizable.[24] In her preface to *A Voice*, Cooper asserts that the "truth from *each* standpoint be presented. ... The 'other side' has not been represented by one who 'lives there.' And not many can more sensibly realize and more accurately tell the weight and the fret of the 'long dull pain' than the open-eyed but hitherto voiceless Black Woman of America" (ii). Rather than being irrelevant, the context of discovery and the knower's lived experience/situation matter (though not in a determinist way) and are taken by Cooper to be epistemologically significant, as one of her most famous statements illustrates. She writes, "Only the BLACK WOMAN can say 'when and where I enter, in the quiet, undisputed dignity of my womanhood, without violence and without suing or special patronage, then and there the whole *Negro race enters with me*'" (31, capitalization and italics original).

Cooper's outlook diverges sharply from the assumption, still powerful today in the Anglo-American tradition, that "social identity" is irrelevant to philosophical inquiry (Alcoff, "Judging" 235). Contrary to prevailing epistemological conventions, Cooper contends, as Linda Alcoff argues, that "perception is not ... mere reportage" but, rather, an "orientation the world": knowing is "historically situated," shaped by context, and "internal to a discourse, or discursive formation, rather than essentially (or potentially) unchanged across historical and cultural difference" (254). To show the extent to which knowledge "cannot be completely disentangled from social location and experience" (245), Cooper unearths theories and practices of racism, sexism, xenophobia, and more in scientific, philosophical, and cultural texts, highlighting systematized opacity, bias, and evasion across multiple sites of knowing.

For example, in her critique of images and "caricatures" (Cooper, *Voice* 186) of African Americans in American literature and culture, from novels by Harriet Beecher Stowe (222–23) and William Dean Howells (203–8),[25] to popular rhymes (216), and later, to musicals such as *Porgy and Bess* and radio shows like *Amos 'n' Andy* ("Negro's" 238–47), Cooper delineates what Guy-Sheftall names "one of the most persistent themes in the intellectual history of the west ... [:] Negrophobia" ("Body" 26). Cooper shows how Howells sees "colored people at long range or only in certain capacities ... as bootblacks and hotel waiters, grinning from ear to ear and bowing ... for the extra tips" (*Voice* 206), while even African American stars like Paul Robeson find themselves pushed to perform the "flavor [they are] expected to create" ("Negro's" 239), an exploitative relation of servitude Trudier Harris later characterizes as "voluntary slavery" (*South* 214).

In arguing that all such stereotyped representations reveal nothing about African Americans but are merely a "revelation of the white man" (Cooper *Voice* 216), tools for "establishing evidences of ready formulated theories and preconceptions" (186), Cooper anticipates the work of Toni Morrison ("Unspeakable" and *Whiteness*), Addison Gayle, Paule Marshall ("Negro"), Barbara Christian ("Images") and others who analyze how Black characters lack interiority, agency, and subjectivity in white-authored, canonical "American" literature: they function primarily as flat, unidimensional screens upon which whites' fears and fantasies of blackness are projected. In other words, like that of many Black authors before her and to follow, Cooper's literary analysis serves as a critique of the "destructive nature and brutality" of white society (T. Harris, *Exorcising* 69) and a refusal of the usual projection of this violence onto Black characters. Given the various ways in which cultural texts operate as tools of social control, Cooper issues a call in *A Voice from the South* for African Americans to create their own literature and to depict their lives and history on their own terms. In making this appeal, Cooper asserts, "No man can prophesy with another's parable" (*Voice* 176).

However, crafting a new "parable" from which to prophesy does not just happen out of the blue or through sheer will. Cooper emphasizes that "a sense of freedom in mind as well as in body is necessary to the appreciative and inspiring pursuit of the beautiful" (223): she advocates for somatic, material, political, aesthetic, and intellectual freedom so that Black culture can flower and prosper in the future. Cooper also insinuates that she too is burdened by the weight of this widespread objectifying imagery and language: as a writer, she must try to extricate herself from its snares and traps. Nevertheless, after recalling the "old proverb 'The devil is always painted *black* — by white painters,'" Cooper suggests, "what is needed, perhaps, to reverse the picture of the lordly man slaying the lion, is for the lion to turn painter" (225, italics original).

Clearly, she intends to paint a new portrait, both of the lordly man and of his slaying, from her perspective. In this regard, Cooper often presents disagreeable facts that her readers might prefer to overlook or ignore. For instance, she points to economic greed and human exploitation as foundational to American democracy ("Ethics" 206–7, *Voice* 193, 216, 239). Cooper also highlights how "virtue" and personhood have been denied Black women, not just in the abstract but also through material deprivation and physical-sexual violence ("Intellectual" 202; *Voice* 91, 111). Yet because "speech is not [an] uncomplicated practice of freedom ... resistance to domination cannot consist solely of opposition, as in the strategy of speaking truth to power" (Samantrai 51). In other words, simply "repainting" or restating the truth or presenting new facts from the viewpoint of the margins — "speaking truth to power" — will not suffice, and Cooper knows it.

In fact, her nonlinear analyses and indirect rhetorical stances suggest that Cooper finds a straightforward, "facts-based" approach on its own inadequate to the pedagogical and political task at hand: transformation both of the imagination and of society. Rather than signaling illogical contradiction or elitist acquiescence on her part, Cooper's oblique angles of analysis suggest she is most interested in *rupturing* the epistemic frameworks that shape dominant understandings of reality and that influence perceptions of (or what even counts as) the "facts" about democracy, history, culture, race, gender, science, theology, or philosophy. For example, in her doctoral exams, just before tearing apart the racist scholarship of her renowned chief examiner, Célestin Bouglé, Cooper wryly stated to the committee, "It is necessary in every case to beware of arbitrary preconceptions" (i.e., Bouglé's bias about the advanced evolutionary development of "Nordic" races making them most suited to egalitarianism) ("Equality" 291).[26]

Cooper's trying to get at and question her audience's underlying assumptions, and her pushing them to acknowledge their own frames of reference, calls to mind Uma Narayan's questioning of "the unreflective and naively optimistic view" of conceptualizing cross-cultural, multicultural learning "primarily in terms of 'information retrieval' — as a simple matter of acquiring information and learning 'the facts'" (Narayan 95), since it leaves aside important questions about power and position, such as how the "facts" have been arrived at or even categorized as "factual." Moreover, because those who are "othered" tend to be commodified, seen as "fascinating" and "mysterious," there are lots of distorted "facts" compiled about "them," but usually without much context or reflexivity (100–1). Narayan therefore advocates a multicultural pedagogy and comparative methodology that account for contextual differences, that are self-conscious (not self-centered), and that acknowledge how asymmetries of power impact perception.

Cooper also disparages objectifying, falsely homogenizing approaches to compiling "data" about group difference and identity. In *A Voice*, she describes how she has "been more than once annoyed by the inquisitive white interviewer who, with spectacles on nose and pencil and note book in hand, comes to get some 'points' about '*your people*'" (111, italics original). Later, in "The Negro Dialect," Cooper argues, "Much of the Negro talk that has burst into the picture since the apotheosis of the 'Type' in post War literature is machine made and crassly overdone. ... For the fact is there is no such thing as Negro dialect *per se* just as there was never such a thing as a unique Negro or African language, understood and spoken *ab origine* by all dwellers on the continent of Africa whose descendents were kidnapped for slavery" (242–3). Much like Narayan, Cooper urges that we think more carefully about what we take for granted as categories of experience, or accept as adequate versions of reality.

Contrary to predominant theories of human agency, histories of revolution, and narratives about the origins of democracy, Cooper's methodological techniques quietly form the basis of an epistemological argument that Black men and women are agents of knowledge, originators of culture, and a driving force of sociopolitical transformation. As a fundamental principle, Cooper assumes the intrinsic subjectivity and capacity for freedom, rationality, and virtue in all of us and asks her readers to do the same. Moreover, in both of her major texts, *A Voice from the South by a Black Woman of the South* and *L'Attitude de la France à l'égard de l'esclavage pendant la Révolution*, Cooper systematically demonstrates that those who have been marginalized have a resistant, insistent "*Singing* Something" ("Equality" 293, italics in original) within that, even if "muted" or silenced, can be tapped into, first on an individual level of self-realization and then on a collective level of group action and coalition.[27]

This "Singing Something" paradigm, present across her body of work, is significant because by presupposing "an ontology of freedom and equality" (Baker-Fletcher 162), Cooper highlights a genealogy of resistance for Black men and women. Shifting her attention beyond the bounds of the United States toward a more diasporic analysis, Cooper argues that African Americans and other marginalized groups are creators of democracy and sources of Enlightenment at home and abroad, not just passive recipients of freedoms "granted" by the powerful or mere imitators of the great philosophers of the Age of Reason. Thus, in her doctoral defense, Cooper excoriates Bouglé's declaration that "'Equality manifests itself only in our Western Civilization'" (Bouglé in Cooper, "Equality" 291). She also mocks his arrogant assumption "that the ideas inherent in social progress descend by divine favor upon the Nordic people, a Superior Race chosen to dominate the Earth," though it "assuredly pampers the pride of those believing themselves the Elect of God" (i.e., Bouglé) ("Equality" 293).[28]

Here, at age sixty-six, we see Cooper as daring as ever — at the moment she requires Bouglé to declare she is a *docteur* of the Sorbonne, she takes him on full force in a public setting (in keeping with custom, her *soutenance* [oral defense] was open to the public). Furthering her analysis about the inherent capacity for freedom, rationality, and agency in all people, Cooper suggests that Bouglé be wary of the limits of his Nordic hypothesis, given the various uprisings around the world that contradict his theory. And, since her dissertation focuses on the dialogic (rather than imitative) relationship between the Haitian and French revolutions, Cooper is also arguing that the Haitian revolution was not anomalous: oppressed groups have been engaged in battles for self-governance and self-determination for centuries.

Thus, Cooper's derisive use of capital letters for the "Superior Race" in her previous sentence shifts to a more serious analysis of the "Surprises" that reveal a priori the equality of all. She warns Bouglé, "But one may as well expect Surprises. For example, note the situation in Russia today[29] [(1925)] little dreamed of 20 years ago, likewise in China,[30] Turkey,[31] in Egypt,[32] [and] the Gandhi movement in India" ("Equality" 293). Cooper's internationalist approach to the question of human agency reveals how her theory of coalition politics and her understanding of the matrix of domination reach beyond the boundaries of the nation. Her cross-cultural attention to resistance movements around the globe highlights the mutually embedded realities (past, present, and future) of differently marginalized or oppressed groups of people. Cooper continually reinforces her vision that "If one link of the chain be broken, the chain is broken. A bridge is no stronger than its weakest part" ("Intellectual" 204).

Moreover, by documenting both in *A Voice from the South* and in her dissertation how democracies usually portrayed as archetypal, the United States and France, attempted to ignore, squash, even permanently silence this "Singing Something" in their midst, Cooper splits open seemingly impenetrable historical accounts and philosophical paradigms to offer a different narrative about the workings of global capital and the practice (or lack) of democratic ideals. As Pellow argues, "Cooper's strength as a scholar was enhanced by her ability to understand issues on several levels. ... [With an] understanding of the world's complexities, of the interconnectedness of the centers of power and finance — particularly those on both sides of the Atlantic — ... comes the knowledge that everything is relative, and that even the racist horrors of the United States were not universal nor even inevitable, but were in fact due to certain inadequacies, omissions, or outright failures" (61).

In a 1902 speech, for example, Cooper challenges our nation's origin story. In contrast to the usual account of Pilgrims, Thanksgiving suppers, and peaceful "settlement," unjustly imposed tea taxes, and revolutionary uprising for full political representation, Cooper inserts a counter-memory, a different point of view. She writes, "Uprooted from the sunny land of his forefathers by the white man's cupidity and selfishness, ruthlessly torn from all the ties of clan and tribe, dragged against his will over thousands of miles of unknown waters ... the Negro was transplanted to this continent in order to produce chattels and beasts of burden for a nation 'conceived in liberty and dedicated to the proposition that all men are created equal'" ("Ethics" 206–7).[33]

Over twenty years later, still critical of expansionist, capitalist democracy doing its "good deeds" of empire around the globe, Cooper parodies self-proclaimed "white" nations who pronounce:

> 'We are the chosen ... and so we enter Africa and forbid the natives to walk except in the middle of the road. We have preempted America — and Lo, the poor Indian! In Australia we say kindly but firmly to the aborigines: 'I need the land. Here is abundance of it. But I am allergic to irritants in my sight. I do not like your complexion. It does not go well with my own. If you are submissive I can serve myself with your labor as a slave. If not, yonder is the exit.' ("Equality" 296)

Through the use of counter-memory, irony, and other narrative techniques, Cooper effectively highlights the arrogant conceit, inconsistency, and denial at the heart of supremacist politics deployed under the pretext of democracy. Her innovative questioning and critique of capitalist, colonial expansion by Western democracies, moreover, is essential to building coalitions and defining liberation beyond the bounds of nation. As Chandra Talpade Mohanty asserts, "historicizing and denaturalizing the ideas, beliefs, and values of global capital such that underlying exploitative relations and structures are made visible" is necessary to forging transnational feminist alliances (485).

While revealing some of these "underlying exploitative relations," Cooper simultaneously highlights the legacies of struggle sustained by those who were enslaved and oppressed. For example, she writes: "The severest persecution and oppression could not kill [African Americans] out or even sour their temper. ...Without money and without price they poured their hearts' best blood into the enriching and developing of this country" (*Voice* 178–9). She also reinforces how, against all odds, Black women resisted degradation to maintain their sanctity of person ("Intellectual" 202): she demonstrates, therefore, that "the experience of slavery provided evidence of the Black woman's moral strength and resiliency" (Giddings, *When* 87). This twofold approach is crucial because it leaves room for Cooper to assert an alternative vision of the margin as other than or more than a locus of oppression — what bell hooks calls "a profound edge" (*Yearning* 49). Cooper's comparative, internationalist, multilevel methodology allows her to expose the relative rather than absolute nature of political structures, historical narratives, philosophical premises, and even scientific theories.

Cooper's foundational differences are significant and visionary. She maintains that all knowers do not have equal epistemic authority, much less equal standing as citizens, because the democratic social contract does not, as generally stated, ensure universal membership in the polity. Rather, it is a contract maintaining a hierarchically ordered ontology of racial and gendered inequality. In addition, Cooper underscores how an epistemology of ignorance functions to obscure these underlying dynamics of exploitation, such that privilege is often an impediment to knowing, whereas oppression can lead to significantly different insights about the world, a standpoint that should be heeded but not romanticized, homogenized, or tokenized. By articulating how marginality is more than a site of domination and how oppression is rarely a total state of being, she emphasizes that a facts-oriented methodology is inadequate: underlying expectations and assumptions must be addressed, while questions of power, lived experience, identity, and emotion must be understood as epistemologically significant. Cooper starts by presuming the inherent subjectivity of all persons and then delineates a longstanding genealogy of resistance and revolution by those assumed to be less than human. Moreover, she advocates an intersectional approach to ontology and a coalitional model of political change that seek alliances beyond the bounds of nation. Clearly, as this brief summary demonstrates, Cooper's premises allow her to "prophesy" with her own stories rather than with "another's parable" (Cooper, *Voice* 176): Why have these methodological innovations and epistemological insights not been more fully appreciated?

"The other is already speaking"[34]: Logic by a Different Measure, Dissent in a Different Voice

Schutte argues that, from the point of view of the "culturally dominant speaker, the subaltern speaker's discourse may appear to be a string of fragmented observations rather than a unified whole" (56). Read "straight," as if they were monological in nature, Cooper's multivocal texts and interdisciplinary methods can seem inconsistent, even inherently flawed, as some have argued (Athey 48, Gaines 148). Yet on the other hand, if we change the ways in which we gauge rationality and begin by presuming that, on some level, Cooper engages in "speaking in tongues" (Henderson), "coding" her ideas to be understood in multiple ways, then a richer understanding emerges of Cooper's methods as in fact radical. As Carla Peterson argues with regard to earlier African American women orators, "If the principles of hybridity ... were inexplicable to the dominant culture in their disruption of fixed hierarchies and binary oppositions, to their own members they were readily comprehensible" (9). By setting aside conventional measures of coherence, Cooper's apparently inconsistent form, voice, or argumentation can be read as (differently) coherent. In other words, because "marginalized people are always socialized to understand things from more than their own point of view, to see both sides of the matter, and to say at *least* two things at the same time, they can never really afford to speak in the singular" (Trinh, *Cinema* 39).

Crafting alternative means by which to assess Cooper's methodology is therefore essential. Otherwise, we risk overlooking many of her important insights and contributions, for "when we deploy the traditional method of studying ideas which searches for links, coherence and integration, regularity and linearity, it excludes from our horizon that which is different" (Bogues, *Heretics* 3). Accordingly, if our measure of adequate and persuasive reasoning, our notion of radical thought, lies not in commensurability, not in coherence, not in (historically violent) expectations for "clarity" (Lugones, "Hablando" 50), and not in the "thingness" of knowledge as mastery of facts, but rather in the modality of spoken, embodied, dialogic narrative — as existing within riddles, stories, and proverbs, as Christian suggests ("Race" 336) — then a different perception of Cooper surfaces.

Clearly seeking responsive understanding and action from her audience, Cooper's manner of writing is quite addressive. She often uses a dialectic model of questioning that reflects both her familiarity with antiphony in church and her educational training in the works of Plato and in classical Greek rhetoric and reasoning. Consequently, Christian's dialogic model of thinking about, crafting, and assessing theory can be understood to be particularly relevant to thinking about Cooper. Christian asserts that the variety, multiplicity, and eroticism of embodied, located theorizing that Black women and men have crafted is often *deliberately* "difficult to control" ("Race" 341), in terms of both form and content. From this perspective, Cooper's playful circumlocutions, sarcastic humor, and rhetorical reversals can be understood as techniques she adopts to allow her to "pivot" or "move" the center (Thiong'o 4).

Much like Anzaldúa's *nahual* or shape-shifter (*Borderlands* 104), Cooper's indirection, juxtaposition, and nonlinear argumentation are generative techniques that allow her to immerse in dominant discourses and simultaneously to critique, even refuse, their foundational rules and premises. Yet Cooper is working with a different set of assumptions about the nature of reality, knowledge, and politics than are many of her readers (by whom she seeks to be understood even as she questions many of their foundational principles). In her writing, therefore, Cooper takes on the difficult task of bridging disparate realities. However, she does not want to become the "bridge" or "back" on which others walk to arrive at critical consciousness (Springer, "Being" 381), a task that women of color continue to be asked to take on disproportionately.

Consequently, Cooper develops her analyses and crafts her philosophy with more of an arc-like movement — a tactic Lorraine Code finds useful for contesting "the limits of imagination." Like Code, Cooper is dealing with the epistemological and political conundrum of readers' "willed unknowings," their "resistance to [the] particulars" of experience and difference, and their desire to "preserve the detached dislocation" of observation, as if the acquisition of facts were paradigmatic of knowing (Code, "Rational" 274–7). Rather than presuppose that all knowers are fundamentally identical and that "real" knowing is "perspectiveless," Cooper, like many feminist epistemologists today, suggests "that situated or subjective understandings of knowledge are more accurate: differing social situations ... produce differing understandings of the world, differing knowledges of reality" (Bergin 198).

In essence, Cooper's interdisciplinary, multilevel method allows her to speak in two or more registers at once, to contest hegemonic thought, and to refuse to be tied down or controlled by her audience(s). Mills explains why unconventional methods are particularly necessary to fighting (racial) stigmatization and oppression: "Because the stigmatization of nonwhites is multidimensional, resistance to it has to be correspondingly broad" (*Visible* 112). Thus, although Cooper's analytic layers individually may seem thin, or even at times conciliatory, in part because of the ambiguity or variation in her voice, I find that her "interdisciplinary methodology has a cumulative effect" (May 83): there is more to Cooper's methods, politically and epistemologically speaking, than she has generally been credited with.

When it is considered as a whole, we can see that across her body of work Cooper wages war on established ideas about knowledge, reality, and personhood; she also offers a multidimensional analysis of the complex workings of power at both macro and micro levels. Thus, rather than happenstance, it is significant, especially in *A Voice from the South*, that Cooper connects her critique of scientific racism to her discussion of capitalism to her examination of democracy's shortcomings to her analysis of stereotypes of Blacks in American literature to her theological critique of the church's role in women's inequality. This technique allows Cooper to demonstrate the ways in which hierarchical thinking and oppressive practices are institutionalized across the board. Rather than focus exclusively on the cultural meaning and function of stereotypes in art or literature, or solely on the economic exploitation that capitalist and imperialist democracies depend upon and sanction, or wholly on the silences and erasures in dominant philosophical and theological texts, Cooper does all of this, and more.[35]

Significantly, this "riffing" from one subject to the next and from one continent to another prefigures the disciplinary and geographic border-crossing found in much contemporary feminist theory, particularly by women of color.[36] Therefore, scholars such as Guy-Sheftall contend that interdisciplinary perspectives are crucial in studying the lives and ideas of Black women (*Daughters* 8), while Stubblefield maintains that any philosophy that seeks to be "post-supremacist" must be interdisciplinary in its method and intersectional in its conception of identity and experience (71–2, 79). Yet despite such urgent calls to shift toward critical interdisciplinary methodologies, Cooper's broad vision, cross-disciplinary connections, and internationalist outlook are perennially underappreciated. If we too quickly reduce the multivocality and layers of meaning in Cooper's work, we not only diminish the wider implications of her ideas but also risk forgetting that Cooper herself is seeking to name, and then reject, the limits of ideas, values, and beliefs that "she did not help to create and that were not created with her in mind" (May 75–6).

By starting from a different set of foundational assumptions and by using an intersectional, interdisciplinary approach, Cooper provides an unusual critical angle on many of her topics, be they theological, educational, historical, political, economic, scientific, feminist, Pan-Africanist, or philosophical. Attending to Cooper's distinctive presuppositions helps us not only to understand her interdisciplinary, border-crossing methods but also to outline in more detail their epistemological and political significance. Cooper's texts and public career embody what Angela Davis characterizes, in recalling her own path to philosophy and activism, as a "philosophical disposition" in which we "contest, rather than simply accept, the given," wherein we do not "assume that the appearances in our lives constituted ultimate realities" ("Conversation" 15, 17). Cooper clearly takes as epistemologically central that which is usually excluded from dominant epistemological models: she finds emotion, lived experience, location and embodiment, power and inequality, and silences or gaps all vital to the knowing process — not secondary, minor, or insignificant.

In addition, Cooper often thinks "from the underside" (Alcoff, "Judging" 257) of an issue. For instance, from Cooper's perspective, to develop adequate theories of freedom it is necessary to understand oppression and think about domination from the point of view of the oppressed while also breaking open ominous silences about slavery, colonization, and domination in prevailing philosophical paradigms and historical debates. This is significant because Cooper brings a sense of situatedness and yearning to her analyses: she refuses the idea that knowledge is ideally "disincarnate" (Mills, *Racial* 53) and without emotion. Going against the grain of culturally powerful "positivist-empiricist" models of knowing (Code, *Rhetorical* 24–25), Cooper instead foregrounds the "subjective dimension of our knowing ... that part of us which is so discouraged by those intent on making us conform to official ... so-called objective 'reality'" (Greene 11). Of course, this is *particularly* risky for Cooper because, as a Black female intellectual/activist, she is already stereotyped as being inherently more subjective, emotional, and even "close — so close — to nature," as she her-self suggests (Cooper, *Voice* 180).

Cooper's pride in the fact that her work is overtly *interested*, subjective, and located is therefore particularly notable. Her approach is decidedly political in its imprint, not "neutral" but feminist, anti-racist, anti-impe-rialist, and diasporic. Like many other feminist and Africana epistemolo-gists, Cooper maintains that objectivity, or truth, is possible, but not via a positivist, disincarnate, remote objectivity. In this regard, for example, Cooper's outlook parallels that of the philosopher and Harlem Renaissance cultural theorist Alain Locke. He wrote, "All philosophies, it seems to me, are in ultimate derivation philosophies of life and not of abstract, disem-bodied 'objective' reality; products of time, place and situation, and thus systems of timed history rather than timeless eternity" (in L. Harris 34).

As we have seen, Cooper's methodology is interdisciplinary, compara-tive, flexible, nonlinear, plurivocal, multilevel, coded, dialogic, and unruly. She finds ways to think beyond the dehumanizing stereotypes, epistemic erasures, and narrow histories foisted upon her. By grounding her analy-ses and philosophy in her own encounters with the world, Cooper invites her audience to question everyday assumptions, to look more closely at established, normative frames of reference, and to examine what we might usually accept as given or true. Yet to be attuned to the nuances of Coo-per's innovative methodology and cadences of her radical voice, we must approach her work with an interpretive frame more intimately connected to some of her groundbreaking ideas, including a "both/and" analytic lens, an intersectional theory of identity, a coalition model of politics, a located and politicized epistemology, and an interdisciplinary outlook. Cooper's insights about the complexities of identity, power, and knowledge come to the fore once we recognize that what may appear to be a fragmented, disjointed, at times conciliatory or contradictory methodology on her part is, in fact, a noncompliant methodology of dissent.

CHAPTER **4**

"Failing at the most essential provision of the revolutionary ideal"[1]

Lessons from France and Haiti's Transatlantic Struggle over Abolition and Égalité

Save for occasional interest in the fact that Cooper was the first Black woman to earn a Ph.D. at the Sorbonne (Figure 4.1) and the fourth African American woman to earn one in the United States, little attention has been paid to the intellectual content of her 1925 doctoral thesis, *L'Attitude de la France à l'égard de l'esclavage pendant la Révolution*[2] (France's Attitude toward Slavery during the Revolution).[3] Yet Cooper was part of a vibrant international Black community in Paris that emerged in the interwar years despite "dogged surveillance" by police to prevent political organizing or protest (Boittin 126). For example, like Cooper, many other African American figures of the Black Renaissance spent time abroad in Paris, including Claude McKay, Walter White, Gwendolyn Bennett, Countee Cullen, Langston Hughes, Alain Locke, James Weldon Johnson, Jessie Fauset, Jean Toomer, and Nella Larsen (Edwards 4). They participated in the creation of a "new internationalism," a comparative approach to diaspora that built on earlier Pan-Africanist and Ethiopianist frameworks from the turn of the century (Edwards 2).

In general, however, women's contributions to a cross-cultural Black modernism have not been acknowledged. Just as the cartography of a Black Atlantic dialectic has been "limited by the fact that [the] theoretical, diasporic 'root' is largely constructed around an elite entourage of African American men," leading to the erasure of figures such as Amy

107

Figure 4.1 Anna Julia Cooper, portrait in her doctoral regalia (likely taken soon after December 29, 1925 upon formal receipt of her Sorbonne diploma at a ceremony at Howard University held by the AKA sorority at its national *boule* or convention).

Ashwood-Garvey and Amy Jacques-Garvey (U. Taylor, "Intellectual" 179–80), so is the usual "narrative of the emergence of Négritude ... a story of 'representative colored men': Senghor, Léon-Gontran Damas, and Aimé Césaire" (Edwards 120), to the exclusion of women like Jane and Paulette Nardal, Suzanne Lacascade, and Suzanne Césaire (Sharpley-Whiting 14–20). Often devalued and characterized as "movement midwives rather than architects" (17), Francophone and allophone Black women in Paris should instead be considered key members of the "'silenced' genealogy of Négritude" (Edwards 122).

In addition to the Nardal sisters, Lacascade, and Césaire, I would argue that to include Cooper even further disrupts this "conspicuously masculine genealogy of ... critical consciousness" (Sharpley-Whiting 12), for she began traveling across the Atlantic to Paris in 1900, then engaged in several years of summer studies at La Guilde Internationale in 1911 before embarking on her Sorbonne thesis in 1924. However, it is not Cooper's merely *being* in Paris that should be "counted" in the history of Black internationalism, but her carefully researched dissertation. In fact, in a December 1927 letter to Alain Locke, Jane Nardal credited Cooper and her research on France and Haiti for helping to raise her own critical consciousness. Nardal had attended Cooper's oral defense at the Sorbonne, and since that time, she writes, "My curiosity, my interest, already captured by other things Nègre, began to awaken" (in Edwards 126–7). The following year Nardal published two articles explicating this new consciousness "awakened" by Cooper's soutenance: "Internationalisme noir," in which Nardal delineates a framework for a cross-cultural race consciousness, and "Pantins exotiques," in which she explores the constraints of being Black and female "in a Paris thirsty for exoticism" (Boittin 121).[4]

Working in the midst of the baldly expansionist U.S. military occupation of Haiti (1914–1935),[5] at the epicenter of French intellectual life, the Sorbonne, and right at the geographical and philosophical heart of French political history as a republic, Paris, Cooper speaks out against past (and, implicitly, present) financial and philosophical rationales for domination, occupation, and imperial expansion. Through her analysis of the dialogic interplay of the Haitian and French revolutions, Cooper demonstrates how accounts of the Enlightenment must be grounded in a transatlantic framework, emphasizes how capitalism emerged out of colonialism as a racially exploitive economic system, and suggests that history must attend to its marginal spaces and silenced stories. By including the Haitian Revolution as part of the Age of Revolution,[6] Cooper contends that the actions of the slaves, the *affranchis* (free blacks), and the *gens de couleur* (free, often propertied, frequently slave-owning people of color)[7] are politically relevant and historically significant both to France and to Saint-Domingue (now

Haiti). As Pellow argues, "Cooper provides us with a unique analysis of diasporean discourse in general and Haiti as a new world narrative of containment in particular. She mapped the intersection of slavery, race, and imperialism ... [and] laid the groundwork for future students of diasporean studies" (61). Moreover, Lemert and Bhan find that Cooper "anticipates by nearly fifty years the key terms of today's dependency theory of global political economy" (269).

Yet more often than not, Cooper's contributions are overlooked.[8] For instance, in his cogent examination of historical silencing, Michel-Rolph Trouillot inadvertently silences Cooper. He writes, "In the United States ... with the notable exceptions of Henry Adams and W. E. B. Du Bois, few major writers conceded any significance to the Haitian Revolution in their historical writings up to the 1970s" (98–9). Mostly, C. L. R. James and Aimé Césaire are lauded as among the first to develop dialectical analyses of French and Caribbean politics; unfortunately, neither James nor Césaire reference Cooper's research in their works, an omission that continues in current scholarship. For example, Bogues cites James for shifting the prevailing interpretive axis of the Age of Revolution, in his well-known 1938 book *The Black Jacobins,* to tell "a different historical tale about the rise of modernity" (*Heretics* 79). Rather than a celebratory narrative about an autochthonous European "miracle" (Mills, *Racial* 33, *Visible* 127), James focuses on how colonialism and plantation slavery were at the root of Europe's accumulation of wealth and economic development (Bogues, *Caliban's* 41–2). Although Cooper develops a parallel argument, Bogues does not refer to her work in this regard. Likewise, Laurent Dubois acknowledges James for his astute analysis of "the potent cross-fertilization between the revolutionary transformations that took place in France and the Caribbean" and points to the importance of Aimé Césaire's observation that Haiti was "where the knot of colonialism was first tied, and where it was first untied" (*Avengers* 2, 3). Even though Cooper offers similar reflections in her thesis, her ideas go unnoticed by Dubois as well.

Granted, such silences are not necessarily intentional, but they do have a cumulative effect. Moreover, following Cooper's rather oblique line of reasoning and somewhat subdued voice in her dissertation can be quite challenging to contemporary readers more accustomed to declarative, overt argumentation. But it is no surprise that Cooper's narrative voice can seem, at times, constrained: she was writing in a second language; she was working with national archives favoring France's view of its own national and colonial history; the Washington, D.C. school board had impeded her efforts to earn her Ph.D.;[9] her original dissertation topic had been rejected by the Sorbonne as "too broad" in scope (Hutchinson 138)[10]; and her chief examiner, Bouglé, charged her with being partisan in her oral *soutenance* or dissertation defense (Cooper, "Third Step" 328).

However, her restrained writing style does not justify our ignoring her ideas: Cooper's forward-thinking study deserves a wider audience. To clarify, in raising the fact that Dubois, Mills, and Trouillot, among other contemporary scholars, overlook Cooper's historical research, by no means do I want to suggest that, for example, James's or Césaire's perceptive analyses should be *less* valued. Neither should we read Cooper through an androcentric, comparative lens to prove that her ideas are just like those of the more widely recognized "race men," nor should we blur important differences among their analyses. Rather, Cooper's work should be considered as part of the conversation, not left in obscurity; her research is central to our intellectual legacy, ongoing scholarly debates, and sense of history.

Cooper's Transnational Analysis of Domination and Exploitation

Cooper cogently argues that the relationship between France and Saint-Domingue was a two-way, interactive dynamic. She writes, "Or, de même que les événements de France réagissaient sur Saint-Domingue, ceux de Saint-Domingue réagissaient sur l'opinion française et sur l'Assemblée Constituante" (*L'Attitude* 66).[11] Accentuating this give-and-take relationship between France and Saint-Domingue, in terms of both the unfolding of political events and the development of ideas and public opinion, Cooper rejects the notion that colonialism and slavery entail a simple one-sided relationship or unidirectional power dynamic. That is, by focusing on the political life of Saint-Domingue as well as the transatlantic circuits of communication and ideas, Cooper stretches the bounds of what constitutes the French nation (i.e., the colony as much as the metropole) and alters the parameters of who should be considered among history's central agents (i.e., *gens de couleur,* free blacks, and slaves, and not just the white political players usually considered the principal "French" characters of this history).

Cooper also departs from a narrower telling of the tale of the French Revolution and of the rise of the republican French state by choosing a different origin story. A more conventional overview of the French Revolution might focus on the rumblings in France against the king, the nobility, and the bourgeoisie that led up to the 1789 storming of the Bastille, the elimination of feudalism, the rise of secularism, the writing of a constitution, the fall of the monarchy, and the creation of an elected, national legislature. In contrast, Cooper opens her thesis with some discussion of the Spanish and Portuguese conquests in the Americas, particularly their unbridled exploitation in the "Age of Discovery," and decries the heinous

rise of racial slavery, after the extermination or genocide of Native populations, to accommodate the voracious European empires (*L'Attitude* 8–9).
She contends that racial slavery in Europe's colonies in the Americas is
uniquely odious because its only founding principle is an "abus de la force"
(abuse of force) that is "sans prétexte comme sans excuse, et seulement
au nom du droit du plus puissant" ("without cause or excuse, and only
according to the imperative of the most powerful/aggressive") (7). The
consequences of such abuses of power were excessive mortality rates for
slaves — nearly triple the birth rate; moreover, for every slave brought to
the colonies, four would die (9).

In addition to stressing the human costs of slavery and conquest in the
Caribbean, Cooper lays out both the political and physical geography of
Saint-Domingue, describing the island's different regions but also the contested and complex ontological hierarchies of race and class at play in the
political and social life of the colony. France's colonial maps do not communicate the island's thorny cartographies of power that Cooper homes in
on (20–22, 25). Moreover, her primary focus in France is on the evolving
political dynamic between the elite and pro-colonialism/pro-slavery Club
Massaic (a political club named after the hotel where members secretly
met in Paris) and the more revolutionary Amis des Noirs (Friends of the
Blacks). Although Cooper's attention to these two groups may not seem
particularly radical, this specific political dynamic centered on debates
over slavery, race, property, and rights; it is not always included in overviews of the French Revolution, nor is it necessarily cited as essential to
understanding the evolution of the French Republic.

Cooper therefore treats history like a hinge, or movable joint, redirect-
ing our attention to the aspects of the narrative she seeks to highlight. She
starts from the basic facts of racial slavery and colonial domination rather
than ignoring or minimizing their historical significance, points to the
subsequent supremacist political, economic, and philosophical legacies of
conquest, and attends to the key role played by political debates about race
in France in fomenting the French Revolution. As a result, Cooper disrupts a powerful and prevailing set of assumptions: "that Europe functions
autonomously from other parts of the world; that Europe is its own origin,
final end, and agent; and that Europe and people of European descent in
the Americas and elsewhere owe nothing to the rest of the world" (Harding, "Introduction" 2).

By pivoting her angle of inquiry, Cooper is better able to highlight
Europe's economic reliance on colonial exploitation and to critique the
ever-increasing gap between democratic *theories* of universal reason and
republican rights and the exploitative *practices* of expansionist capitalist
empires dependent on slave and colonial labor (*Slavery* 70). Specifically,

she emphasizes that this theory/practice gap grew exponentially in the eighteenth century with the emergence of the lucrative sugar trade and its devastating exploitation of slave labor. For instance, although the population of slaves in Saint-Domingue had nearly tripled between 1687 and 1700 (from 3,358 to 9,082), the rise of the sugar plantation required an inordinate amount of slave labor. As Dubois documents, "by midcentury there were nearly 150,000 slaves and fewer than 14,000 whites, and on the eve of the [Haitian] revolution, 90 percent of the colony's population was enslaved" (*Avengers* 19). Cooper's focus on what Trouillot names the ongoing "encounter between ontological discourse and colonial practice" highlights the myriad ways in which, ironically, as Enlightenment ideas of universal rights became more widely accepted, the slave trade and colonial sugar economy grew by leaps and bounds; to put it mildly, the "gap between abstraction and practice grew" (78).

This disconnect — or "vast gulf" as Cooper vividly describes it (*L'Attitude* 60) — led to a drawn out and rather circular political situation, both in France and in Saint-Domingue, in which property rights (including plantation owners' slaves, slave labor, and subsequent profits) kept butting up against the question of citizenship rights, with no obvious resolution in sight. In fact, the predominant pattern of political behavior outlined by Cooper is inaction, delay, and evasion: she highlights the incessant deliberations without resolution and perpetual quarrels with no action (e.g., *Slavery* 86). This political impasse reveals a "profound tension" (Dubois, *Colony* 3) in the ideology of rights with which France was unwilling to come to terms; Cooper critiques both the politicians and the *philosophes* for their naive (or willful) neglect of the need to address slavery if the principles of *égalité* were ever to come to fruition.

Cooper is particularly wary of theories that deal only in abstract universals cut off from the realities of inequity and iniquity. For example, the main goal of the Amis des Noirs was mostly to ready public opinion for the *idea* of emancipation in the abstract; they did not seem to have any concrete action in mind beyond the ideational or philosophical (Cooper, *L'Attitude* 58), nor had they ever "expected that one thing would lead to another so quickly." Moreover, "the Friends of the Blacks were always cautious as to the moment when abolition must take place" (*Slavery* 78). The few "idealists" and "enthusiasts" whom she identifies as having honestly embraced "the question of the emancipation of the slaves" were shortsighted: they "had only seen a problem to be resolved by human sentiment and theory where in fact thorough preliminary groundwork was needed" (*L'Attitude* 106).[12] To Cooper, France's endless debates resulting mostly in evasion illustrate that abolition was thought about primarily as a theoretical conundrum or an economic crisis, not really as a human problem and moral quandary.

To counter this interpretation, Cooper highlights how enslaved blacks in Saint-Domingue are a flesh-and-blood "*living* negation of [France's] noble principles" (*Slavery* 35, italics added): slavery as an institution is not an abstraction, and slaves are *human,* not inanimate property. Cooper suggests that the living contradictions between theory and practice, and the ensuing paradoxes and disconnects, should be considered among our core philosophical and political problematics. The ideals of liberation must connect to the exigencies of lived experience; these should be engaged with a sense of urgency, not dealt with in the abstract. Further, she argues that without transforming the colonial slave economy and its attendant human hierarchies or social ontologies, no amount of theorizing about freedom or philosophizing about universalism would transform the reality of a racially divided, inherently exploitative, profit-driven polity.

Cooper therefore highlights how the *structural* economic and political relationships in place worked against, and directly undermined, philosophical ideas about universalism and political goals of republicanism. A key issue inadequately addressed by the *philosophes* and the politicians was that in the French Caribbean, as well as in France, systems of "work and profits" were organized around slavery (*L'Attitude* 14). Capitalism's profits, which helped to spur change in the class and political structures in the metropole, relied on conquest and slave labor in the colonies: France's emergent democracy depended on the most extreme forms of exploitation.

Cooper argues that the reason such contradictions were consistently ignored was that "the colonists, the rich merchants, had too much to gain from the shameful traffic in slaves to be willing even to consider the possibility of suppressing slavery. Since the time of Colbert, too many French ports had been developed and enriched by the [slave] trade. Bordeaux, Saintes, Marseilles and le Havre prospered" (*Slavery* 37); trade with Saint-Domingue, in fact, represented almost two-thirds of France's total trade (66). Moreover, the plantations of Saint-Domingue did not just supply France; almost all of Europe depended on the sugar produced by the 200,000 slaves working sugar plantations alone (*L'Attitude* 19). In other words, Cooper points to the fact that "African slavery and sugar are critical points for locating the Caribbean in the racialization of global politics. This is where race became part of the process in which the social relations of production developed around plantations in which slaves and their descendants ... produced sugar and other agricultural commodities for the world market. The Caribbean was a pivotal starting point in the making of the capitalist world system" (Watson 462).

She also homes in on the paradox that, with the rise of republican ideals, what held more sway than egalitarianism was "that absolutely corrupt principle of forced labor, labor forced by the whip ... for a whole class of human beings, outrageously exploited." Cooper asserts it was the slaves' labor (not unmatched European genius) that "made their fortunes," both in Saint-Domingue and France (*Slavery* 57). Her focus on the slaves as an exploited class is radical in that they were represented in political argument, philosophical debates, and in the popular culture of the time as incapable of being truly exploited: as Cooper points out, slaves were regarded merely as "bêtes de somme" (beasts of burden). She highlights the slaves' extreme alienation and exploitation, for they were forced "au travail qui ne fructifiait que pour autrui" ("into work that profited only others") (*L'Attitude* 23). Cooper also shows the *colons'* worldview to be primarily one informed by class pretensions and an outright refusal to face the reality in front of them (23): hubris and ignorance, ironically, seemed to rule the day in the Age of Reason.[13]

Although Cooper frames as a class struggle the political conflicts that arose in both France and Saint-Domingue over race, property, and rights, her intersectional method does not reduce race to class, or vice versa. After all, many of the *gens de couleur* were propertied: as Joan Dayan documents, "By 1789, they owned one-third of the plantation property, one-quarter of the slaves, and one-quarter of the real estate property in Saint-Domingue, as well as competing in commerce and trade" (297). The *gens de couleur* also "comprised 47 percent of the colony's free inhabitants in 1788" (Garrigus, "Blue" 233). Cooper underscores that their interests as plantation owners and slave owners shaped their struggle for equal rights as people of color in particular ways; they sought equality with propertied whites, not universal rights for all (*Slavery* 91–2). Cooper's intersectional approach highlights how race and class operate as constantly shifting yet entangled factors: the twists and turns of power in Saint-Domingue and in France cannot be adequately understood if the clash over rights, the ensuing revolution, and the eventual Haitian independence are framed only as struggles of class or race in isolation.

Consequently, Cooper's study offers what Mills would characterize as a "fundamentally *different* understanding of the political order, pointing us theoretically toward the centrality of racial [and class] domination and subordination" ("White" 272, italics original). By arguing that political and philosophical issues of exploitation are historically central, Cooper shifts the focus back to France, but with a decentered eye. For instance, she is careful to emphasize that an economic reliance on and rationalization of slave labor was not just at work in the colonies: major French ports and maritime regions profited from the slave trade and the sugar trade slave labor supported. This highly profitable financial system entailed an "unbridled waste of resources," "oppression and excessive despotism" (Cooper, *Slavery* 43) and influenced the shape of daily life and political ideas in both the colony and the metropole. Repeatedly, she shows how events in Saint-Domingue affected France, and not just the reverse.

In redefining the bounds of nation by attending to its margins, Cooper refuses to accommodate the patronizing notion of a unidirectional relationship between (active, enlightened, and beneficent) colonizer and (passive, backward, and dependent) colonized/enslaved person. Despite the fact that French influence on Haiti/Saint-Domingue is often underlined, Cooper subtly shifts gears to delineate how actions by blacks, slaves, and *gens de couleur* in Saint-Domingue affected debates in France about the nature of the polity vis-à-vis race and pushed France's nascent democracy forward. Accentuating a reciprocal relationship between Saint-Domingue and France, Cooper implies that the "democratic possibilities imperial powers would claim they were bringing to the colonies [as a 'gift'] had in fact been forged ... through the struggles over rights that spread throughout the Atlantic empires" (Dubois, *Colony* 4–5).

Cooper therefore interrupts the usual "*writing out* of the polity of certain spaces [and people] as conceptually and historically irrelevant to European ... development" (Mills, *Racial* 74, see also 122). Her redrawing of the geographic boundaries of French politics and her reframing the philosophical genealogy of what is often characterized as simply "French" intellectual and political history illustrate that without the uprisings and collective action of the *gens de couleur,* the *affranchis,* and the slaves in late eighteenth century Saint-Domingue, French revolutionary universalism and subsequent republican polity might not have turned out to be as inclusive, pluralistic, or democratic as they eventually became. As Dubois asserts, "Had it not been for the revolt that soon erupted in Saint-Domingue, the French Revolution would probably have run its course, like the American Revolution, without destroying the massive violation of human rights at the heart of the nation's existence" (*Avengers* 89).

For instance, slavery would not have been abolished in France and in all French colonies so early, nor would universal political rights without distinction of race or property necessarily have come to fruition (and not just the recognition of "natural" rights with a gradualist approach to the political rights of citizenship). Moreover, a radically new juridical order in which the colonies and the metropole became united as one polity with one set of laws (Dubois, *Colony* 172) would have been out of the question. As Cooper emphasizes, the *colons* and *petits blancs* preferred to sidestep the French constitution and be exempt from the revolutionary "Rights of Man," an evasion Cooper was particularly sensitive to and deeply critical of given the egregious inequalities made legal in the United States under Jim Crow after *Plessy*. The *colons* wanted "special" laws for Saint-Domingue, given the "unique conditions" and different climate and geography of the colonies; they argued against a unified jurisdiction with France in the name of needing to secure the colony's political and social order (i.e., slavery). They sought a "special code" (Cooper, *Slavery* 65), arguing "it would be necessary to modify the French constitution in favor of the colonies, according to their localities" (77) and that "laws incompatible with local customs ... should not be imposed" (80).

The white *colons* and elite Club Massaic were not the only ones with inflexible attitudes toward change, for many of the *gens de couleur* were interested only in a limited degree of political and social transformation: they sought, initially, simply to be equal, as free landowners, to the white *colons* (79). As Cooper reminds us, many of the *gens de couleur* thought of themselves primarily as "colonists of color" (64) and saw no allegiance between their cause and the lives and rights of free blacks or slaves. They were not necessarily interested in abolishing slavery or in restructuring the colonial economy from which they profited; it was only later that the *gens de couleur* and *noirs* would ally to overthrow the French state. In addition, the Amis des Noirs generally advocated a gradualist approach to abolition that did not include full citizenship. Cooper reproaches the French for this cowardice and compromise: "The French legislators were certainly wrong to think as the American legislators did that time and future laws would provide an inoffensive and effective remedy" (113).

Not only are gradualist approaches to social change ineffective, but in the case of abolition, they also entailed a distinction between an abrogation of "natural rights" and any guarantee of political rights, a division Cooper did not accept. As Dubois explains, Enlightenment "thinkers saw clearly the daily resistance of slaves through poison, suicide, abortion, as well as *marronage*[14] and revolt, and the violent response of the planters formed a cycle that had to be stopped before it spun out of control. [However, they] were not particularly antiracist and certainly not anticolonial. ... Enlightenment critiques of slavery attacked the institution as [only] a violation of the natural rights that all human beings shared" (*Avengers* 58). Thus, many of the Friends of the Blacks who supported gradualist abolition often still accepted the idea that there was an inherent hierarchical scale of humanity, with some groups of people more culturally advanced, intellectually superior, and politically developed than others; from this point of view, protection of natural rights is distinguished and divorced from any guaranty of (or capacity for) political rights of citizenship (*droits de cité*).

Cooper's technique for untying this knot of power dynamics is perceptive. By using an intersectional approach to class and race politics, both in

France and in Saint-Domingue, she shows that to comprehend the political forces at work, questions of class interests and racial domination can neither be collapsed nor placed in a hierarchy in which one is subsumed to the other. Otherwise, the class interests of the *gens de couleur,* in which they sought their own rights but wanted to maintain slavery and keep their plantations profitable, would be obscured. In addition, the "excessive and mistaken patriotism" (*Slavery* 35) equating capitalist gain with democratic good, or collapsing whiteness with concepts of the French nation — both of which Cooper emphasizes as problematic — would fade into the background. For example, the tricolor National Cockade (*L'Attitude* 48), a patriotic symbol worn on hats, lapels, or shoes, was illegal for the *gens de couleur* to wear, revealing a collapse between racial identity (whiteness) and French national identity. In addition, the patterns of compromise, delusion, and widespread acceptance of human exploitation that Cooper so meticulously explores would not be captured by an analysis focusing on one system of domination over another.

By shifting the genealogy of French republican ideas and politics to encompass France's colonial history, Cooper shows that without a history of slavery and colonialism, our understanding of the culture of citizenship developed during the French Revolution remains incomplete. Thus Cooper counters what Sibylle Fischer characterizes as an entrenched "Eurocentric bias against considering issues of colonialism and slavery relevant to the high history of the metropolis," a bias so deep, Fischer finds that even the "new interpretations of the French Revolution that emanate from the bastions of higher learning in France[15] continue to ignore the issue to this day" (215). In other words, although Cooper's transatlantic repositioning may seem rather small or inconsequential, Mills contends that such tactics have larger implications: "In radical oppositional political theory ... a crucial initial conceptual move is often the redrawing of the boundaries of the political itself, and the corresponding entry of new, hitherto unrecognized actors onto the theoretical stage" ("White" 271). Cooper's different point of departure allows her to identify the agency and subjectivity of the non-white political actors in this transatlantic epic drama and thereby to shift the operative parameters of both the political and the philosophical.

"Un incendie que rien ne pourrait plus éteindre" ("A fire that could no longer be quelled")[16]

Plainly, a foundational assumption shaping Cooper's research is that there is no intrinsic hierarchy among humans, no natural rank order of cultures or nations: those that exist, past and present, are socially created and maintained, not innate and immutable, for "the democratic sense is an inborn human endowment" (Cooper, "Equality" 293). In terms of the Haitian Revolution, then, Cooper illustrates how "The principles of liberty, equality, and fraternity finally triumphed, because these were *immortal* principles inherent in human nature. The Friends of the Blacks did not introduce Africans to democratic principles but helped awaken them to a priori principles they already possessed" (Baker-Fletcher 55). To accentuate this inherent agential capacity, Cooper sometimes uses the phrase "tous les esprits" (*L'Attitude* 30)[17] to mean all people or humankind, rather than the more secular and common phrase "tout le monde." Cooper also highlights the notion of spirit and its role in equality of all persons in her oral *soutenance* or exams before her doctoral committee. There, she chastises "aggressive usurpers" to remember that "the divine Spark is capable of awakening at the most unexpected moment and it never is wholly smothered or stamped out" ("Equality" 293).

Since the "Spark" or "urge-cell" (293) can *never* be fully extinguished, Cooper emphasizes that domination is never total: even in the most extreme state of subjection, the capacity to resist remains and can be ignited at any time.[18] It is in this sense that Cooper artfully invokes the dual meanings of *l'incendie* to suggest that although the physical fires lit in battle can be doused and the flames smothered, the metaphysical "fire" within each person, the incendiary desire for freedom that causes a political *bouleversement* or revolutionary upheaval, cannot be. She concludes, "*a priori* ... we ought to admit for all peoples the possibility of establishing [free, egalitarian] institutions." Moreover, the "concept of Equality ... [the] inherent value in the individual derived from the essential worth of Humanity must be before all else unquestionably of universal application" (293, 297).

However, not all historians of the Age of Revolution or of Enlightenment philosophy start with the basic working premise that full subjectivity and agency are intrinsic capacities held by all people. Whether overt or implicit, conscious or not, assumptions of cultural, racial, or national supremacy often shape interpretations of events in both Haiti and France. In fact, many "French historians continue to neglect the colonial question, slavery, resistance, and racism more than the revolutionary assemblies ever did. ... The list of writers guilty of this silencing includes names attached to various eras, historical schools, and ideological positions. ... Even the centennial celebrations of French slave emancipation in 1948 did not stimulate a substantial literature on the subject" (Trouillot 101–2). Fischer concurs, and remarks, "If one were to believe standard [historical] accounts, neither slavery nor the colonial question had any impact on the events in Europe" (215). She concludes that this ubiquitous disavowal of the Haitian Revolution, this "suppression of a struggle" for "racial equality and racial liberation" (274) is central to the "modernity that took shape in the Western Hemisphere" even if its presence is hidden, its role denied.[19]

Moreover, in terms of the general public, the fact that slaves, free blacks, and people of color formed flexible coalitions, shifted allegiances, and negotiated with various European states (France, Spain, and England), and brought slavery to an end throughout the French Empire remains relatively unknown, and to some incomprehensible. This is not all that surprising when one considers that, when not left out of historical accounts altogether, the Haitian Revolution's significance or meaning is often qualified or explained by external influences: it is frequently characterized as simply an unsophisticated imitation of France's Revolution or thought of as begat by the French (i.e., the origin lies in France) (Dubois, "République" 23; Reinhardt 107; Trouillot 103).

Thus, scholars' wording often implies that the origin of political revolt and the root source of liberation are European. For example, John Garrigus explores pedagogical and curricular concerns for "students trying to understand how the French Revolution produced a slave revolt of such lasting power in the Caribbean" ("White Jacobins" 265): the "revolt" in Saint-Domingue was *produced by* France. Consider also Williams-Myers's assertion that the Haitian Revolution was a "child" of the French Revolution (382), a phrasing that invokes the parental metaphors (and paternalism) of the colonial "family." In addition, we can infer that, given his theory of the greater "natural" capacity of "Nordics" to *égalité*, Cooper's own chief examiner, Bouglé, might not have thought the Haitian Revolution all that significant; at best, he might have conceded that the story of the *noirs* (blacks, both free and enslaved) and *gens de couleur* illustrated their derivative capacity to copy the French.

Moreover, the Enlightenment is often regarded as taking place only within the bounds of Europe proper, rather than in an Atlantic context of cross-fertilization; therefore, "struggles surrounding political forms — citizenship, rights, the Republic — ... are still powerfully associated in the minds of many with European political and intellectual history" (Dubois, *Colony* 6). In contrast, Cooper argues that although the French Revolution certainly provided a fruitful environment or, as Bogues puts it, a "permissive context" (*Heretics* 82) for the Haitian Revolution, it was not the sole origin: the French Revolution was one cause, she writes, but not *the* cause (*L'Attitude* 18). Again, *the* foundational source of revolt in Saint-Domingue is, for Cooper, the "divine Spark" inherent in all people, everywhere; this inimitable quality is what makes humankind unique. Therefore, although the *noirs* were, for all intents and purposes, almost completely overlooked by politicians in France and by the *colons* in Saint-Domingue, or, if acknowledged, dehumanized and maligned, this does not mean that they did not play a significant political role in French politics, at home and abroad. Cooper concludes, "Ils n'allaient pas manquer d'être un élément actif d'insurrection" ("they would not fail to be an active [i.e., not passive or merely imitative] element of the insurrection") (*L'Attitude* 22–3).

Brilliantly relying on the double entendre embedded in the word *l'incendie*, Cooper not only accentuates the fire, or spirit, burning within all persons; she also calls to mind the use of fire as a weapon of resistance by the Black armies in Saint-Domingue under the leadership of Toussaint Louverture, Henri Christophe, and Jean-Jacques Dessalines, among others. In fact, the Haitian Revolution began and ended with fire. For instance, the massive 1791 slave insurrections involved a carefully orchestrated burning of "all manifestations of slavery," including the slave quarters, and of all the mechanisms of the sugar economy, including the sugarcane fields, the mills, and the machinery (Dubois, *Avengers* 92–6). Thirteen years later, the successful battles resulting in Haitian independence also involved extensive burning as a combat tactic. Although a focus on fire when discussing the Haitian Revolution is not that unusual, Cooper's interpretive frame is quite different: she does not scandalize or sensationalize Black resistance.[20]

However, when the destruction of human life and property caused by these fires and battles is referred to in documents of the time and by historians, it is often done in a way that ascribes horrific and extreme violence only to the Black perpetrators. Dubois explains: "Since the moment slaves rose up in Saint-Domingue in 1791, accounts of the revolution have focused a great deal on its violence. The fact that some of the atrocities in the Haitian revolution were committed by insurgent slaves, and later by Black officers and troops, has made them the object of fascination." Rhetorical appeals to shock and alarm have made violence perpetrated by the *noirs* in Saint-Domingue hypervisible while the "ideas and ideals generated" by Black resistance have been generally avoided or suppressed (Dubois, *Avengers* 5, see also 110). Meanwhile, the atrocities committed by whites engaged in revolution are often interpreted simply as the (rational but unfortunate) cost of engaging in just forms of war, not as symbolic of whites' lesser human status or incapacity for civilization.

In contrast, Cooper inverts this rhetorical frame and turns the imperial gaze back on itself. Using a *volte-face* technique (a sudden rhetorical about-face), Cooper suggests that it is those who support slavery who are "uncivilized," much like those who support U.S. policies of imperial expansion and conquest (what Cooper names the "equilibrium of the jungle" at work in the epicenters of "civilization") in the present day ("Equality" 297). Moreover, she argues that the whites, particularly the *colons*, were unsuited to freedom and to the responsibilities of democracy. Not only were they ill prepared to legislate (*Slavery* 70), but they remained "unworthy of the liberty which was accorded them or the confidence shown in them" (72). Nevertheless, France continued to be "too indulgent with the turbulent colonists" (73) despite the fact that "they were the real foment-ers of the troubles" in Saint-Domingue (74). Here, Cooper indirectly takes on Condorcet and the other *philosophes* who proposed a gradualist approach to abolition. He argued that "'the slaves of the European colonies have become incapable of fulfilling the duties of free men'" (Condorcet in Dubois, "République" 25). Despite his status as a founding radical of the Friends of the Blacks, Condorcet "wrote a history of slavery as an institu-tion that had left the slaves incapable of living responsibly with freedom" (Dubois, "République" 25). In response, Cooper reverses Condorcet's con-clusions: she argues that, taken as a whole, the white *colons'* obstinacy with regard to questions of race and rights, their arbitrary abuse of power, and their calculated political manipulations of France's greatest fears (i.e., the loss of the lucrative colonies via massive upheaval and violent slave revolts) demonstrate a conspicuous incapacity on their part for liberty and *égalité*.

Of course, there are limits to the effectiveness of Cooper's inversion, for it leaves intact the operative dualism between those "capable" and "inca-pable" of the responsibilities of citizenship, albeit reversed. However, one can imagine Cooper may well have gained some satisfaction in transpos-ing the dominant logic, documenting the inhumanity of those usually deemed "higher" in the rank order of peoples and cultures. In particular, we can speculate that she may have delighted in upending Bouglé's Nordi-cist theory of "Occidental" *égalité*.[21] In spite of the limits of inversion as a method, Cooper successfully shows that owing to the prevailing ontologi-cal assumptions about the greater (political, cultural, intellectual) advance-ment of white/European peoples, the slaves were not really thought of as a political force; they remained an abstraction to most of France and to the dominant classes of both *colons* and *gens de couleur* in Saint-Domingue.

In contrast, Cooper presumes the inherently equal capacity of all humans, no matter their politically and historically constructed status (e.g., as a slave). Not only does she recognize Black agency and subjectivity where others ignore or suppress it, but she also highlights the oppressive actions and assumptions of those with more power. For example, France's own archival materials document that slaves and maroons had been openly resisting for over a century: prior to the uprisings of 1788–1791 were those of 1679, 1691, 1703, and 1758[22] (Cooper, *L'Attitude* 22). Cooper also uncov-ers references to widespread work stoppages on plantations (104). More-over, she shows that the French knew that slave resistance was not isolated to Saint-Domingue: the Colonial Committee, for instance, wanted to "slow down a revolutionary movement menacing the whole of the West Indies" (*Slavery* 66). Later, as the Haitian Revolution picked up momentum, General Rochambeau was sent to the colony "to try to put down the rebellious Negroes, whom nobody had been able to defeat" (*Slavery* 93).[23]

Yet despite the wide array of evidence to the contrary, Cooper finds that hardly anyone in France could imagine that the blacks would claim citizenship, even after Toussaint Louverture and his army of over 20,000 *noirs* fought successfully time and again (*L'Attitude* 72). In fact, "Theories assuming chaos under black leadership continued even after Louverture and his closest lieutenants fully secured the military, political, and civil apparatus of the colony" (Trouillot 93). Cooper therefore has to work against racist stereotypes and pervasive ontological assumptions built into historical analysis and embedded in her archival materials. For instance, she challenges the idea of colonized and enslaved people as imitative but ultimately naive outlaws or "brigands" not really capable of the responsibilities of citizenship. "Brigand," which Cooper always places in quotes (e.g., *Slavery* 91, 95), is a derogatory word (meaning bandit, thug, thief, felon, or robber) commonly used to describe uprisings by slaves, the *affranchis,* and the *gens de couleur.* The term diminishes the significance of Black resistance in Saint-Domingue, reducing it to criminally deviant, isolated outbursts, whereas the more positive and overtly political term "revolutionary" would connote organized collective political action.

Cooper is particularly careful to use positive adjectives to describe Black military commanders in Saint-Domingue: she refers to Jean-François and Biassou, for instance, as "great leaders" (*L'Attitude* 102), and shows General Michel to be rather cunning in his back-door negotiations with the French commissioner Sonthanax (*Slavery* 104). She also characterizes the Black army's successful revolt under Louverture, Dessalines, and others as a "coup d'état" (104), emphasizing both the Black army's military prowess and that the events in Saint-Domingue should be thought as much a part of the Age of Revolution as the American or French revolutions. The clearest examples of Cooper's admiration for Black leadership, however, lie in her descriptions of Toussaint Louverture, who was born a slave on a plantation in Le Cap in 1743. Cooper emphasizes that "he was the son of an African Negro of Guinea and a Negro woman; he had not a drop of white blood in his veins" (101). This brief passage is particularly significant, for here Cooper rejects any hint of race supremacy in the history of revolution. Pellow explains: "When describing the heroic achievements of Toussaint Louverture in the struggle for liberation in Haiti, she is emphatic in pointing out that he was of unmixed African descent, so that his intelligence and accomplishments could not be attributed to any admixture of Saxon blood, as whites would often claim" (65).

Cooper repeatedly accents Louverture's military brilliance, excellent leadership (*Slavery* 101), and shrewd insight, all of which were "much admired" (102). With maximal freedom for all Blacks in mind, Louverture skillfully maneuvered shifting alliances between European states and built up his political base, rising to power in Saint-Domingue; his leadership and success were not due "chance or caprice" (101), for he "had always known how to keep himself informed about European movements and what they meant" (106). And, although his persistent "political sagacity" (105) may have "never occurred" to French leaders, Cooper remarks that it should have been patently clear that "Toussaint Louverture knew how to see and foresee" (102). Moreover, when the French captured this "strong and cunning foe," he and the other Black leaders did not truly surrender: Cooper points to their dissemblance, remarking that "in all cases" they just "appear[ed] to surrender" (109). Louverture "held himself aloof, inoffensive in appearance but watching events"; even in apparent defeat, "his intrigues and his conspiracies provoked constant uprisings" (110).

While underscoring the overlooked agency of slaves, free blacks, and leaders like Louverture, Cooper meticulously documents the excessive regulation of the status quo on the part of whites, both in Saint-Domingue and in France. Of course, the Code Noir (Black Code) played a major role in this. For example, it "designates slaves, only to negate them. Its rigorous logic does not permit the slave to play any role in the arena of law and rights. Slaves exist legally [as persons] only insofar as they disobey" (Dayan 288); otherwise, slaves are defined in the Codes solely as objects of property. Contrary to declarations by the *colons* and French merchants that the "dependence in which [the slaves] live is a hundred times easier[24] than that in which live a great portion of French individuals" (*Slavery* 119), Cooper documents how intensely cruel working conditions (*L'Attitude* 24) led to extremely high slave mortality rates: the countless dead say more about the realities of the life of the slaves than do the insincere declarations of the slave-owning *colons* (9). Cooper also emphasizes how whites and *gens de couleur* used fear, torture, and cruelty to keep the slaves in a state of subjection (23), suggesting, of course, that if slavery were so beneficent, "sweet," and "natural," then such violent and brutal techniques would be unnecessary.

Moreover, even though they were free, myriad constraints were placed upon free blacks and *gens de couleur* because they "'still bore on their foreheads the mark of slavery, [and therefore] had to be reminded constantly of their origin, through the weight of scorn and opprobrium and the breaking of their spirits'" (Boissenade in Cooper, *Slavery* 45). This "breaking of their spirits" occurred through the law, which determined viable professions, housing segregation, and anti-miscegenation decrees (Cooper, *L'Attitude* 22), as well as through ontological degradation or social shaming as "pariahs" (21). For example, the "white colonist-proprietors and even the 'petits blancs' took pride and pleasure in humiliating the mulattoes, in scornfully referring to them as dogs, ugly ones, big bellies, quarter-breeds, half-castes, and so on" (*Slavery* 44).

These derogatory naming practices outlined by Cooper arose in conjunction with additions to the *Code Noir* "to exclude or segregate persons of any African descent from white colonial free society. Notaries, priests and other officials were required to fix racial labels to all families of mixed European and African descent. ... African ancestry ... became a permanent 'stain'" (Garrigus, "Colour" 26). Dayan adds that "The techniques of degradation depended on social segregation and judicial inequality, all of which read as if they were castigated for the sin of blurring the 'demarcation line' between castes (that is, between colors) in Saint-Domingue. The ritual of naming, so central to enslavement, was now brought to bear upon the free people of color. ... [T]he new onomastics reminded *libres* of their origins" (296). In addition to legal codification of the public sphere according to racial status, to prevent the spread of radical ideas and abolition literature, free blacks and *gens de couleur* were prevented from returning to Saint-Domingue once they left (Cooper, *Slavery* 48, 59); even their transatlantic correspondence was opened and checked for reasons of "security." Strict censorship prevailed over "everything coming from France," particularly the "correspondence of the colored men in France with their brothers in Santo Domingo" (63).[25]

Thus, whites in Saint-Domingue and in France spent an inordinate amount of time and energy creating and maintaining an ostensibly "natural" state of submission and degradation of the nonwhites, enslaved and free. They constructed a perverted race supremacy, and then deluded themselves into believing it was innate and eternal (*L'Attitude* 43). Even when what Cooper names "The Revolution in Saint-Domingue"[26] (82) was well under way, the majority of slaves were still referred to as, apparently, inclined to "submission," at least according to the king's proclamation, which declared that nothing had changed in the state of "obedience" that the slaves had "always" shown their masters (82, fn. 3). Letters and archival materials also contain statements such as "I do not believe that there is any insurrection of the Negroes" in Saint-Domingue (*Slavery* 121). Such patent denials of reality are not all that surprising. As Trouillot argues, "Built into any system of domination is the tendency to proclaim its own normalcy. To acknowledge resistance as a mass phenomenon is to acknowledge the possibility that something is wrong with the system" (84).

Despite the whites' desire to reassure themselves that the colonial social order was viable and that the slaves were happy and content, Cooper shows the ridiculousness of these everyday observations, political assertions, and royal declarations by juxtaposing contradicting archival evidence. Two pages after Cooper writes that the slaves were reported in the Assembly to be as obedient and submissive as ever, she quietly shifts her focus to archival materials from the Assembly about the Artibonite revolts (*Slavery* 67) and to correspondence about other ongoing and massive uprisings by both *noirs* (free and enslaved) and *gens de couleur* (71–2). Later, Cooper slyly characterizes the *noirs* as "surexcités" (*L'Attitude* 74), which Keller translates as "aroused" (*Slavery* 79). However, this term has other meanings, including being in a state of political agitation (protest) and being in a state of exaltation (joy, exhilaration).[27] In other words, it is a turn of phrase that aligns perfectly with Cooper's idea about the "divine Spark," universal human agency, and desire for freedom: the *noirs'* being so easily moved to a state of "surexcitation" suggests that they were *not* content with a state of domination, despite the *colons'*, the king's, and the merchants' delusional declarations to the contrary.

On occasion, nonwhite subjectivity *was* acknowledged by whites, but usually only to incite fear, to fuel a race panic or "l'affolement" (Cooper, *L'Attitude* 45) about the "dangerous" future if nonwhites (even those already free and propertied, the *gens de couleur*) were to gain any rights whatsoever. For example, "all the letters of the time from the colony to Paris sounded the same note of rising alarm" (*Slavery* 80). Plantation owners warned that any spread of republican ideals to the Antilles would "cause torrents of blood and tears to flow in the colonies" (120). Via inflammatory and openly prejudiced correspondence, the *colons* sought to influence French affairs and political decisions in their favor (i.e., to retain slavery and the slave trade, and to maintain a white-only definition of citizenship) by raising the specter of imminent and total chaos in Martinique, in Guadeloupe, and at Le Cap on Saint-Domingue, playing on French fears of losing all its colonies in the Caribbean (*L'Attitude* 68). In regard to the *gens de couleur*, the marquis de Gouy d'Arsy declared that "the whites of his island in fact viewed the mulattoes as enemies whom they must leave in their low condition if they wished not to have reasons to fear them" (*Slavery* 54). In addition, the "nature is destiny" card was played to justify slavery and to manipulate racist fears of black "assassins." For example, M. Legorgne, secretary of the National Civil Commission, argued that "nature ... seems to intend[28] the African to wear chains and that to break them too precipitously is to make him an assassin, or to become his accomplice!" (149, fn. 123).

Thus, the stereotypes and "evidence" about slaves and *gens de couleur* shifted according to political expedience, from the supposedly happy, obedient, willing, and even fortunate slaves, or the ostensibly tranquil and submissive *gens de couleur*, to hordes of monstrous, violent outlaws. One set of controlling images rationalized slavery and validated the whites' unyielding attitude toward the *gens de couleur*'s claims to the full rights of citizenship as property holders, diminishing or even ignoring resistance by focusing on supposed compliance and insisting upon the harmonious rightness of the existing social order. In contrast, the second set of controlling images focused on resistance, not as a sign that slavery might be wrong but to gain support for suppressing "savagery" and maintaining slavery by any means necessary. Both types of imagery served the same purpose: to maintain the economic and ontological status quo.

"Scientific" rationales were equally as mercurial. At first the slaves and *gens de couleur* were considered related by "blood" (such that all blacks, enslaved or free, were equally "black" — much like the "one drop" rule in the United States). According to this logic, the *gens de couleur* could not have the rights of citizenship because their blood ties to the slaves overrode any of their blood ties to the whites and made them "natural enemies" who must be kept in abjection (Cooper *L'Attitude* 36–7). However, as the political climate changed in Saint-Domingue, the white *colons* feared losing the colony and their profitable plantations entirely: the increasing insurrections by *gens de couleur* and widespread revolts by *noirs* (blacks free and enslaved) could no longer be ignored (41). The *colons* then decided that the *gens de couleur* were, on balance, closer to whites, hence their greater "perfectibility" and potential as reliable allies. *Gens de couleur* deserved their rights after all, but only if they would help maintain slavery and the colonial economy (*Slavery* 88).

Many influential *gens de couleur* followed this lead and declared in letters and speeches that they were in no way in favor of abolishing slavery. Cooper cites several examples of such expedience, but she is particularly critical of the well-known planter of color Julien Raimond, who made his fortune in indigo.[29] She writes, "To anyone who studies the correspondence of Julien Raimond it is evident that he never ceased to urge his brothers to endure everything in order to preserve tranquility in the colony and to allow the whites all that they wished" (*Slavery* 64). Later, Raimond's resolute pro-slavery attitudes would prompt Louverture to oust him from Saint-Domingue for a time. Through fixed "elections," he sent "Raimond to France; he was guilty of ... never having favored freeing the slaves, and of always having separated the question of slavery from that of political liberty of men of color" (105). Cooper castigates Raimond even further, emphasizing how he had "carried this separation to the point of totally refusing to favor the liberty of the blacks, letting it be known that his fortune, that of his family, and that of all the colony as well, were based on slavery" (105).[30]

Raimond is not the only one whom Cooper disparages: she exposes General Rigaud's conceit and prejudice, for example, in choosing to take his "'elite corps' of mulattoes ... to Cuba rather than surrender to a black" (i.e., Louverture) (*Slavery* 106). However, in focusing on Raimond's and Rigaud's colonized imaginations, Cooper is pointing to a larger, more systemic problem. A supremacist metaphysic going back to the Spanish-Portuguese conquests was so deeply entrenched in the colonies that it molded the perceptions of the *colons*, the *petits blancs*, and the *gens de couleur*: few could see beyond it. She explains that "color prejudices ... had grown so deep that they were even stronger than all the other social distinctions made between the free man and the slave since ancient times, to the point where a mulatto slave would have refused to obey a free [Black], even if the latter had the audacity to buy him" (114). Cooper decries this institutionalization of human hierarchy and systemic collusion with the "right" of might and profit over human rights such that, in order to prove their true "Frenchness" and full humanity, and to demonstrate patriotism, the *gens de couleur* had to show a willingness to dominate the *noirs*, both free and enslaved (*L'Attitude* 96). Paradoxically, the French republican ideal required an oath not to liberty, brotherhood, and equality but instead a promise to maintain an ontological hierarchy among humans so that the profits of a colonial, slave economy would not be disturbed.

"Can we — ought we to — analyze human society as if it were a question of minerals or of vegetation?"[31]: Cooper's Historiographic Method

In addition to stretching the parameters of who and what "counts" as historically significant, rejecting an internalist framework in favor of an Atlantic model of analysis, and advocating an intersectional approach to race and class exploitation, Cooper employs several other methodological techniques to unpack the story of the French and Haitian revolutions. For example, she approaches her research from a situated standpoint, not an objectivist position. Although "Modern [Western] thought has often conceptualized objectivity as achieved by transcending particularities of social position and experience, abstracting from them to construct a standpoint outside and above them that is general rather than particular" (Young 113), Cooper asserts that truth and meaning can be found in the situational particulars of lived experience. Decrying the limits embedded in a method of "pure reason" (Cooper, "Equality" 292), Cooper chooses to delineate the significance of "differences of social position, structural power, and cultural affiliation " (Young 81). Cooper remarks, for example, "It goes without saying that the white colonists viewed things with a different eye" (*Slavery* 88). Occasionally breaking away from the detached narrative voice commonly believed appropriate for historical analysis, Cooper declares that she "makes no pretensions to scientific sanctions on either sociological or psychological grounds" ("Equality" 295). In fact, she finds the idea of "scientific" abstraction in social and historical analysis almost ludicrous, "as if men and societies reacted like chemical atoms" (295).

Just as Cooper distrusts the "rational" arguments presented in the eighteenth century for maintaining slavery, she is equally skeptical of the much-lauded "objectivity" practiced in the social sciences. Since ostensibly pure detachment often meant, in actuality, a cruel indifference to those who had been marginalized or disenfranchised, Cooper sought a narrative strategy that would allow for a more dimensional understanding of history, that would account for a view from the periphery. Yet traditionally, much of Western historical research has assumed a positivist method in which "the role of the historian is to reveal the past," simply to uncover it. Moreover, "within that viewpoint, power is unproblematic, irrelevant to the construction of the narrative" (Trouillot 4–5). Of course, Cooper is not interested in transcending questions of power: power is *the* core problematic shaping the story of the Haitian and French revolutions, influencing how (or whether) it is told, and to what end. The meaning and role of slavery and colonialism, for France and for the Age of Revolution, is often minimized if not suppressed, just as the significance of Black people as historical agents is often circumscribed if not ignored; Cooper, however, believes in the centrality of people, places, and events that others relegated to the margins of history.

And yet, here she is, in the midst of one of Europe's most powerful empires, going against the grain of much French historical writing. Cooper must determine how to tell some of history's suppressed stories and offer a different interpretation of world events even with a definitively Eurocentric data set as her primary resource. Keller documents that the parliamentary archives are, to put it mildly, imbalanced: "Of the thousands of published cahiers in the Archives parlementaires, there are only thirty-seven which formulate demands for any action favoring the Negroes [sic]. Of these eleven demand the eventual abolition of slavery. Twelve ask for improvement in the condition of the slaves, but are indefinite as to what should be done. ... [O]nly one cahier expressed concern with the condition of free Negroes [sic]" ("Perspective" 20). It is no wonder that Cooper characterizes the powerful suffering of the *noirs*, and particularly the slaves, as silent (*L'Attitude* 23).

Immersed in France's military and political archives, Cooper culls from the extensive documents to capture the shifting race and class alliances criss-crossing the Atlantic. She also highlights the agency and influence of the slaves and free blacks — those who had an "unsuspected power" and were "endowed with remarkable qualities of intelligence and dignity" (*Slavery* 45), even though in the historical records Cooper has as her resource, they are *never thought of* at all (50). Noting the gaps, oversights, and omissions built into her materials, Cooper examines them from a decidedly different standpoint: not only does her research negate the logic of many of the carefully collected speeches, letters, laws, pamphlets, royal decrees, and political arguments rationalizing slavery, her very presence in the archives as a scholar also controverts bigoted proclamations about Black women's supposedly "naturally" inferior intellectual capacity.

To coax a different sense of history out of these documents that violate her very being, Cooper highlights history's "debatability" (Appadurai in Trouillot 8). She brings together widely divergent voices, opinions, outlooks, and ideologies to present history as a situated, contested conversation. Cooper draws from a range of eighteenth- and early nineteenth-century materials, including private and state correspondence, colonial reports, military records, voting records, inflammatory political pamphlets and speeches, assembly debates, and political club minutes, as well as scholarship and analyses from the period about slavery, colonialism, Saint-Domingue, and the French revolution in general. However, like any dialogue, history as conversation has its omissions, its array of voices with differing degrees of authority or "hearability," its uneven rhetorical space. As Paget Henry argues in his introduction to Afro-Caribbean philosophy, "the contradictory tendencies and patterns of communicative inequality that characterize our intellectual tradition derive from the colonial nature of the cultural system that institutionalized it" (*Caliban's* 9). Issues of communicative inequality and archival power are particularly relevant for Cooper's resources: she fully realizes that the "general silencing of the Haitian Revolution by Western historiography ... is due to uneven power in the production of sources, archives, and narratives" (Trouillot 27).

Accordingly, despite the mountain of materials made available to her in Paris, Cooper remained ever wary of the bias and incommensurability of power at the heart of archival work. In fact, Cooper suggests that the elite status of many of the white colonists and members of the Club Massaic, whose "association ... was very much richer" (*Slavery* 48), led to their materials being safeguarded in history. Actually, the archives are so full of the Massaic's documents that Cooper finds she has been unable to exhaust them in her extensive research (48). She even remarks, in her footnotes, that the archives are replete with minutiae, such as trivial complaints about carriage street noise interrupting Massaic meetings (144, fn. 23), implying that a power imbalance has helped create an archival imbalance.

Further alluding to the fact that she has reservations about her primary sources, Cooper describes some of the pamphlets as "shaded by inevitable prejudice" (48) and refers to reports written "from a point-of-view as favorable as possible to the white colonists" (75–6). It is not just the primary sources that are biased, but also other scholars' historical research, including that of Garran-Coulon[32] (149, fn. 139) and Stoddard.[33] She therefore advises that "caution is necessary" when reading Stoddard because of his "constantly obvious prejudice against the mulattoes and the blacks" (147, fn. 102). Sometimes Cooper includes remarks about the partial and prejudicial nature of her sources in her footnotes or in her *pièces justificatives* (supporting materials). For example, she writes, "Many papers, letters and memoranda from the Massaic Institute tend[34] to prove that the [*noirs*] are not unhappy, that they have not asked for ... liberty ... [and] that the [slave] trade ... is preferable to the fate which awaits them in Africa" (128).

As Cooper's embedded critical comments reveal, "Most of what we know about [the Haitian Revolution's central protagonists'] actions and ideals comes from the writings of (often quite hostile) witnesses, whose views about slavery and slaves profoundly influenced what they wrote" (Dubois, *Avengers* 6). Occasionally, Cooper overtly introduces doubt into the telling of history by using phrases such as "if we are to believe the documents of the period" (*Slavery* 87), or "If we believe an undated, unsigned memorandum" (93). She is cautious about accepting without question the analyses and arguments preserved in France's military and political archives, and with good reason. As Trouillot argues, "Official debates and publications of the times ... reveal the incapacity of most contemporaries to understand" the mere *idea*, much less the reality, of a slave revolution because they could only perceive the world around them with their "ready-made categories" or lenses, which preclude this possibility (73). As both Trouillot and Cooper document, the French were totally incapable of imagining the Haitian Revolution, much less a Black-run republic.

Thus, another key analytic technique used by Cooper is to focus on the fissures in people's thinking. She pinpoints instances of whites' utter inability to understand the reality unfolding before their own eyes: even after several successful slave revolts, "people thought, superficially enough, that an alliance of the whites and the mulattoes would be sufficient to put down the revolt of the blacks" (Cooper, *Slavery* 87). They simply could not realize that the *noirs* would never agree to continued degradation because they never *had* "agreed" to it in the first place! The concept of Black agency, spirit, or will, seems completely out of the realm of possibility; ironically, it turns out that it is the whites, particularly the *colons*, who came to believe in the artificial race supremacy they had created and maintained by force. Cooper homes in on how they crafted their own "apparently unassailable truths — the indefatigability of 'whites,' the 'natural' subhuman status of 'blacks'" (Munro 2) — and could not imagine any reality beyond the world they had constructed. Despite the fact that the colonial system based on slavery was wholly untenable (Cooper, *L'Attitude* 55), the repeated slave uprisings continued to be characterized as anomalous: their meaning and import was unfathomable.

The problem is not only that the slaves were underestimated as a political force; the key issue, as Cooper identifies it, is that they were not really thought of at all. For example, while discussing the Legislature's discussions about "the status of persons in the colonies," Cooper inserts a rather sarcastic parenthetical statement: "(It is never a question of the slaves)" (*Slavery* 88). Again and again, the Assembly acts "without ever giving a thought to the condition of the slaves" (94). In Saint-Domingue, "they complained bitterly of the devastation of their properties [(which included "damage" done to slaves)], but the question of slavery appeared secondary" (97–8). How is it that the French could espouse Enlightenment philosophies of universal rights and instigate a revolution to create a republican democracy, yet never think of slavery as an abrogation of their most deeply held beliefs and principles? How is it that repeatedly, they opted for economic interests over all else, choosing to maintain the status quo system of exploitation in the name of profit?

Exploring the Politics of Conciliation and the Pitfalls of the "Common Good"

Cooper's dissertation seems a rather straightforward comparative study of the political debates between opposing political interest coalitions, the Friends of the Blacks (who advocated, to varying degrees, the rights of citizenship for free, property-owning *gens de couleur*) and the Club Massaic (the club of *colons*, merchants, and others who opposed the rights of the *gens de couleur*, who were pro-slavery, and whom Cooper characterizes as a "strongly organized pressure group serving class interests" [*Slavery* 49]). Obviously, the Friends and the Massaic were very different in terms of both outlook and political base. Cooper does not ignore these differences in motivation or political ideology, but she does ask us to attend to a surprisingly consistent pattern of overlap and general accord among the vast majority of political players in France.

Cooper carefully juxtaposes archival materials from these political rivals to highlight extensive similarities in spite of outward differences. Specifically, both groups continually ceded ethical and philosophical principles of *égalité* in name of the "common" interest of property rights and economic profit; the "general interests of French commerce" predominated (*Slavery* 67). As Catherine Reinhardt contends, "Evoking the economic ruin of the colonies was the most effective way of lobbying against the application of egalitarian ideals to non-whites" (111). Cooper's supporting documents, or *pièces justificatives*, reveal how defense of "the welfare and prosperity" of France regularly got equated with being "defenders of the Commerce and of the Colonies" (*Slavery* 124), not defenders of liberty and human rights. Slavery was justified as one of the unfortunate but necessary "costs" of doing business and remaining strong as a nation.

Ironically, the noble-sounding "'perfect understanding which must reign among all citizens,'" referred to by Julien Raimond and others in their plea for the rights of *gens de couleur* before the National Assembly (*Slavery* 131), turns out to have its basis in monetary arrangements, although Raimond's discursive emphasis on virtue and rationality directs attention away from this fact. The apparently dignified "wonderful brotherhood" between *gens de couleur* and propertied whites actually rests on the "foundations of common prosperity" rather than universal humanity and rights (122). As Cooper frequently reminds us, in France and in Saint-Domingue the primary goal was to retain the colonies, even if that meant maintaining slavery (*L'Attitude* 59). The remarkable ease with which a metaphysic of domination was regularly acceded to, with little to no debate, reveals the tenacity of the old social, economic, and racial order. Cooper shows that the greater part of France was, when it came down to it, of a similar mind when it came to defining the prevailing "common interest" of the nation as financial profit, not equality and freedom for all. In fact, at one point she characterizes the nation's accord over slavery in the name of profit as so harmonious that the members of the Assembly "walked" as if they were "one man" (54).

However, a historical method highlighting the political contest between the Massaic and the Friends, and upholding the premise that they are indeed "opposite," runs the risk of obscuring the degree to which all of France, and indeed much of Europe, was deeply reliant on the sugar trade and thus basically dedicated to the continuation of slavery. Cooper presents her study as tracing the conflict between these two factions, but there is much more to her analysis. If she was only interested in the political to-and-fro between the Massaic and the Friends, Cooper would not bother raising the larger issue at hand: how colonialist capitalism's seductive profits oiled the machinery of political negotiation in ways that compromised, even negated, France's foundational ethics and core ideals, ironically all in the name of the nation's best interests.

Moreover, by focusing on the series of compromises over slavery arrived at in France's national assembly, Cooper suggests that unity and consensus do not necessarily embody the democratic ideal. In examining the twists and turns of events in France and in Saint-Domingue, and in outlining the political negotiations between the Massaic and the Friends, Cooper queries: "Comment concilier des points de vue si contraires?" ("How to reconcile such divergent points of view?") (*L'Attitude* 67). She raises this key political and philosophical question in good faith and not only rhetorically, for the French seemed at a loss as to how to proceed. But there are also larger questions raised by the particulars she examines. For example, is it possible, or even desirable, to "reconcile" those arguing for the economic interests of slave labor based on an ontological hierarchy with those arguing for the human interests of universal human rights? Obviously, these diametrically opposed paradigms cannot really be brought together in any meaningful way, nor should they be. Cooper clearly advocates abolition as the only means of living up to the ideals and premises of the French Revolution: the French *must* connect theory and action in order to realize the full potential of liberty, she argues. But instead, they focused on pecuniary gain.

By bringing up the issue of reconciling contrary worldviews, Cooper suggests that conciliation may not, in fact, be the best way to arrive at the common good. She implies that there are dangers in a deliberative democratic ideal and in common-interest arguments, since deciding the general welfare of the people is often arrived at with a very limited definition of who "the people" are and with a constrained notion of what the general "good" is as well. In the case of Haiti, Césaire later would conclude that France's universal ideal of the good of the nation amounted to a "faux universalisme" in which "le droit de l'homme" is in fact merely the right to liberty and equality of (particular, not universal) European Man (343). Similarly, Young maintains that today, in the case of common interest arguments, "there tends to be a reinforcing circle between social and economic inequality and political inequality that enables the powerful to use formally democratic processes to perpetuate injustice or preserve privilege" (17). Thus, paradoxically, "the idea of a common good or general interest can often serve as a means of exclusion" (43). In the case of France, as Cooper shows, to validate their predilection for profit and downplay their flagrant violation of universalism, the French majority accepted a supremacist ontology in order to enhance the economic good. Not only does financial gain, ironically, supersede all other factors, but those who are dispossessed and disenfranchised disappear from view as part of the equation.

Yet there are risks in Cooper's analytic method. By using juxtaposition to highlight commonalities between sworn political enemies, she can seem strangely neutral toward those whom we might expect her to denounce. Consider, for instance, her treatment of Barnave, chair of France's Colonial Committee, who favored the Massaic and the merchants: Cooper even acknowledges that he has been accused of "repugnant partiality" (*Slavery* 66). Although she points to problematic gaps in his decision making, such as his determination to accord rights to the *gens de couleur* but to retain slavery (*L'Attitude* 76), Cooper seems unwilling to hang the failures of the

French to live up to Enlightenment ideals on the Massaic Club or on people such as Barnave. She seems to go out of her way *not* to focus on Barnave's shortcomings and biases (56). Upon a first reading, this can seem rather odd. After all, we *know* Cooper is not one to absolve those who perpetuate domination, and yet Barnave agreed with the Massaic Club's politics and colonists' interests. What is going on?

Although Cooper's take on Barnave seems rather confusing at first, I find, in the end, that she is not keen to focus solely on the infringements or biases of individuals like Barnave, or even on the collective oversight or failures of particular political coalitions such as the Massaic. Instead, Cooper argues that the facts show a much more sinister situation: the archival materials illustrate that all of Barnave's adversaries, including Grégoire,[35] Brissot,[36] and Pétion,[37] were fundamentally of the same opinion as he — they favored gradualism, never the abolition of slavery, and fully accepted an ontological distinction between full humanity and lesser human status to justify this (*L'Attitude* 57). As Aimé Césaire would later comment, "L'abolition de l'esclavage ... la Constituante, c'est un fait, avait reculé devant elle, unanime" ("Abolition... It's a fact that the Constituent Assembly recoiled from it, unanimously") (134, ellipses in original, translation mine). Moreover, Barnave and the Colonial Committee's motion to keep the lucrative colonies at all costs, even if it meant retaining slavery, was received favorably in the Assembly, indicating a majority opinion or mindset (Cooper, *L'Attitude* 58). Cooper therefore concludes, "Few legislative assemblies have proceeded with so substantial an agreement and so much unity. ... The majority went forward as one; ... only in theory was the Assembly ever favorable to slaves" (*Slavery* 67).

Later, the question of the political rights of Blacks could easily have been raised, but it was sidestepped and hesitated over as much by the Amis des Noirs as by anyone else (*L'Attitude* 61–2). Cooper reveals a pattern of cowardice and prejudice as pervasive in France as in the colonies. For example, when it came to the May 15, 1791 decree (according some rights to some *gens de couleur*), everyone seems to have tolerated making the law a "dead letter" in the name of colonial profits (77). Later that year, the French assembly would try to wash its hands of ever having to confront the "problem" of race and rights again by creating an unalterable article of the constitution giving all discretion over the status "des mulâtres et des esclaves" to local colonial assemblies and the king (78–9). They built ignorance and evasion into the constitution in an attempt to avoid dealing with the obvious contradictions in their republican ideals and in Enlightenment theories of universal rights.

In other words, Cooper does not excuse the actions of the Massaic Club or of Barnave and the Colonial Committee, but she does not want to isolate these ways of thinking to just a few obvious "villains" of history. Doing so would draw attention away from the larger picture of *general* accord with exploitation that she seeks to paint. She writes, "Barnave's attitude ... was in accord with the thinking of the entire Constituent Assembly, with all thinking Frenchmen of the time, and it is unjust to blame him personally" (*Slavery* 67–8, see also 83). By focusing on the legislature's mantra, "il faut garder le *statu quo*" ("we must maintain the status quo") (*L'Attitude* 58), Cooper shifts our attention to the widespread and deeply entrenched problem of class and race exploitation at work, as well as the concomitant ongoing inability to engage with questions of race and rights in any meaningful way. She wants her readers to understand domination as a *systemic* issue, not an individual foible, and as a structural and institutionalized problem, not just a theoretical or attitudinal one.

Again and again, the questions of slavery, abolition, and full citizenship were tabled, avoided, or ruled on with ambiguity by the Assembly: hesitation, evasion, delusion, and a pervasive silence over issues of rights and the "colonial question" are the key factors Cooper highlights (*L'Attitude* 62–5). Further, she suggests that the French were not really capable of transforming their economy or following through on the full implications of Enlightenment ideals because they were too deeply invested, literally and metaphorically, in ontological hierarchies, an iniquitous polity, and an exploitive economy. Cooper argues that France had created "une plutocratie incapable de voir autre chose, dans Saint-Domingue, qu'une source d'exploitation" ("a plutocracy incapable of perceiving, in Saint-Domingue, anything other than a source of exploitation") (126). Moreover, an acceptance of human exploitation in the name of profit was not unique to France, for it had not seemed to bother what she sarcastically refers to as the "big consciences" of George Washington and Thomas Jefferson in the "birthplace" of political independence, the United States (57).

Although the immediate application of ideas of liberty and rights did not seem possible to the majority of whites, it was obviously both plausible and desirable to the nonwhites who rose up, revolted, and clearly had freedom and full citizenship in mind as their end goal (60). Once the *gens de couleur* and *noirs* realized that a return to a full-blown slave economy was imminent under Napoleon, who had declared that once again "the colonies would be governed by special laws, in conformity with their geographic and social position" rather than in accord with France's constitution and declaration of rights (*Slavery* 108), the final stages of the Haitian Revolution took place. "Finally triumphant," the Blacks under Dessalines "proclaimed the independence of the island, to which he gave back its [Native] name of Haiti, so that there would no longer be reminders of the European occupation" (111).[38] To reinforce this symbolic shift in identity, from colony and slave economy to an independent, postcolonial state, "Dessalines proclaimed that policy of the exclusion of the white race which would remain the essential foundation of Haitian politics" (111).

Cooper points out that the French were indeed foolish to think that they could "temporiser" (delay) or "tergiverser" (procrastinate) when it came to freedom (*L'Attitude* 110). How could the French be so visionary, on the one hand, and so insular and small-minded on the other? Perhaps the problem here is that, as Trouillot puts it, "Worldview wins over the facts: white hegemony is natural and taken for granted; any alternative is still in the domain of the unthinkable" (93). In fact, Cooper maintains that widespread resistance to colonialism is not just in France's distant past, but is still to come because rule by "might" is always untenable. While Cooper celebrates some of France's forward-thinking ideals and points to a somewhat better situation for Blacks in France, she also clearly suspects that, in 1925, it continues to be the case that France's "ontological presuppositions lead to historical amnesia" (Mills, *Racial* 69). Cooper therefore offers her Sorbonne committee a warning in her footnotes. She rightly concludes that French colonies in the "Pondichéry" (in India) and in "l'Afrique orientale" (eastern Africa) will be overthrown via collective uprisings and revolt; the people there "will not fail to protest" (*Slavery* 146, fn. 71). In her conclusion Cooper reiterates this key point and forewarns, "It is impossible to retreat on questions of liberty" (115).

Global Politics: Self-Determination as the Right of "the human family, all the several"[39]

With her usual attention to irony, Cooper explores the paradoxical twists of fate that play out in history. Just as the French Revolution was thought impossible by the ruling elite and nobility in France, so the Haitian Revolution was not conceived of as a viable threat by the French public, who had just risen up to transform France from an absolute monarchy to a republican and secular state. Given their own recent political upheaval, the French might well have appreciated that no matter how skillfully those in power seek not to know or not to understand the reality before them, no matter how vociferously the dominant classes seek to rationalize oppression, those who are exploited and disenfranchised will eventually resist. For instance, could the French really not remember how the more the king sought to stifle the French Revolution, the more he fueled it? Similarly, the more France sought to maintain a slave economy in Saint-Domingue, the more it energized the Haitian Revolution. Just as the rigidity and unyielding attitude on the part of France's *ancien régime* led to its demise, so did the absolutism and what Cooper calls the "criminal obstinacy" (*Slavery*

45) of the ruling whites vis-à-vis *noirs* and *gens de couleur* help ensure the end of colonial rule in Saint-Domingue.

From their own experience, the French ought to have realized that human will and freedom cannot be suppressed: the more one seeks an absolute and irrational control over others, the more inclined they are to fight back, particularly once the "spark" of consciousness becomes lit. Cooper focuses on how the French public quickly abandoned their ideals and hastily forgot the portent of their own immediate past: France's inability first to acknowledge and then to bridge the gap between theory and politics was its Achilles heel, for as Cooper asserted in 1902, "a nation cannot long survive the shattering of its own ideals. Its doom is already sounded when it begins to write one law on its walls and lives another in its halls!" (in Hutchinson 115). Thus, the relationship between France and Saint-Domingue was unstable and unsustainable because its basic foundation, slave exploitation, is inherently indefensible (Cooper, *L'Attitude* 73). France's static attitude toward slavery reveals a narrow outlook shaped by prejudice, arrogance, and a well-practiced refusal to acknowledge the basic humanity of all persons; it is this basically unaltered ontological worldview that was the key cause of France's "loss" of Saint-Domingue, Cooper argues (*Slavery* 113).

Moreover, Cooper shows that some of the most groundbreaking transformations of the Age of Revolution occurred in the Caribbean and were instigated by people of African descent, both free and enslaved. In addition, she argues that several of France's visionary ideas about a democratic, inclusive polity came about because of the *gens de couleur* and the *noirs* in Saint-Domingue/Haiti. In fact, Cooper's repeated emphasis on the stagnant state of affairs in France can be read as a subtle yet ironic inversion on her part of the colonizer's normative and powerful stereotype (used as a rationale for conquest) of the culture of non-Western "Others" as static, timeless, and dependent. Here, it is France and its citizens who are quietly revealed by Cooper to be unchanging, rigid, and reliant, rather than the enslaved or the colonized.

Consequently, Cooper suggests that too great a degree of likemindedness is dangerous, leading not only to political stagnation but also to a lethal ossification of ideas. At the heart of the matter is France's constrained national imagination: a worldview based on a system of human exploitation that is utterly "égoïste" — fundamentally self-centered and self-interested, rather than other-oriented (*L'Attitude* 12). Truly democratic communities account for and consider "l'autrui" (others) and not just the self. Yet when it came to France's relations with Saint-Domingue, self-interest prevailed, and the pull of financial gain took precedence. To Cooper a society's regard for the interests of others (both "others" within its bounds and internationally) is the way to measure its "greatness," not its capacity to conquer, exploit, or overpower other peoples or nations. Moreover, capitalist gain should not be equated with democracy, for the "span of the circle of brotherhood [sic]" reveals much more than the "things [a nation] makes and uses. Things without thoughts are mere vulgarities" ("Ethics" 206).

Cooper therefore emphasizes that France's fixed attitudes toward slavery and reductively defined national good reveal a lack of understanding of the true nature of democracy and freedom, because they posit racial and cultural differences as problems: human variety is equated with the need to contain difference via hierarchy, an approach Cooper deplores. So how can the common good be crafted in ways that account for and benefit "the human family, *all the several*" ("Souvenir" 339, emphasis added)? Cooper's answer lies in her politics of difference: to arrive at a more accurate and inclusive definition of common interest, society must draw its premises "from myriad sources and under myriad circumstances and conditions" (339). In contrast to a deliberative ideal of consensus as the basic building block of democratic rule, Cooper views multiplicity and pluralism as key factors in a thriving democracy; differences and "heterogeneity" are not "obstacles" but a necessary "contribution," for multivocal "harmony" can only be arrived at via "variety" ("Equality" 298).

Engagement with difference and an other-oriented ethos, in Cooper's analysis, are the catalysts of freedom, whereas false unity and egotism are more often than not means of retaining privilege and holding back social and political transformation. In her oral defense, Cooper pointedly underscores how "human equality is the result of the final equilibrium of all the human forces of the entire world." The idea of *Égalité* therefore "operates not between such and such places [or] such or such shape of the cranium" ("Equality" 297). In other words, the capacity to practice egalitarian principles and the ability to author philosophies of human equality are not restricted to particular regions, cultures, races, or hemispheres. Moreover, Cooper does not support an equilibrium created by means of force either, "where one concedes the equality of another only when he cannot crush or exploit him" (297). *Égalité* can be arrived at only via an equilibrium of differences, not by means of false unity or narrowly defined parameters of who "counts" as the citizen whose "good" must be protected. By emphasizing the need to balance "all the human forces of the entire world" (297), Cooper implicitly advocates a radical reordering of international relations, pointing to the need to develop a global symmetry of power and resources among diverse regions, cultures, religions, and peoples.

CHAPTER **5**

Mapping Sites of Power

Cooper's Redefinition of "the philosophic mind"[1]

Across her body of work, Cooper offers an important contribution to philosophical explorations of both domination and resistance. Deftly, she connects structural domination (inequality formalized or built into the nation's institutions) with both psychological coercion and ideological control. Using interdisciplinary analysis to identify how power operates in many locations simultaneously, Cooper exposes dehumanizing knowledge practices at many different levels of American society. For example, she links together the workings of derogatory stereotypes, internalized subjugation and dominion, biased research methodologies, and structural inequality. Cooper also shows that scientific or democratic discourses that seem virtuous because of rhetorics of rationality or of "the greater good" can still be both destructive and violent. Moreover, she emphasizes repeatedly the need to think systematically about oppression. By making the connections among varied mechanisms of power visible, Cooper invites her readers to actively question the social order; she does not take the world before her — its categories of being, its hierarchies, its exclusions — as natural, fixed, or immutable. Instead, she highlights its constructed and changeable nature while she holds out hope for a truly inclusive, fundamentally democratic, and radical form of universal freedom.

Notably, Cooper gives special emphasis to epistemological components of oppression, casting doubt on widely accepted epistemic norms employed to construct expertise and authority, to extend social control, and to reinforce hierarchy. She demonstrates, in other words, how "conceptual practices are a tool of ruling" (Harding, "Socially" 30). Within institutional, methodological, ideological/cultural, and emotional/psychological contexts, Cooper identifies objectifying ways of knowing used by scientists, politicians, educators, lawyers, statisticians, writers, and artists to construct overly simplistic and homogenized categories of racial and gendered otherness. Persistently, she illustrates how misrepresenting and pathologizing marginalized groups is a requisite tactic of coercion. Sexist and racist images in popular culture, religion, philosophy, literature, and the natural and social sciences are not innocent or random: they have a pernicious ideological function in that they stress the lesser humanity of the "other" while ascribing positive value to dominant groups. Moreover, Cooper illustrates how seemingly innocuous metaphors and analogies "accumulate social legitimacy" (Harding, *Whose* 210).

It is not only social institutions, discursive techniques, or epistemic conventions that Cooper identifies as problematic: she also explores the politics of "knowing" other people, questioning in particular the role of emotions, both positive (e.g., altruism, admiration, or benevolence) and negative (e.g., selfishness, hatred, or arrogance), in reinforcing a psychology of domination and subordination. For example, at the level of the individual, Cooper describes having to puzzle through the conundrum of being defined chiefly as a "problem" or object of study. She also identifies the burden of having one's person and body be thought of primarily as a lightning rod for other people's preconceived ideas, a screen for their projected stereotypes. In addition, Cooper suggests that bias and presupposition go beyond interpersonal relations or individual perceptions; they also affect the development of scientific and philosophical truths, social policies, and the law. In other words, hierarchies of human value have been institutionalized: the law (including legally sanctioned lynching and rape), education, religion, and science are institutions that enforce power for some at the expense of others and that encourage us to be passive and accept the status quo as given, to not question or challenge the world around us.

Contrary to dominant theories of her day, however, Cooper illustrates, for example, how the natural and social sciences are "inside" culture, not apart from it. By showing the many ways in which the observer, researcher, or scientist is always *located* in a sociohistorical context, Cooper demonstrates that many of the "discoveries" or "findings" about the nature of reality, seemingly just "happened upon" (e.g., see Gannett 328 and Harding, "Socially" 33), are more often than not the outcome of ready-made assumptions about the "natural" social order, about inherent and immutable differences in kind between groups of humans, and about the ability to measure and quantify biological superiority or inferiority. Cooper argues that scientists' theories about race are therefore "not simply scientific"

— they are "not simply driven by the data they're working with" (Evelyn Hammonds in Adelman, Episode 1).

To counter powerful scientific and social research about ostensibly innate differences and their implications, Cooper offers a social and historical analysis of gender, race, and class categories and roles, showing supposedly intractable "traits" to be variable and changeable across time and space. By demonstrating how gender and racial inferiority are socially constructed, she discredits theories of biological determinism to argue that inequality is culturally maintained and institutionalized, not "natural," preordained, or inherent. Yet despite the fact that Cooper finds hope in a constructivist analysis, she is not naive. Bias and prejudice cannot be "annihilated" only by "rhetoric," argues Cooper (*Voice* 232): these are "folly to rail at ... For as a rule the narrower the mind and the more circumscribed the experience, the greater will be the exaggeration of accidents over substance, and of circumstance over soul" (231). Thus Cooper underscores that the socially constructed nature of the world and its artificial distinctions and inequalities are not always easy to grasp or to articulate; forceful cultural practices come into play to naturalize differences in power, reinforce prejudices, and silence resistant voices.

As Whitten explains, even if we come to recognize that the dominant "point of view is partial and distorted, it nevertheless structures social relationships and determines values in society. This means it cannot be simply dismissed as false" (362). Moreover, on an individual level, we often adopt these oppressive beliefs; thus, internalized oppression, internalized arrogance/dominance, and a passivity before the status quo are major political hurdles and personal obstacles that must be understood and addressed. Cooper therefore emphasizes that a transformed self (on the part of both oppressed groups and dominant groups) and a transformed model of knowing — one that is action-oriented rather than passive and accountable to a wider community rather than only to the individual "facts"/data — are essential elements of social and political transformation.

The problem of being a "'puzzling' case"[2]

Although today W. E. B. Du Bois is usually remembered for posing the question, "How does it feel to be a problem?" at the beginning of *The Souls of Black Folk* (3), Cooper had already raised the question of problematized existence and analyzed the notion of a "race problem" over a decade earlier in *A Voice from the South*. Throughout her lifetime, Cooper objected vehemently to marginalized groups of people being "sized up and written down by others" (*Voice* 225), characterized as a "mystery" (iii), a "problem," or an "interesting case" ("On Education" 252) to be studied and generalized about (*Voice* 186, 179), though "seldom consulted" as knowers, experts, or even as human subjects (i). Almost a century later, in introducing her radical anthology *The Black Woman*, Toni Cade Bambara would express her own fundamental "impatience with all the 'experts' zealously hustling us folks for their doctoral theses or government appointments" ("Preface" 10). Likewise, Cooper specifically abhorred being defined, first and foremost, as an inanimate thing to be "reasoned about *en masse*" by "experts" ("On Education" 250, italics original). She was wary of sweeping generalities about "authenticity" (*Voice* 204–6), scientific human taxonomies (102), and overdetermined labels (260) about the "Soul of a Folk you have never seen before at closer focus than the outer rim of some epidermic cells" ("Negro's" 246–7).

But in contrast to the much-lauded aperspectival "view from nowhere" (Harding, "Socially" 26) in which affect, bias, and cultural context are ostensibly transcended, Cooper emphasizes the "hidden subjectivities" (Code, *Rhetorical* 28) behind the presentation of the "facts," highlighting the degree to which artists, writers, scientists, lawmakers, ministers, and social do-gooders "have taken up the subject [of the Negro] with a view to establishing evidences of ready formulated theories and preconceptions ... [and] have altogether abjured all candid and careful study" (*Voice* 186). She therefore takes a stand against "Every journeyman tinker [who] thinks he can tell you what to do with the Negro; what sort of clothes he should wear, what sort of meat he should eat, what sort of books he should and should not study: in short, just what ... is sane, sensible, and 'practical' for one of his texture of hair and hide" ("On Education" 250).

Further, Cooper argues that an objectifying, top-down approach to educational and social policy has been harmful to oppressed groups. She writes: "It has been a misfortune that too often our program has been handed down from above, along with the cash. ... The Negro, being an 'interesting case,' all the good old ladies in the country have had a hand in prescribing his medicine, and they mean to see that he takes it. No fumbling with the bedclothes and trying to spit behind the bed! Down it must go" (252). Instead of a condescending, infantilizing approach, a more participatory, community-based methodology that does not objectify but is "in touch" with its subjects should be used (*Voice* 36, 41). In other words, Cooper suggests that knowledge practices do in fact "*distort*, manipulate, [and] constrain their objects" of study; they are not neutral "tools" irrelevant to the knowledge produced (Grosz 190, italics original).

Basically, Cooper argues that dominant epistemic norms systematically hinder marginalized groups and devalue, even denigrate, alternative knowledge claims produced by such groups. Moreover, she emphasizes that prevailing knowledge practices have a history — they do not come out of nowhere. For example, Cooper traces the entrenchment of objectification as an instrument of domination back to the slave trade and to the subsequent legal machinations created to justify slavery when it came under fire, particularly the 1850 *Dred Scott* decision. *Dred Scott* stated that "the slave was a chattel (a 'thing,' not a person)" ("Legislative" 300), a legal finding that, Cooper points out, willfully runs counter to the wording of the Constitution, which refers to slaves as "'persons held to service or labor,'" and not as things (300). Criticizing Chief Justice Taney, Cooper excoriates his proclamation that "neither a slave nor a descendant of slaves could have the rights of citizens; that they could neither sue in the courts nor be recognized under the law save as chattels, i.e., property or possessions of a master — *not* as persons or individuals" (303, italics original). As in her criticism of France's eighteenth-century compromises over slavery and human rights,[3] Cooper finds fault with a reading of the United States as a democracy defined not by the protection of liberty but by the protection of profit and property. Thus Cooper further critiques Taney for alleging "that one of the functions of the Congress was the protection of property rights; that slaves had been recognized as property by the Constitution and the Congress was bound to uphold slavery" (303), over and above any consideration of slaves and their descendents as persons.

Cooper argues that this foundational ontological divide did not become a "dead letter" (*Voice* 106) in the law even after the overturning of *Dred Scott* and the abolition of slavery. The legal bifurcation between persons and subpersons, or subjects and objects, continues on in Jim Crow's "separate but equal" statutes ("Angry Saxons" 259), which resulted in what Cooper sarcastically describes as "Special kinds of education, special forms of industry, special churches and special places of amusement, special sections of our cities during life and special burying grounds in death" ("Ethics" 209). The effects of Jim Crow, in other words, infiltrate and shape all aspects of daily life, including segregationist church leadership (*Voice* 33–42), feminist organizing (81), public transportation (94, 111), recreation ("Equality" 294), unequal education (*Voice* 113, "Equality" 294), "denial of the franchise" ("Equality" 294), and housing discrimination (*Voice* 208).

The law also ignores numerous outright violations of the few basic rights it supposedly *does* recognize in the case of African Americans: for instance, they were offered no protection by the courts after the collapse of the Freedman's Savings Bank ("Ethics" 211). More perniciously, because the law overlooks violent hate crimes against Black men and women, it in effect sanctions brutality as a means of social control to enforce allegedly natural inequalities. In this regard, Cooper cites the "recent Wilmington massacre[4] when the accumulations of a lifetime were wantonly swept away and home loving, law abiding citizens were forced into exile, their homes and little savings appropriated by others" (211). Moreover, in the case of lynching, the law "makes sheer mockery of Equality," as does the profit-driven practice of "Peonage, a system under which prisoners from the State Penitentiary are farmed out to private landlords into worse than slavery and exploited without remedy" ("Equality" 294).

Likewise, the endemic crimes of rape and sexual violence perpetrated against Black women by white men, which Cooper does not name directly but clearly alludes to, are ignored by the courts. This leaves women of color in a state of vulnerability "before the fury of tempestuous elements" (*Voice* 25), facing "snares and traps" that other women do not face (32). They are pushed into situations of violent "forced association" (111), leaving "the mothers of the next generation" in a state of "imminent peril." Cooper therefore insists, "Negro sentiment cannot remain callous" about "wronged sisters" (32). Moreover, she reminds us, despite lack of protection Black women have always resisted, often fighting to the death for their own bodily self-determination. Cooper writes, "All through the darkest period of the colored women's oppression in this country her yet unwritten history is full of heroic struggle, a struggle against fearful and overwhelming odds, that often ended in a horrible death, to maintain and protect that which woman holds dearer than life" ("Intellectual" 202).

But it is not only legal interpretation or willful oversight of violence and inequality that trouble Cooper: the economy, the church, and education are other sites of institutionalized oppression that she identifies for their role in naturalizing socially constructed human hierarchies, in regulating narrow gender roles for women and men, and in enforcing a circumscribed "place" in the nation for African Americans. For example, the U.S. economy, argues Cooper, requires a surplus population of underemployed and impoverished citizens to reap maximal profits (*Voice* 130), a pattern of molding and using Black people primarily as "machines or as manikins" (37) established with the country's early reliance on slavery (216). In addition, as the economy is structured, women's work at home is both unpaid and unrecognized as labor, while women's labor in the paid workforce is not given a fair or equal wage; women in general, and "colored" women in particular, argues Cooper, are doubly discriminated against when it comes to wage considerations ("Wage Earners"). As Frances Beale would argue a century later, "the oppression of women acts as an escape valve for capitalism" (94).

Like the law and the economy, the church has played its part in perpetuating oppression. For example, in contradiction to Christ's teachings, Cooper contends, the church set up sexist relations of chivalry between men and women (*Voice* 13), establishing a form of misogyny masquerading as "respect" (14) that erroneously imputed impurity and ascribed lesser status to women under the guise of paternalistic protection (15). As Hilde Hein explains, "Moral and spiritual weakness is projected upon woman as 'the weaker vessel,' and she is incarcerated and mummified to forestall the greater temptations of man" (441). Cooper also challenges the church for institutionalizing racism between white and black believers and church leaders (*Voice* 42), formalizing relations of race supremacy in the church rather than universal equality before God. Using mockery to admonish "believers in a white Christ and these preachers of the gospel, 'Suffer the little *white* children to come unto me'" (192, italics original), she suggests there is a lack of true faith in "Christians who cannot read the golden rule across the color line" (199).

Education is yet another site of institutionalized racism and sexism explored by Cooper. She maintains that women should not be denied an education or relegated to an inferior, less rigorous "Ladies Course" (49); rather, every woman should be allowed access to a full education "so that she may ... stamp her force on the forces of her day, and add her modicum to the riches of the world's thought" (61). In addition, a racially segregated, separate and unequal education, especially one designed by "efficiency experts" ("Angry Saxons" 260), is, Cooper argues, detrimental to the individual and deleterious to the nation. Connecting eugenics with allegedly innocuous social science methods of assessment, she categorically rejects the "'postwar Machine Method of tests and measurements to single out the unfit'" (Cooper in Gabel 79).[5] Moreover, Cooper maintains that an educational system that merely makes someone a "'hand'" without attending to and nurturing both head and heart, is pernicious, for it aims to "suppress or ignore the soul" ("On Education" 251); instead, "education should have regard to the whole [person]" ("Angry Saxons" 258).

Structural domination, Cooper demonstrates, is a key aspect of socially constructed inequality, as is the asymmetrical distribution of resources. She therefore argues, "The clamps and irons of mental and moral, as well as civil compression must be riven asunder" (*Voice* 39). But, Cooper suggests, domination cannot be fully understood without also examining epistemic norms, for these comprise a key site of objectification that intertwines with the structural and material dimensions of oppression. Thus, she explores how the problem of being defined as a "'puzzling' case" or object by the law, the church, education, and the nation-state also plays out in the reductive methods used to (mis)represent or "know" the Other in the natural and social sciences, the arts, and the popular imagination. To better appreciate and then change institutionalized inequality, she maintains we must also grasp the connection between our social institutions and our knowledge practices, particularly the "epistemological manufacture of Otherness" (Goldberg 156) in which difference becomes reduced to deviance.

"Angry Saxons,"[6] Scientific Authority, and Social Construction

Cooper points out that the findings of natural and social scientists and the data gathered by statisticians can be hard to question, in large part because of the attendant aura of impartial neutrality and total objectivity, as if researchers are untouched by cultural practices, social inequalities, and historical realities. As Stephen Jay Gould's research outlines, biological determinists, who since the time of Plato have argued "that social and economic roles accurately reflect the innate construction of people," often invoke "the traditional prestige of science as objective knowledge, free from social and political taint" to help prove their determinist theories (20). By revealing how "objective" data are manipulated not only by scientists but also by politicians, educators, social workers, and labor union leaders, Cooper challenges those enamored with "measurement" to question their use of quantitative data to reinforce biased preconceptions under the guise of objectivity.

Moreover, Cooper suggests that the context of discovery (how knowers decide what to research, which questions to ask, what the key issues or concepts are, and which methods to use) is as epistemologically significant as the context of justification. In other words, rather than being nonrational, subjective, and irrelevant, the researcher's social context, cultural values, historical beliefs, and even unexamined assumptions are, for Cooper, meaningful and relevant to the knowledge produced; they should be examined as closely and carefully as the findings, the "facts" or outcomes. By refusing the conventional "fact/value" distinction[7] in science, Cooper implies that science, like all knowing activities, is a process: rather than being outside culture or historical context, it is a "socially contingent knowledge-seeking activity," which means that the facts do not exist in a bubble completely isolated or apart from politics (Fausto-Sterling 1, 10).

However, these sorts of epistemological assumptions were not the norm for Cooper's time. Scientific methods, in which large amounts of data were collected about race, gender, sexuality, class, and disability (because all were presumed to be measurable biological phenomena), had a lot of cachet at the turn of the twentieth century with the rise of science and medicine, of sociology and anthropology, as well as of philosophical movements such as logical positivism (Collins, *Fighting* 95–123, Stanfield 218–21, Tanesini 76–77). As a leading educator, Cooper was particularly wary of the increased use of educational testing, I.Q. assessment, and school accreditation "standards," most of which were overtly eugenicist in impulse and, obviously, extremely harmful to Black students, educators, and schools. For example, Rutledge Dennis's research illustrates that intelligence testing came about at a time in which politicians, scientists, and policymakers sought methods and measures to validate popular scientific explanations of "natural" white race ascendancy, including Francis Galton's hereditarian theories of white superiority and Frederick Hoffman's "extinction" predictions for African Americans owing to their "innately infirm" biological make-up.[8] Dennis concludes that "Just as Social Darwinist theories were used to justify European imperialism and colonialism, the thesis of Anglo-Saxon supremacy, buttressed by test results, justified racial and ethnic oppression and exclusion in the Unites States" (247). Gould's research likewise demonstrates that "What craniometry was for the nineteenth century, intelligence testing ... [became] for the twentieth" (25).

Cooper suggests that both the scientific method and quantitative forms of measurement, especially statistics and assessment testing, often serve as masks for biased preconceptions and bigoted cultural assumptions. Science is not, in other words, the "citadel" it appears to be (Martin 26): the supposed "view from nowhere" (Code, *Rhetorical* 24) used to buttress biologistic accounts of reality is as "situated" (Haraway 581) as any other form of knowledge. Not swayed by science's mystique, Cooper is clearly suspicious of objectivist methods, particularly "the habit of generalization and deductive logic" employed by "Statisticians and Social Science Research compilers" (Cooper, "Racial" 237). She implies that "quantitative data are as subject to cultural constraints as any other aspect of science ... [and that] they have no special claim upon final truth" (Gould 27). In other words, Cooper tears off what David Theo Goldberg characterizes as the "scientific cloak of racial knowledge, its formal character and seeming universality" (154); she uncovers stereotypes and presuppositions in supposedly impartial research and highlights the role of emotions and bias in the most revered of knowledge practices.

For example, Cooper calls into question the mantle of emotional detachment and neutrality assumed by proponents of biological determinism, showing repeatedly that seemingly neutral perception is patently biased (*Voice* 292–3, "Ethics" 210, "Equality" 291–2). Using her typically dry humor, Cooper emphasizes how the "Anglo Saxons" are, in actuality, "Angry Saxons," not dispassionate observers ("Angry Saxons" 259): their claims to objectivity and neutrality are both insincere and bogus. She also renames Social Darwinist theory "survival of the bullies" in place of "survival of the fittest" (*Voice* 118); astutely drawing attention to potential for abuse of power in science, her semantic shift also discredits the premise of natural and inevitable domination of one group over others implied in notions of "fitness." Moreover, Cooper's derision of "blue-bloods" as power-hungry, xenophobic nationalists (157–63) is daring and reveals the depth of her commitment to protesting the misuses of knowledge to perpetuate domination. Many years later, Cooper would argue that a passive belief in pure reason is dangerous, for it lays the groundwork for fascism and lethal race supremacy ("Hitler" 263–4).

Contrary to popular and powerful scientific theories of her day, Cooper maintains that biological differences in "blood" are invented fantasies, not innate: they are illusory creations of the observer designed to reinforce the status quo. To illustrate, Cooper describes crossing the border into Canada, where she traveled to Toronto as part of a Black teacher-exchange program (Hutchinson 107). Patricia Hill Collins argues that "invoking the authority of lived experience" has been a key way in which "African-American women confronted seemingly universal scientific truths" (*Fighting* 48). Here, through personal anecdote (albeit generalized as that of "the Black Woman of the South" [*Voice* 88] but obviously her own), Cooper shows how supremacist hierarchies are not fixed or innate, but variable and, therefore, changeable.

Just a short way north across the border, Cooper enters another world in which she is treated with respect and where she no longer fears violence, be it attitudinal or physical. In Toronto, unlike the outright hatred and fear of bodily harm and violent attack, including sexual assault, Black women must constantly navigate in the Jim Crow United States (*Voice* 89–91), Cooper describes discovering a sense of bodily freedom in an egalitarian public sphere. She explains how she enjoys a "uniform, matter-of-fact courtesy, a genial kindliness ... — a hospitable, thawing-out atmosphere everywhere — in shops and waiting rooms, on cars and in the streets." After some time, Cooper finds that she began to shed her "old whipped-cur[9] feeling," and when that feeling "was taken up and analyzed she could hardly tell whether it consisted mostly of self pity for her own wounded sensibilities, or of shame for her country and mortification that her countrymen offered such an unfavorable contrast" (*Voice* 88–89).

By showing this instant transformation of supposedly inherent racial and gendered "essences," Cooper quietly debunks arguments in support of biological determinism. In addition, she discredits theories of geographical determinism (i.e., that one's geographic place or "climate" of origin determines one's traits and capacities and that different regions/peoples can be ranked on a geographic hierarchy of being; see "Equality" 297, for example). Such "environmental" theories were equally racist but more indirect; they appeared to have a gentler veneer than other prominent theories of eugenics and biological heredity in this period, such as Galton's statistical approach to biometrics or Mendel's laws of heredity. In Cooper's experiential anecdote, because Canada and the United States are on the same continent, the supposed "biological" distinctions in kind and lived inequalities between Blacks and whites are clearly cultural constructs, not geographic or "racial" qualities.

To further discredit geographical arguments about "natural" human taxonomies, Cooper reminds her readers of the violent experiences of rape and lynching experienced by African Americans in the United States; these realities reveal how brutality exists equally as much in America as in Africa (*Voice* 91). Thus, rather than ascribe "degeneracy" and "barbarity" only to certain parts of the world, particularly Africa (a common "scientific" practice that helped to justify imperial expansion and economic development policies in the early twentieth century), Cooper emphasizes that violence and hatred exist the world over: no geographic locale is free of domination. She writes that there "are murderers and thieves and villains in both London and Paris. Humanity from the first has had its vultures and sharks, and representatives of the fraternity who prey upon mankind may be expected no less in America than elsewhere" (91–2). She points to Americans' disingenuous "horror" at atrocities carried out in *other parts* of the world while ignoring the many hate crimes committed here at home. In the United States, even if she were hungry and alone, Cooper reminds us she would be told, "'We doan uccommodate no niggers hyur.' And yet we are so scandalized at Russia's barbarity and cruelty to the Jews!" (97).

Cooper argues that hierarchies of difference between the powerful and the "weak," the intelligent and the "ignorant," men and women, whites and Blacks, or the "Occident" and the "Orient" are not innate qualities or immutable "facts." Rather, these "sweep[s] of [a] generalizing pen" (52) are socially constructed: difference and what we make of it, finds Cooper, lies in the eye of the beholder. Thus, "race, color, sex, condition, are ... the accidents, not the substance of life" — they result from "mere circumstance," and are not fixed (125). Although few over the centuries have been able to see beyond such socially enforced distinctions between peoples and cultures, Cooper wryly suggests that science could learn something about the natural world from two eminent teachers, Buddha and Christ. She writes, "Christ was the first of democrats ... a teacher who proved that the lines on which worlds are said to revolve are *imaginary*, that for all the distinctions of blue blood and black blood and red blood — *a man's a man for a' that*. Buddha and the Christ, each in his own way, sought to rend asunder the clamps and bands of caste, and to thaw out the ice of race tyranny and exclusiveness" (*Voice* 154–5, italics original).[10]

In emphasizing the *imaginary* nature of biological and cultural differences, Cooper develops a constructionist analysis of social roles and identities. She focuses on the fact that a social group's "weakness" or "strength" is "socially enforced," not inherent. Cooper therefore discredits the idea that the shape of the "cerebrum" determines a propensity for "lunacy" or "criminality" (289), and finds ample evidence to suggest "there is nothing irretrievably wrong in the shape of the black man's skull" (26). Cooper also argues that oppression plays out on the body, affecting rates of illness or morbidity (247) as well as rates of mortality (248). The obvious reason behind large disparities between Blacks and whites in rates of death, disease, and infant mortality is environmental racism (including poverty, lack of adequate housing, employment, and nutrition [250]), not any built-in deficiency, fundamental biological difference, or preordained extinction.

Thus, although she identifies a problem of "persistent poverty" for African Americans, the root cause, Cooper contends, is unequal "chances," not intrinsic "indolence" (253); after all, "the original timber as it came from African forests was good enough" (238), argues Cooper. Moreover, widespread poverty for African Americans and the concomitant comparative wealth of white Americans (216) has a *past*: "two hundred and fifty years" of slavery (239). There are also causal factors of poverty in the present, including underpaid domestic and laundry work for Black women (254) with few other avenues for employment, and exclusion from the trade unions (255) and from government jobs for Black men.

While refuting scientific racism, Cooper simultaneously debunks biological determinism as it relates to gender. For example, if it turns out that, in the present time, men seem to have more "intelligence" than women, it is because of their having received a *superior education*, not because men are inherently more intelligent than are women (74). Mocking the idea that "higher education was incompatible with the shape of the female cerebrum" (65), Cooper argues that women's secondary status is constructed and enforced (44–5), not innate. In an attempt to delineate an international perspective on sexism that accounts for different forms of misogyny cross-culturally, Cooper maintains that women's inferior place in the world can be traced to differing but interconnected practices across cultures, including chivalry and Christianity in the "Feudal System" (13), Chinese foot-binding, and silences in the Koran, for in Cooper's (ethnocentric) reading, "Mahomet makes no account of woman whatever in his polity" (9).[11] Across various cultural contexts, and within Christian, Buddhist, and Islamic traditions, Cooper maintains, women have been *kept* in an enforced and unnatural state of passivity (39) and infantilized "ignorance" (56), glorified only for being "lisping, clinging, tenderly helpless, and beautifully dependent creatures" (66).

Men, suggests Cooper, have incorrectly argued that woman is a lesser being lacking a soul, and have selfishly concluded that "it was, or ought to be, the sole end of woman to glorify man" (65). Moreover, women have been taught that they have no "work" or "value" in the world, no "duty to self": their role as a "mere toy" for men has been constructed as entirely other-oriented, their value construed as simply "relative," measurable by their "pleasure-giving" capacity (65). In this regard, the one area in which women have been tutored ad infinitum is in practicing the verb *amo*, "I love," "since that is already the ground and limit of their intuitive furnishing" (48). With limited avenues available, women have been encouraged mostly to become a "domestic statue" (122), a "help-meet" (68), or merely a "mirror" of man's greatness.

Woman, argues Cooper, has been wrongly "compelled to look to sexual love as the one sensation capable of giving tone and relish, movement and vim to the life she leads" (68–9). In addition, women have been denied an education, made dependent on the marriage relationship for their own wellbeing (68), and refused the right to own property (although, ontologically, they could *be* the property of their husband and thus become totally indistinct from him before the law [58–9]). In advocating for new responsibilities and opportunities for women at large, and for a heightened political consciousness and role for African American women in particular, Cooper anticipates the call by many other Black women for "getting into the larger life," as Amy Jacques Garvey would put it, now that the "doll-baby type of woman is a thing of the past, and the wide-awake woman is forging ahead" (Garvey 92, 94).

Dull Blocks and Shuffling Bootblacks, Wiggling Prostitutes and Threatening Rapists: Cooper's Analysis of Race-Gender Stereotypes

In addition to Cooper's astute appraisal of the ways in which narrow definitions of "the race" or of "woman" are used to circumscribe race and gender roles, and to make these constrained roles appear as if they were the result of fixed natural traits, she also highlights how race and gender ideologies are not independent from one another, but always intertwined. Using an intersectional approach to race and gender politics, she asserts that African Americans "are the heirs of a past which was not our father's moulding ... [and] of a manhood and a womanhood impoverished and debased by two centuries and more of compression and degradation" (28). One particular method of "compression and degradation" explored at length by Cooper is the use of "long-distance stereotypes" (206), evidence of "malice prepense" ("Negro's" 245) in the arts, popular culture, and the natural and social sciences. She shows how visual ideology, a tool of justifying and normalizing socially created inequality, has played out in specific ways for Black men and women.

Cooper meticulously documents how African Americans' "character" has generally been "prejudged by formula" as "shiftless" ("Ethics" 208), "sullen" (214), unsophisticated, close to nature (*Voice* 180), "simpleminded," "child-like" (179), and "ludicrous" ("Negro's" 245). Such reliance on a careless and irresponsible "economy of stereotype" to convey meaning (Morrison, *Whiteness* 67) can be found not only in the arts and popular culture, Cooper argues, but also in the sciences. Consider the work of Louis Agassiz, a prominent nineteenth-century American anthropologist who, with Samuel Morton, developed the theory of "polygeny" (the theory that the "black race" was an entirely different species). Agassiz argued that "blacks' 'eminently marked' dispositions are submissiveness, obsequiousness, and imitation." The data analyst, Morton, then "set out to establish relative rank on 'objective' grounds" (Gould 47). Gould's careful analysis of Morton's and Agassiz's data sets and research method proves definitively what Cooper suggests: without a doubt, their data reveal "a patchwork of fudging and finagling in the clear interest of controlling a priori convictions" (Gould 54).

Like Lorraine Hansberry, who would maintain that African Americans have only been "allowed to exist ... in the form of repository of all the suppressions the dominant society found unseemly" (*To Be Young* 209), Cooper asserts that African Americans have been conceptualized, in the popular imagination, as a "nightmare vision" (*Voice* 222), or what Audre Lorde would come to name as "your most deeply cherished nightmare," a "roach" "scuttling through the painted cracks / you create to admit me" ("Brown Menace" 149). Although Cooper argues that these projections are merely "revelations" of white people's limited imaginations (*Voice* 216) and have "no objective reality" whatsoever (222), they are nevertheless powerful tropes that carry "sedimented historical meaning" (Collins, *Black Sexual* 120).

In addition to critiquing such "hideous phantasm[s]" (*Voice* 222) about African Americans as a group, Cooper examines the nexus of racist and sexist ideology to uncover the specific ways in which Black women and men have been objectified in popular culture. For example, she argues that Black women have been characterized as outside the realm of the ideal (white) "lady" (*Voice* 32, 94–6, 108). As Cooper highlights in her famously sarcastic and insightful "*Whimodaughsis*" analysis, there is a presupposition of whiteness built into many (white) feminists' working concepts of womanhood; this results in the category "woman" being duplicitously used as a false universal, since nobody had "calculated that there were any wives, mothers, daughters, and sisters, except white ones" (81). Through humor, Cooper insightfully "encapsulated the Janus face of the conventional definition of womanhood" (Carby, *Reconstructing* 105).

Cooper points to how, in contrast to ideologies of white femininity, Black women are represented as the obverse — as unladylike: they tend to be characterized either as unattractive, asexual, working bodies (defined as objects of labor) or pigeonholed as oversexed bodies exuding forbidden and even "savage" desires. For example, she criticizes stereotypes of Black women as ugly, with "cat-fish mouths" (202) — mere "brutes" (Mayo in *Voice* 204) and "dull block[s]" whose 'natural' role is heavy labor ("Intellectual" 202).[12] Likewise, Cooper deplores trite descriptions of African American women ostensibly wallowing "'half conscious'" in a "'slough of unchastity'" that is the "'double inheritance of savage Africa and slavery'" (Mayo in Cooper, *Voice* 204).[13] Like later African American feminists who would also find "the Negro woman ... struck in the face daily by contempt" (McDougald 83), pushed up against "a solid wall of grave misconceptions, outright distortions of fact, and defensive attitudes" (Beale 90), Cooper wages a textual war against Black women's dehumanization and seeks to dismantle a violent "hieroglyphics of the flesh," or what Spillers characterizes as "the grid of associations, from the semantic and iconic folds buried deep in the collective past, that come to surround and signify the captive person" ("Mama's," 61, 65).

To defend Black women's virtue against supposedly neutral scientific observations and anthropological theories about African women's animalistic sexual nature, Cooper maintains that Black women in Africa are widely known to be among the most "chaste" and virtuous in the world (*Voice* 238). Importantly, Cooper also emphasizes how cultural and "scientific" stereotypes of Black womanhood and manhood interconnect and play out in the legal control and treatment of their bodies. For example, she describes riding on a train in the South. Because of Jim Crow, Cooper must change to a separate train car. She describes how a railroad employee remarks, "'Here gurl,' (I am past thirty) 'you better git out 'n dis kyar 'f yer don't, I'll put yer out'" (*Voice* 95). Alluding to Ida B. Wells's 1884 forcible removal from a first-class "Ladies" train car by a conductor,[14] Cooper recalls "instances of personal violence to colored women ... forcibly ejected from cars, thrown out of seats, their garments rudely torn, their person wantonly and cruelly injured" (91), and then switches train cars "voluntarily."

After moving cars, Cooper describes what she sees out the train window: "I see from the car window, working on private estates, convicts from the state penitentiary, among them squads of boys from fourteen to eighteen years of age in a chain-gang, their feet chained together and heavy blocks attached" (95–6). Her observations about imprisoned Black men condemned to forced labor circle back to the legally legislated and enforced distinction between "ladies" and "colored people" that Cooper must navigate upon exiting the train (96). Without collapsing the very real differences here between her moving and scholarly (because writing) self and the incarcerated prisoners as equally or analogously constrained, Cooper's shifting back and forth between her observations inside and outside the train car quietly highlights that there is nevertheless a link between acts of physical coercion toward "unladylike" Black women and the incarceration and exploitation of Black men presumed more "naturally" criminal.

Generally, argues Cooper, Black men are portrayed in one of two ways: as submissive or as threatening. Either way, their "lesser" status and deficiency are reinforced: each trope buttresses the other. If portrayed as deferential, it is to signal African American men's lack of appropriate or normative masculinity, whereas if painted as aggressive criminals, it is to represent their less "civilized" and more animal-like capacity. Anticipating in many ways twentieth-century analyses of "ethnic notions" of Blackness in American visual culture (Riggs, *Ethnic*), Cooper denounces prevalent stereotypes of Black men as "bowing," "groveling," and "humble" (*Voice* 222–3). Further, she wonders why so many popular white American authors only seem capable of peopling their novels with Black male characters who are either subservient "bootblacks" or "grinning porters" (206) ready to serve and happy to stay in their "place."

Moreover, Cooper points out that it is not just powerful white men who are guilty of this epistemological coercion: white feminists, with a tendency to portray themselves as "pure-minded and lofty souled," advocate for *their* rights alone by stooping to characterize "the great burly black man [as] ignorant and gross and depraved" in order to try and win political favor from white men (123). Cooper admonishes white feminists for pursuing a narrow vision of liberation, and for seeking to maintain the power and privileges accorded whites in a supremacist society. Naming the collapse between white femininity and ideologies of nation (108), Cooper crafts an anecdote about "miladi" (88), the "queen of the drawing room with penciled brows ... [who] signifies who may be recognized and who are beyond the pale," to illustrate that supremacy is taught, and that white women can be complicit in domination, teaching it to their children and fellow citizens by example (87). Moreover, although Cooper knows that "Mrs. Mary A. Livermore[15] ... was dwelling on the Anglo-Saxon genius for power" when, in a public address, she took pride in not caring that an "unoffending Chinaman" was beaten on the streets because he was perceived as effeminate and weak (53–4), Cooper has a more radical vision of liberation in mind that does not "disparage what is weak," glorify brutal patriarchy or white supremacy, or seek to gain the rights of a few at the expense of other dispossessed groups (117).

In addition to critiquing white women's gross manipulation of stereotypes of minority men to gain political advantage, Cooper deplores how African American men are depicted as if they were "vicious" (253), cast as illiterate criminals by the federal government (269) and as chicken thieves by prominent American authors (211). Worse, they are portrayed as the "devil" (225) incarnate, sexual "monsters of lust and vindictiveness" ("Ethics" 211), full of "savagery" and "tropic heat" (Thompson in *Voice* 212). Cooper remarks that they have been wrongfully cast as murderous rapists (*Voice* 198, "Ethics" 211) by the real sexual predators: white men (*Voice* 25, 32, 102–3, "Ethics" 207). Daringly, Cooper asserts, "the overtures for forced association in the past history of these two races were not made by the manacled black man, nor by *the silent and suffering black woman!*" (*Voice* 111, italics original).

Cooper also explores how, over time, dehumanizing roles are not just ascribed to African Americans by whites: for example, she later finds Paul Robeson "impersonating" the stereotypical "shuffling, sprawling, crap shooting, chain gang Negro" while singing "Water Boy" and questions the racism built into *Porgy and Bess*'s predictable, obligatory (and wholly artificial) "Negro Dialect" ("Negro's" 244). Although Cooper emphasizes that she appreciates Robeson's obvious artistry as a musician and actor, her linguistic and cultural analysis also reveals a degree of ambivalence. Cooper feels that Robeson's visibility in such roles is a mixed blessing and would prefer he had other choices as an artist; but, given the narrow choices he has, she wishes that he would choose *not* to sing songs or perform roles that reinforce negative stereotypes (244).

However, there are other instances in which Cooper is unequivocally critical: she accepts no derogatory, sexist-racist imagery of Black women, no matter the author or context. Her palpable indignation suggests that she sees such imagery as reinforcing deviance models of Black sexuality and personhood used to buttress both white supremacy and white somatic and gender normativity. As Collins explains, "Early on within sociological treatments of race, Black women became associated with crime and fertility, the theme of a Black deviance constructed around a degenerate sexuality resulting in prolific fertility" (*Fighting* 98). Collins adds, "For Western sciences that were mesmerized with body politics, White Western normality became constructed on the backs of Black deviance, with an imagined Black hyper-heterosexual deviance at the heart of the enterprise" (*Black Sexual* 120).

Thus, when a black newspaper, the *Washington Tribune*, published a poem about a sexually hungry "colored" prostitute by the well-known author Langston Hughes, Cooper was outraged. Although Lemert and Bhan find her letter to the editor a sign of Cooper's old age and suggestive that she was "somewhat of a moralistic crank" (308), I see this letter of protest as a logical continuation of her intersectional analysis of sexism and racism. Cooper objects to Hughes's stereotypical, or as Cooper calls it, "nauseating," portrait of a "Shameless gal" prostitute: "Pretty baby / You want lovin' / And you don't mean maybe" (Hughes in Lemert and Bhan 341). Cooper asks how a paper "which condemns *Amos 'n' Andy* as pernicious propaganda and a vicious caricature of the race, should allow [Hughes's] 'Midnight Nan' to 'strut and wiggle'" across its pages (Lemert and Bhan 342). How is it that denigrating portraits of black *men* are considered by the paper's editors to be irredeemably racist and destructive to the community, but stereotyped images of hypersexed black women are acceptable for promoting African American culture and upholding the future of "the race"? One can be sure, Cooper implies, that the *Tribune* would never publish a "light" poem about Black male hypersexuality; subtly, she is protesting here what Angela Davis would later identify as the "inseparable companion" image to that of the Black male rapist, "the image of the Black woman as chronically promiscuous" (*Women* 182).

With her usual sharp wit, Cooper gives Hughes a dressing-down, and not just the paper's editors. She writes, "My criticism is not against Hughes for writing about whatever he sees and happens to know" (342). Her searing words, suggesting that she cannot help it if he frequents prostitutes but would prefer not to read about it in the *Tribune*, are not simply the ranting of a cranky old lady. Just as she objects to the assumed whiteness built into the falsely universal category of "woman," Cooper refuses to accept the presumed masculinity built into normative conceptions of blackness. Cooper's analysis here, which begins with the assumption that eradicating sexism *is* part and parcel of eradicating racism, falls in with a long line of Black feminist theorists who object to widespread sexism in Black popular culture, particularly reductive treatments of Black women's sexuality as a crude commodity and Black women's bodies as exploitable objects. As Cole and Guy-Sheftall maintain, "We must pose the difficult question of whether all forms of artistic license are socially acceptable if they threaten our basic humanity" (203).

In this vein, Cooper's letter to the same paper regarding Richard Wright's *Native Son* (Lemert and Bhan 342–3), in which she excoriates the popularity of the novel's protagonist, Bigger Thomas, could also be understood as informed by Cooper's intersectional feminist politics. Since "Devaluation and violence are twin enemies of Black women" (Cole and Guy-Sheftall 202), rather than stemming from prudish moralizing, Cooper's outright condemnation of Bigger Thomas might well be connected to the fact that in the novel he murders a white female character, Mary Dalton, and rapes his black girlfriend, Bessie Mears, while she screams "don't, don't, don't" (Wright 219), before murdering her by smashing her face in with a brick (222). Although I do not necessarily agree with the line of distinction Cooper draws between art and politics in this letter, she can nevertheless be interpreted as rejecting any wake-up call to the nation about racism that hinges on misogynist violence to make its point.[16]

The Problem of the "Stultified" Self

In criticizing sexism within Black politics and creative culture as well as racism among women and in white feminist organizing, Cooper argues for the merits of an intersectional or "both/and" approach to race and sex domination. She also emphasizes the dangers of internalization and thus the psychological dimensions of oppression, the daily "spirit murder" (P. Williams 73) engendered in a social conditioning process that presents denigrating images as "authentic" and unequal opportunities and structural oppression as natural. Cooper highlights the cumulative destruction that results from these countless derogatory images and from the patently biased data based on gross distortions about those thought to be "inferior" because different. She advocates developing a resistant consciousness, self-love, and counter-hegemonic ways of knowing as viable strategies to combat these pervasive, and perverted, ideologies.

In addition to the problem of hypervisibility of negative images, and their repercussions, Cooper explores how omnipresent cultural stereotypes of Black men and women have their ideological counterpart in more indirect but equally pernicious modes of epistemological violence or annihilation: silencing, invisibility, and erasure. African Americans remain "overlooked" and forgotten in general (*Voice* 254), having been avoided in the Constitution ("Legislative" 300), erased from the federal patent logs (*Voice* 270), silenced by "persecution" (178), and made "voiceless" by lynching ("Sketches" 226). Rather than accept these "disquieting lacunae" (Spillers, "Mama's" 71), African Americans have kept alive an "unwritten history" (Cooper, *Voice* 101) to challenge this willful obliteration. However, argues Cooper, Black women have a particular and unique unwritten history ("Intellectual" 202). She asserts, "The colored woman ... is confronted by both a woman question and a race problem, and is as yet an unknown or unacknowledged factor in both" (*Voice* 134). Black women, she maintains, have a specific kind of "voicelessness" and occupy a distinct space of incomprehension (i) that stems from having survived indescribable experiences (90).

Cooper raises the complementary issues of invisibility and hypervisibility because she fears that such silences and erasures will come to be accepted, the resistant voice forever "muffled," and the ubiquitous, harmful images believed as natural and accurate. In this regard, Hansberry would later write, "*The acceptance of our present condition is the only form of extremism which discredits us before our children*" (*To Be Young* 222, italics original). Cooper therefore shows how those marginalized by sex or by race can find their sense of self "snubbed and chilled" (*Voice* 199) by a hostile climate; she warns of the risk of being "lulled" into accepting the status quo, withdrawing from the world's "ridicule" and even finding glory in inferiority (64). This, remarks Cooper, is why many women have worked hard to fit into the narrow parameters of their subjugation and assiduously embrace a secondary position in society. Sadly, they have asked themselves only this question for their life's pursuit: "'How shall I so cramp, stunt, simplify and nullify myself as to make me eligible to the honor of being swallowed up into some little man?'" (70). Similarly, race prejudice "like stones between our teeth and like iron in the marrow of our bones" ("Ethics" 215) can have dire consequences: one may come to accept one's own "subjection," a peril faced by African Americans since slavery, she contends (*Voice* 102).

Internalizing externally imposed and distorting stereotypes as if they were "facts" and meekly accepting the status quo are not viable survival strategies, argues Cooper. Although seemingly the easier path, submissiveness in the face of violent misnaming leaves one mired in "the twilight of self-doubt" and burdened with "a sense of personal inferiority" (McDougald 80). Cooper maintains that uncritical passivity is yet another means by which we perpetuate our own and others' oppression. For example, in decrying the lack of attention to the education of African American women, she remarks that the "atmosphere, the standards ... do not afford any special stimulus to female development" (75). Further, Cooper wonders why it has come to be that a state of kept ignorance (56, 63) has been rationalized as sufficient for African American girls. Despite Black men's visionary ideals for the race in general, she writes sadly, "When they strike the woman question they drop back into sixteenth century logic" (75). Or, as Frances Beale would observe a century later, "When it comes to women, [the Black male] seems to take his guidelines from the pages of the *Ladies' Home Journal*" (92).

Drawing from her own life experience, Cooper points out that while boys, even those with "shallow ... pretensions," are encouraged to study theology, girls are discouraged from pursuing an education and are left to "struggle" and "fight " on their own, with little to no support (*Voice* 77). In a similar vein, bell hooks would later write about her own upbringing, "Had I been a boy, they might have encouraged me to speak believing that I might someday be called to preach. There was no 'calling' for talking girls, no legitimized rewarded speech" (*Talking* 6). Cooper therefore homes in on the specific impact of racist-sexist ideas upon Black women and warns that Black women might become so "hampered and shamed" that their contributions to the world of ideas, to labor, to politics, to education, will be squashed (*Voice* 135).

Moreover, Cooper underscores that survival, although important, and not a given, should not be equated with true freedom and liberation. She writes, "To feed is not the chief function of this [human] material. ... There is the hunger of the eye for beauty, the hunger of the ear for concord, the hungering of the mind for development and growth, of the soul for communion and love. ... And every man owes it to himself to *let nothing in him starve*" (257, italics original). Likewise, Barbara Smith would later contend, "An ability to cope under the worst conditions is not liberation, although our spiritual capacities have often made it look like a life" (xxvi). Cooper therefore argues that as a community, African Americans will suffer the consequences of unidimensional thinking about race and gender, as will the nation at large (*Voice* 78). Moreover, she asserts that both intraracial and interracial relations are hindered and distorted by succumbing to derogatory ideologies of race and gender (218).

Cooper urges her readers to learn to question norms and to begin to think and feel against the grain. Akin to what Chela Sandoval describes as an "emancipation of the imagination" (184) through love as a "hermeneutic" of social change (140), Cooper specifically appeals to African Americans to love themselves, even if the greater world does not: she seeks a fundamental "revolution in the self" (Bambara, "Roles" 101). As Collins explains, a calling to "engage deep feelings in searching for justice suggests a complex redefinition of the personal" by connecting it to collective struggle (*Fighting* 244). Cooper therefore proposes that love (self-love and loving other persons) can go beyond the level of a personal or individual emotion: it can be a site of moral reasoning and a source for the collective struggle for liberating "*all*" persons, not just some (*Voice* 100, italics original).

Thus, rather than think of love narrowly, as romantic love or even as the legal dependence otherwise known as marriage (68), Cooper discusses how love, as "heart power" (131) or "Heart Talent" ("Equality" 297), can be a source both of collective resistance and of "*loving service*" to humanity (*Voice* 197, italics original). By "service" Cooper does not mean servitude, or "being used" ("Racial" 236). Rather, she has self-determination in mind. Cooper exclaims, "Keep true to your own ideals. Be not ashamed of what is homely and your own. Speak out and speak honestly. Be true to yourself" (*Voice* 226). Moreover, she insists that being true to oneself does not require denigrating or destroying anyone else's person or culture: "Men will here learn that a race, as a family, may be true to itself without seeking to exterminate all others" (168). In particular, Cooper highlights ethical principles of interdependence, mutuality, and reciprocity. To her, these are not mere abstract ideals: they are building-blocks for realizing lived realities of cross-cultural "equilibrium" and "balance" that begin from an other-oriented, rather than egocentric, ethos of recognizing and engaging with differences. Even if, at this time, these different ways of thinking and new modes of being together in the world seem improbable or even impossible, Cooper nevertheless insists that they are possible.

And yet, at the same time, Cooper is also quite skeptical about the realm of emotions; she clarifies that her outlook is not grounded in a "Polly-Anna" attitude ("Racial" 236) and that in strategizing for change, she does *not* endorse superficial forms of philanthropy that objectify via coercive empathy (*Voice* 28). Cooper's wariness about the misuses of care is highly significant: she suggests that empathy, seemingly a positive emotion, has the potential to be used to impose "meaning on someone else's existence from a position removed from it, or ignorant of and indifferent to its specificities" (Code, *Rhetorical* 125). Cooper also advises her readers not to buy into a bootstraps ideology in which the victims of oppression are blamed for their lowly status, lack of education, and poverty (*Voice* 28, 208; "Ethics" 209), as if these are freely chosen. Remember the "hideous handicaps" and "inequalities of environment" faced by many, she insists, and transform society rather than disparage the disenfranchised ("Social" 217).

She therefore advocates a bottom-up approach to community "uplift," not reliance on external forces (*Voice* 29), for other people's "benevolent wisdom" (38), no matter how pious or well-intended, can be both shortsighted and patronizing. People, she emphasizes, are not "sheep" to be "superintended" by others (39). Thus the "magnanimous" gestures of those with more power should be treated with suspicion (67), as should altruism, since it can simply be motivated by "selfishness," which is frequently just a "highly cultivated" form of egotism (137). Later Cooper builds on this insight and asserts that international acts of state "benevolence" in the form of the "White Man's Burden" are an especially odious form of ostensible assistance ("Equality" 298). We should remember, warns Cooper, that those who offer to "help" are often the ones most in need of being "cultivated" themselves; with sarcasm, she remarks on the "need of missionary teaching to 'elevate' the white race" (*Voice* 204). She concludes, "If the cultivated black man cannot endure the white man's barbarity — the cure, it seems to me, would be to cultivate the white man" (210).

Situatedness, Solidarity, Accountability, and Action: Cooper's Criteria for a Socially Relevant Philosophy

Cooper uses her sharp wit effectively to mark her observations as located and embodied. In other words, she daringly writes "her body into the text" such that her words "stand in a new space between the first-person confessional of the slave narrative or spiritual autobiography and the third-person imperative of political [or philosophical] essays" (Alexander 338). In addition, in her use of first-person observations to back up her analyses (e.g., *Voice* 76–77, 89–90, 94–96), she demonstrates that one's own lived experience is an important source of knowledge. As Elizabeth Alexander contends, "Cooper posits an African-American woman's lived experience as evidentiary." Cooper refuses the erasure of her own embodiment and uses phrases such as "I confess" and "I would beg" to propel her arguments (344). In drawing on and theorizing from her own lived experiences to interrogate oppression, Cooper, like later Black women writers, sought to do more than simply "testify" in an individualist or egocentric way; rather, she sought to "alter the consciousness of [her] readers" (Perkins 24–25).

Without apology, Cooper emphasize how what can be known is contingent: thinking is embodied within *particular* rather than universal bodies, spaces, and historical moments. For Cooper, situated knowledge claims are not to be dismissed as mere opinion because *all* knowledge claims are partial and contextual; what you see and also come to value, she argues, "depends on where you plant your standard" (*Voice* 195). Cooper maintains that close attention to the meaning of our social identities and to the contexts in which we live and think is not detrimental to the truth, as is often claimed. Similarly, theorizing from the lived experience of marginality is not, she argues, any more myopic, narcissistic, or emotional than supposedly disembodied, universal, and objective forms of knowing, though it is often characterized as inherently limited by its locatedness and therefore as fundamentally flawed.

To the contrary, she insists that a reliance upon and focus on abstract generalization tends to impede sufficient understanding and to undermine adequate knowing (186). Cooper suggests that acknowledging the locatedness of knowledge practices and reflecting upon the context of discovery can help us to achieve what might today be called "strong objectivity" (Harding, "Rethinking" 69–72, May 78). She explains that, "paradoxical as it may seem, instead of making us narrow and provincial, this trueness to one's habitat, this appreciative eye and ear for the tints and voices of one's own little wood serves but to usher us into the eternal galleries and choruses of God" (*Voice* 177). Thus, for Cooper, what she calls infinite truth exists, but, she reiterates, it can never be "encompassed and confined by one age or nation, sect or country — much less by one little creature's finite brain" (298). As a Black woman, then, Cooper does not claim to have a privileged perspective in totality; rather, because her knowledge, as in the case of all knowing, is partial, it must be shared with others and pieced together with other partial truths.

As is apparent in her critiques of biologism or of racist and sexist stereotypes, Cooper amply demonstrates that those who claim to rise above socio-political contexts or seek to purge all affect or embodiment from their observations cannot fully succeed. And, in their fervent attempts to deny their locatedness, such knowers actually undermine the knowing process. The body, Cooper illustrates, is not "always or simply a drag on theory" (Alcoff, "Unassimilated 258). However, this is the general argument usually presented to counter claims derived from openly "embodied" knowing (258). In questioning the validity and normative status of aperspectival knowledge models, Cooper therefore knows that she is going against the grain. For instance, she emphasizes that her "conviction[s], wrought in by hard experience" are considered by society's "experts" as "too apparently audacious to be entertained even as a stealthy surmise" (*Voice* 99). Nevertheless, Cooper stands by her situated knowing and suggests that other Black women do the same.

Cooper affirms how "social identity makes epistemic differences in what is noticed, understood, meant, and, thus, known" (Alcoff, "Judging" 244). She describes the "calm elevation" of the Black Woman, a "thoughtful spectator who stands aloof from the heated scramble" (*Voice* 137), and emphasizes women's "peculiar coigne of vantage" (138). Generally speaking, argues Cooper, men do not see the world from women's standpoint (122), nor do Black men, in their "busy objectivity" (ii), necessarily understand the world as Black women see it. Cooper writes, just "as our Caucasian barristers are not to blame if they cannot *quite* put themselves in the dark man's place, neither should the dark man be wholly expected fully and adequately to reproduce the exact Voice of the Black Woman" (iii, italics original). She adds, "Our men are not perhaps to blame if they see everything colored by the light of those agitations in the midst of which they live and move and have their being" (136). Further, Cooper argues that, like the chemist's distilled water necessary for good laboratory testing, African American women are a "touchstone" of reliable observation and insight (93): here Cooper develops an argument for the epistemic value of an "outsider-within" standpoint.[17]

Yet, as we have seen, differences in social identity are, for Cooper, not innate or biological. Rather, they stem from diverse and even divergent experiences of reality that are the outcome of socially created inequalities (including asymmetrical educational opportunities, unequal legal standing, lack of employment options, and experiences of systemic gender- and/or race-based discrimination and violence). Cooper maintains that these differences, while constructed, are nevertheless lived and real: they affect one's daily experience of the world and shape one's conceptions of the self. In other words, although Cooper is not determinist, she also wants to emphasize the knowledge and wisdom to be found in the margins. However, her operative concept of marginality is flexible, not fixed, for "locations on the periphery ... move and slide along the circumference"

(Peterson 7), as Cooper's analyses of simultaneous privilege and oppression amply illustrate.

Moreover, although Cooper claims epistemic privilege based in race-gender marginality, she does not suggest that the cognitive authority arising out of marginalization and struggle is natural or inherent. Rather, it is a learned critical capacity: mere group membership is not sufficient. If it were, the dangers of internalized oppression, which Cooper outlines at length, would neither merit attention nor pose any threat to liberation. Thus, while it is not impossible to learn to understand the insights and outlooks of those who experience the world in fundamentally different ways (*Voice* 60–61), privilege and power can be an impediment to knowing that must be accounted for. Critical consciousness is not, in other words, a given: it is achieved, and never assured.

Similarly, freedom is neither constant nor guaranteed. In fact, the false "peace" of "suppression, which is the passivity of death" (149), threatens daily to keep in check collective freedom for all. Although basic "freedom in mind and body" (223) are, obviously, necessary, Cooper maintains that the most meaningful liberation is achieved via an interrogative and reflexive application of those freedoms, not by adhering to absolutisms or "unspeculative belief" (287). She writes, "We look within that we may gather together once more our forces, and ... address ourselves to the tasks before us" (27). Cooper further explains that "deciding how best to use ... [the] present ... is a question to be decided each day by every one of us" (26). Thus Cooper urges her readers to "live into" rather than "brood over" the world — to be accountable to others and to engage with the world's problems (285, 303).

By advocating a model of "living into" the world, Cooper is asking that we attend to the moral dimensions of knowing and that we hold ourselves accountable to others. Philosophy, she argues, is not for lifting us "above the toils and anxieties the ambitions and aspirations of the common herd" (287) by dwelling only in the "high ground of generalities" (73). Moreover, philosophy must be fundamentally other-oriented, not egocentric: it has a social role, argues Cooper — "uplifting your less favored brethren," which entails pouring "the oil of human kindness and love on these troubled waters" (287). Repeatedly, Cooper emphasizes linking theory with action and the related need for solidarity and coalition, for "If one link of the chain be broken, the chain is broken. A bridge is no stronger than its weakest part, and a cause is not worthier than its weakest element" ("Intellectual" 204).

Cooper maintains that rather than "mistake individuals' honor for race development," we must always remember the collective whole. "A stream cannot rise higher than its source," she adds, and "A race is but a total of families" (*Voice* 29). Here and elsewhere, Cooper seeks to redefine what racial and gender solidarity might mean as well as what might "count" as a "race issue" or "women's issue." In other words, she "disrupts dominant constructions of identity that define differences in competitive, antagonistic terms" (Glass 38). For example, she forcefully reminds Black men that trying to "build up a ... manhood without taking into consideration our women" is as futile and as impossible as trying to "grow trees from leaves" (*Voice* 78).

In thinking about the race as a whole, they should abandon this one-dimensional vision of the future and of the race; instead, African American men should strive to be their "*Sister's keeper*" (32, italics original). Here I interpret Cooper to be advocating collective consciousness and a gender coalition based on parity or equal status, not patriarchal and condescending forms of "keeping" or protection, which she abhorred. Cooper emphasizes that African American men must realize how the concerns and needs of African American men are *linked* with, but not always the *same as*, those of African American women. Black men, argues Cooper, are not the synecdochal stand-in for the collective whole — they alone do not "represent" the "race."

Similarly, instead of the widespread "disparagement" of those who are vulnerable and powerless shown by many white women activists and feminist leaders, Cooper advocates the "due consideration" of all persons (117). "Woman's cause," asserts Cooper, should never be reduced to a "bluestocking debate or an aristocratic pink tea" (123). By adhering to a coalitional model of social change, Cooper argues, women's "'rights' will mean the final triumph of all right over might" (125–6). Later, Cooper reiterates that "the colored woman feels that woman's cause is one and universal. ... Woman's wrongs are thus indissolubly linked with all undefended woe" ("Intellectual" 205). Robin D. G. Kelley identifies this coalitional approach as a constant of Black feminism (5–9, 135–136), as do Guy-Sheftall ("Evolution"), T. Denean Sharpley-Whiting and Joy James (1–7), the Combahee Collective (272–82), and many others. Kelley writes, "Radical black feminists have never confined their vision to just the emancipation of black women or women in general, or all black people for that matter" (137).

Thus, across her body of work, Cooper repeats the need for collective accountability, or "mutual succor and defense" (*Voice* 102). She concludes that one-dimensional thought lends itself to supremacist "monomania" and violence (219), whereas multiplicity in thought and in culture serves to ward off not only dull "monotony" but also the dangerous "limitations produced by exclusiveness" (156). Cooper suggests, in other words, that the criteria for an egalitarian polity and for a socially relevant epistemology overlap: "All interests must be consulted, all claims conciliated" (164), and differences in identity, power and position must be acknowledged and accounted for, not denied.

Difference, from this approach, is no longer understood as a problem to be smoothed over or controlled; rather, it is a valuable resource. She asserts that "no one is or can be supreme" and that "universal reciprocity" is the only viable model for adequately recognizing difference and for fostering a multicultural and democratic society (164, 165). It is not only the case that "No finite mind can grasp and give out the whole circle of truth" (183), but also that those who have had more power accorded to them should not have the right to speak for the oppressed. Rather, those who have been silenced, denied both voice and power, must have their say: the "truth from *each* standpoint" should be represented by "one who lives there" (ii, italics original). This precept of Cooper's remains a constant in Black feminist theorizing; as the 1,603-member collective "African American Women in Defense of Ourselves" would assert in response to Clarence Thomas's confirmation hearings, "We pledge ourselves to continue to speak out in defense of one another, in defense of the African American community and against those who are hostile to social justice no matter what color they are. No one will speak for us but ourselves" (272).

Furthermore, Cooper illustrates that socially responsible knowledge practices cannot rely on the findings derived from monological methods or mechanical "cast-iron formulas" that are then hailed as the "TRUTH" (*Voice* 298, capitalization original). As Christian would later explain, "Many of us are particularly sensitive to monolithism since one major element of ideologies of dominance ... is to dehumanize people by stereotyping them, by denying them their variousness and complexity" ("Race" 341). Cooper therefore insists that the ideal "philosophic mind" is not "narrow"; rather, it seeks to understand the interconnection of "all prejudices" and strives for "recognition" of the other in her difference (*Voice* 117). Guy-Sheftall similarly argues there is no illogic or contradiction in this multilevel, matric approach ("Evolution"). Rather, unsound reasoning lies in fragmenting political analysis and action along the lines of atomized, supposedly competing identities or groups — a futile strategy that Cooper thoroughly ridicules and dispenses with (*Voice* 123).

Again, an intersectional metaphysics and political philosophy like Cooper's refuses a hierarchy of oppressions and therefore rejects choosing between either "race" *or* "gender" solidarity (and the false universalization of group experience and identity that entails) in favor of a "both/and" model of coalition.[18] Further, Cooper insists on a global analysis of domination that accounts for imperialism, colonialism, and war.[19] From this standpoint, "sex, race, country, [and] condition" must all be accounted for — and none must be favored over any other ("Intellectual" 204). As participants, including Cooper, in the 1900 Pan-African Congress would conclude, this means that each country shall have the right to self-determination; the oppressive forces of empire and the pernicious ideology of the "white man's burden" must be overthrown (Pellow 67–8). Later, by invoking the Gospel according to Matthew regarding the judgment of nations at the close of her doctoral exams (25:40, King James version), Cooper reiterates the need to measure the success of our ideas and practices not according to the values of the powerful but, rather, by holding ourselves accountable to the lives and to the judgment of those who are oppressed both at home and abroad: "Inasmuch as ye have done these things to the least of these my brethren ye have done it to Me" ("Equality" 298).

Cooper's cross-disciplinary analysis of the ways in which all knowledge practices are partial, contextual, and marked by power relations is insightful, as is her discussion of the entangled nature of epistemic, material, and structural forms of inequality. Importantly, Cooper identifies the interrelated problems of objectification and internalization and discusses the psychological and emotional elements of coercion and domination. Her outlining of alternative epistemic practices is also noteworthy. Cooper presents a theory of situated, embodied knowing that is intersectional in its analytic approach, that resists both objectification and a fact/value distinction, that is oriented toward coalition and acknowledges partiality, that requires reflexivity on the part of the knower, and that calls for the recognition of the other and for an engagement with difference as its ideal rather than generalizations that suppress difference.

These insights on Cooper's part merit further debate and discussion. In other words, I am not suggesting that Cooper's theoretical premises are incontestable or without fault, but I have sought to outline them more fully because she has not been adequately recognized for the range of her philosophical contributions. Cooper's insistence on the need to connect mind with body, self with other, reason with feeling, and theory with action to help realize a loving and politically radical vision of the world is a redefinition of the "philosophic mind" worth paying much more attention to.

CHAPTER 6

Tracing Resistant Legacies, Rethinking Intellectual Genealogies

Reflections on Cooper's Black Feminist Theorizing[1]

Throughout this volume I accentuate the visionary nature of Cooper's intersectional politics, her interdisciplinary methodology, and her reflexive, embodied, and socially accountable model of philosophy. Consciously, I have focused more on Cooper's foresight than on her oversights not because I want readers to view her as a stereotypical Black feminist "cipher of transgression" (Philip), a critical superheroine who busted down walls right and left. I recognize and refuse the "superficial attractions of strength" (T. Harris, *Saints* 10–11) that continue to predominate both in fictional representations of Black women and in critical analyses of Black women's ideas. My claim is not that Cooper is beyond critique, nor that she should be thought of in this way: this would flatten out her legacy and belittle her ideas. But I have emphasized methods for identifying Cooper's insights and for further understanding the innovation in her work because the critical and interpretive terrain has been uneven; the rhetorical space into which Cooper spoke and continues to be read is asymmetrical rather than equal.

Unlike that of countless major thinkers to whom critics have accorded room for error and whose life work has been approached as complex, evolving, and multifaceted, Cooper's later work as a scholar and educator remains obscure. Her extensive theoretical contributions in *A Voice from the South* have not been given their due, and her lifelong activism and advocacy have been virtually brushed aside as if they were afterthoughts separate from, rather than informed by, her perceptive analyses. As Michelle Wallace emphasizes, more often than not Black feminist intellectuals, writers, and activists "are not allowed to establish their own intellectual terrain, to make their own mistakes, to invent their own birthplace in writing" (*Dark* 172).

To appreciate adequately the intricacies and textures of Cooper's work as a "birthplace" of self-invention and of a new and different imaginary requires more than merely acknowledging her ideas, only then to assimilate them to preexisting methodological, chronological, or theoretical paradigms, be they in the disciplines or in interdisciplinary fields. An "add and stir" technique does not rupture or transform normative epistemological tenets or prevailing political assumptions; moreover, a tokenizing or "cosmetic" inclusion is itself a "posture of domination" (Alarcón 357, 364). As Henderson argues, "the self-inscription of black women requires disruption, rereading and rewriting the ... canonical stories, as well as revising the conventional generic forms that convey these stories" (131).

Individually and collectively, it is time to heed Cooper's call for "retrospection, introspection, and prospection" (*Voice* 26–27): an intensely personal and political rethinking of our past, present, and future. Attending to the implications of Cooper's expansive insights necessitates that some accepted frames of reference be abandoned while others are shifted or "bent" to be more flexible and porous, less fixed and rigid (K. Holloway 623). The criteria for methodological and epistemological adequacy must change radically, in other words, and not simply stretch a little. Cooper illustrates this need, for example, by highlighting a wide range of encounters with concealment, some structural and institutional, others cognitive and emotional. As Toni Morrison would later suggest, "certain absences are so stressed, so ornate, so planned, they call attention to themselves; arrest us with intentionality and purpose" ("Unspeakable" 34). Similarly, Cooper does more than merely document the existence of such opacities, particularly in *A Voice from the South* and in *L'Attitude de la France à l'égard de l'esclavage pendant la Révolution*. She examines their "intentionality and purpose" — their role in helping to maintain the status quo, their function as part of a deeply embedded epistemology of ignorance.

To help bridge gaps in perception and to span these myriad fissures or "vast gulf[s]" (Cooper, *L'Attitude* 60) that characterize our reality, Cooper contends, for example, that different notions of trauma and histories of resistance must be developed so that Black women's "yet unwritten history" ("Intellectual" 202) of invisible struggles and "*silent ... suffering*" (*Voice* 111, italics original) can be recognized, even though this "cadenza" has been willfully "uncomprehended," "little understood," and made "voiceless" (i). In connecting seemingly individual or isolated incidences of exploitation to systemic forms of domination, Cooper asserts that our national origin stories have to account for their heretofore evaded realities and shades of nuance. By employing tactics of critical "re-memory" of the past (Christian, "Somebody" 226), or "counter-chronicling" (V. Bell 16), Cooper renames historical periods. For instance, the Progressive Era becomes "the most trying period of all [colored people's] trying history in this land of their trial and bondage" ("Ethics" 207–8) or, as Herbert Gutman would later christen it, the "retrogressionist" era (531–2).

Furthermore, whether writing about the United States or France, Cooper homes in on the fundamental paradox of democracies built on slavery and genocide and the ongoing implications of this past in present forms of empire building and capitalist exploitation. She refuses to push these contradictions aside as anomalies or tragic errors, for doing so simply takes the dominant group as normative, the standard point of reference. As Spelman explains with regard to discussions of slavery in the United States, "to acknowledge the situation of slaves by linking it to the tragic limitations of whites ensures that Blacks are not talked about independently of whites. The suffering of slaves remains the property of the tragically flawed characters and institutions that caused it" (*Fruits* 57–8). Cooper therefore insists on shifting to paradigms that do not simply use either whiteness or Europe as their "normative interlocutor" (Shohat 6).

Likewise, Cooper upsets Eurocentric notions of the Age of Revolution. In her dissertation, she develops a comparative historiographic model. Through tactical repositioning, Cooper illustrates how the Haitian Revolution should be considered as much a part of the history of revolution as the uprisings in France or the United States. Arguing that the seeds of the Haitian Revolution were sown in the moment of Portugal's beginning the slave trade in West Africa in the fifteenth century and in Columbus's arrival on Hispaniola, Cooper quietly proposes a revised genealogy of resistance in the Caribbean and highlights a long-standing transatlantic circuitry of knowledge. She debunks the idea that the ongoing uprisings in Saint-Domingue and across the Caribbean were anomalous, meaningless, or merely imitative of European Enlightenment political philosophies and movements.

In addition to highlighting the need to conceive temporal and analytic categories in ways that approach history from its "undersides," a rethinking of the operative "origin stories" in the field of education is also requisite. For example, figures such as John Dewey or Jean Piaget are well known for their advocacy of constructivist pedagogy, and the influence of the Frankfurt School of philosophy is frequently associated with the later work of critical pedagogy theorists such as Paulo Freire and bell hooks. However, the efforts and ideas of Cooper and other early African American feminist educators are rarely discussed as shaping either field,[2] even though Cooper

and many of her contemporaries worked to reshape the meaning of education as "the practice of freedom" (hooks, *Teaching* 13). Persistently, they
did this labor not merely for a select few — not just for the "talented tenth,"
as Cooper is so often charged with — but equally for the disenfranchised
whom Cooper described as the "submerged tenth" ("On Education" 250).[3]
In other words, further study is needed to explore how Cooper and other
educators, in Washington, D.C. and across the nation, advocated "teaching
to transgress," as hooks would call it, or a "pedagogy of the oppressed," as
Freire would name it, in the fifty-year period between the 1890s and the
1940s. In curricular design, educational leadership, pedagogy, and educational advocacy, Cooper clearly refused eugenicist ideas of cultural, moral,
or intellectual "unfitness" and rejected the notion of a biologically inherent pathology or underclass.

Similarly, our timelines for marking out the history of community advocacy for multicultural education and for culturally relevant, inclusive curricula often begin with the education movements of the 1960s and 1970s;
occasionally they go back to Carter G. Woodson's work in the first quarter of
the twentieth century to have the history of Black America incorporated into
the public consciousness (via what is now Black History Month). However,
what of the fact that teachers at Dunbar High, such as Cooper and Simpson,
were teaching about Toussaint Louverture and the Haitian Revolution in
French classes, or that Cooper translated her doctoral exam research to be
used as world history curricular materials at Frelinghuysen — for that very
"submerged tenth" not thought by many others to be worth educating at all,
much less introduced to a critical, Black Atlantic model of history? What of
Frelinghuysen's offering an education for adult "retarded learners" in the
1930s — how might more knowledge of this endeavor shift our understanding of the intersecting politics of race and disability in education?

These small bits of information suggest that there is much more to
uncover: a new mosaic history of our oppositional educational legacies
needs to be crafted from such fragments. Cooper's rejection of racially
denigrating textbooks, her fight for equal access to an equitable and fair
education at the secondary and college levels for all persons, no matter
their economic, gender, race, or disability status, and her push for more
active, less didactic, and essentially constructivist models of learning as
a corrective to passivity-inducing top-down models of teaching all negate
the commonly held assumption that these are relatively recent developments in American education. Cooper's work shows us that the fight to
address issues of power, culture, and authority in our educational system
is at least a century old.

Whether in linguistics, history, social work, educational leadership,
philosophy, literature, theology, labor analysis, or political organizing,

Cooper speaks from the margins to develop and deploy an interstitial political and analytic method. She pushes us to draw new cartographies of resistance that do not reinforce the worldview of the metropole and to craft innovative methodologies that do not simply replicate an epistemological stance of dominance. Cooper argues that asymmetries of power, at the level of the individual and the structural, in philosophy and in politics, must be transformed. To account for Cooper's substantial contributions to our understanding of both social movements and social philosophy, different conceptualizations of what forms of activism are considered valid and what kinds of writing or theorizing are designated to be philosophy "proper" must be developed.

Unfortunately, many of our prevailing conceptual models remain both constrained and inflexible. It seems that dominant perceptual screens are so tenacious, so resistant to shifting or bending, that Cooper's roles as a philosopher, an activist, a civil rights leader, and a feminist continue to be routinely diminished or studiously ignored. Like Black feminists before and after her, Cooper refused to cede the rights (both her own and that of other women of color) of entry to and ownership of the domains of critical theory, philosophy, feminism, civil rights, education, and more. In fact, the flowering of Black feminist theory and criticism in the 1980s and early 1990s "would further establish ... a continuous black feminist intellectual tradition going back to the publication of Cooper's *A Voice from the South* a hundred years earlier" (Guy-Sheftall, "Evolution" 19). Nevertheless, these contributions are repeatedly disregarded, even dispensed with.

Consider, for example, that a new philosophical anthology of feminist theory (Cudd and Andreasen) includes the ideas of Mary Wollstonecraft and John Stuart Mill as foundational, but the only Black feminist theorists' writings included in the 430-page volume are those of bell hooks and Anita L. Allen, while no work by, or about the work of, any other women of color feminist theorists/philosophers seem to have made the cut at all, despite a wide array of existing and relevant material. This double tactic of tokenism and exclusion is as unjustifiable today as when Cooper and others critiqued it well over a century ago. In other words, more than mere oversight, it must be considered evidence both of an ongoing (and willful) opacity about the lives and contributions of women of color in general and of Black women in particular (Lorde, *Sister* 66–71, 110–13, 160) and of a steadfast "unrelinquished authority" (duCille, "Occult" 251) over feminism and philosophy on the part of white feminist theorists.

Masculinist forms of "unrelinquished authority" have also been at work in both Africana studies and in civil rights discourse. Figures such as W. E. B. Du Bois, Carter G. Woodson, and Alain Locke are readily cited for their forethought and innovation, while Cooper's work, for example, is rarely pointed to, much less acknowledged in a substantial way. Partly this is the case because such men were able to publish more, and more widely, and all three held highly visible roles as public intellectuals in their own time. But of course, the very fact of their visibility was (and is) due in part to their masculinity. At the same time that they were instrumental advocates of the work of many African American women, they also gained greater access to and accrued more power in the public domain as men.

Thus, while Du Bois, for instance, has been rightly admired for his incipient advocacy of Black feminist ideas and ideals, as Giddings illustrates in her work on Ida B. Wells-Barnett's "vexed relationship" with the NAACP, it is also the case that when highly visible and widely admired Black women activists like Wells-Barnett wanted to be considered more than mere props for the civil rights establishment, they were explicitly pushed aside ("Missing" 1–2), in terms of both scholarly endeavors and organizational practices (14). To be included in the workings of national civil rights organizations (instead of cast out), Black women were asked to fill subordinate, even filial roles: rather than be outspoken and taken seriously as a leader, one had to agree to play the puerile part of an underling, minion, or dutiful daughter to be brought into the fold.

This model has also affected theoretical pursuits. Still too frequently, the assumption that "All the Women Are White, All the Blacks Are Men" (Hull, Scott, and Smith) remains axiomatic. Obviously, this should be considered an untenable approach to tracing a radical philosophical tradition, for it silences Black feminist intellectual and political contributions. On some level, conscious or not, I would argue that this unsustainability is actually known and understood, for the reluctance to engage with African American feminist thought is not necessarily stated outright or overtly; rather, it is evidenced via glaring omission, indicated in the marked exclusion of Black feminists' voices and ideas. In this case, one must turn to what James Baldwin aptly named "the evidence of things not seen" to understand the meanings behind such theoretical absences and to comprehend the damage done by these sites of avoidance that are often so eloquent and persuasive that it is hard to name or identify the gaps and silences in the work.

Consider, for instance, the recent scholarship of the Black philosopher Charles V. Mills, groundbreaking work that is most powerful and insightful, on the one hand, but relatively impervious to Black feminist theory on the other. For example, in *Blackness Visible*, Mills's lineage of Black philosophy includes only men, ironically while in the midst of challenging the willful opacity and exclusionary "official ontology" of the dominant philosophical tradition with regard to race (71). Paradoxically, this newly proposed ontology of Black philosophy suppresses, even erases, the existence of Black feminist thought, while it encompasses the work of an array of Black male theorists, including David Walker, Martin Delaney, Frederick Douglass, W. E. B. DuBois, Marcus Garvey, C. L. R. James, Frantz Fanon, and Martin Luther King, Jr. (17). Unfortunately, such mystifying "conceptual erasures" (*Racial* 97) of Black women's contributions persist, signaling an overlooked yet fundamental characteristic (and not a secondary attribute) of the very racial contract and "cult of forgetfulness" (98) Mills critiques.

Other recent texts and anthologies in Africana philosophy do more fully consider the ideas and work of a wide range of Black feminists, including Maria Stewart, Anna Julia Cooper, Ida B. Wells-Barnett, Angela Davis, Sylvia Wynter, and many others (e.g., Bogues *Heretics*, Gordon, Henry, Lott and Pittman, and Yancy). However, this exciting work also occasionally reverts to a masculinist explanatory framework, implicitly privileging the contributions of male Africana thinkers. For example, although Lott and Pittman anthologize the work of a range of Black feminist scholars in their groundbreaking collection (including essays by Hortense Spillers, Anita Allen, Patricia Hill Collins, Joy James, Annette Dula, Angela Davis, and Trudier Harris), in their preface to the volume they identify this philosophical tradition as arising out of the "social movements of black people themselves" without ever explicitly naming Black feminism as key among these various movements or sites of philosophical inquiry (xii). Other scholars rely on the masculinist metaphor of "Caliban's Reason" or "Caliban studies" to trace Afro-Caribbean and Africana philosophical traditions (e.g., Henry; Gordon, *Existentia* 3; Bogues *Caliban's* 15–16). Thus there remains the overarching problem of conceptualizing Black and/or Africana philosophy via subtly exclusionary timelines of radical action or via the androcentric metonym of Caliban: it does more than imply that radical Africana or Black philosophers are male, it subordinates women's various contributions under the rubric of seemingly "universal" masculine genealogies and bodies.

Likewise, Black modernism is a transnational phenomenon in which Cooper participated, though she has rarely been mentioned in histories of this movement. Fresh genealogies of Pan-Africanist and Black modernist discourse must be traced, the timelines and boundaries of the era shifted to include the work not only of Jane and Paulette Nardal, Amy Jacques Garvey, Amy Ashwood Garvey, Suzanne Lacascade, and Suzanne Césaire, but also that of Black feminist educators like Cooper, Anna H. Jones, Emma Merritt, Georgiana Simpson, and many others who did not merely engage in transatlantic travel but sought to identify and articulate a cross-cultural race consciousness. The imaginative borders of the Harlem or Black Renaissance must also be newly rendered, the trajectories reconceived. Again, it is not simply about "adding the women" into preexisting androcentric models of the Black Atlantic, of Black modernism, or of Négritude: it is about transforming the fundamental epistemological assumptions and methodological techniques so that a different evolution of these philosophical and cultural movements can emerge.

Of course, Cooper's work also suggests that the "origin story" for comparative feminist thought across the bounds of nation must be thoroughly revised. Not only does Cooper identify the harmful effects of sexism on African American women's lives, she attempts to draw comparisons between seemingly distinct forms of sexism at home and abroad.[4] Moreover, as part and parcel of her comparative approach to the politics of gender and race, Cooper refuses to devalue *métissage*, hybridity, or *mestizaje*: rather than advocate a "pure" Black feminist stance, Cooper is clear that her multifaceted philosophical and political outlook stems from her mixed-race heritage as Black, white, and Native American. In the *Washington Tribune*, a Black newspaper, Cooper wrote the following: "The part of my ancestors that did not come over in the Mayflower in 1620, arrived, I am sure, a year earlier in the fateful Dutch trader that put in at Jamestown in 1619. ... I believe that the third source of my individual stream comes ... from the vanishing Red Men [sic]" (n.d., in Hutchinson 3). Cooper defies the eugenicist claim that a "mixing" of "blood streams" leads to contamination, decay, and the death of "civilization"; in her work, she argues that differences are not only vital to innovative thought and culture, but also the building blocks of an intersubjective ethic of connection and mutual recognition. By articulating that her worldview is grounded fundamentally in the simultaneity of her identities, Cooper advocates major paradigm shifts not only at the level of national or international politics, but also within the resistance movements in which she was active.

Whether the context was Pan-Africanism, feminism, civil rights, temperance, child development, housing, healthcare, incarceration, or education, Cooper enacted intra-community critiques of what Deborah K. King would come to name the "politics of expediency" in which white women "trade upon" their race privilege and African American men their gender privilege (305). Like later Black feminists who were "aware of their own erasure from the annals of history" and who sought to "chronicle the achievements of their sister-activist-thinkers" (Guy-Sheftall, "Evolution" 24), Cooper reminds her readers of critically aware "but hitherto voiceless" (*Voice* ii) African American women and asks that she and her sisters "in the service" (140) be recognized by both civil rights leaders and by feminists as agents of history and not just as a convenient surplus activist labor pool to be drawn on or exploited, when convenient, for modes of political action defined by others.

Moreover, Cooper thoroughly rejects the idea of subpersonhood or "partitioned social ontology" (Mills, *Visible* 7) as well as a "pop-bead" approach to metaphysics (Spelman, *Inessential* 15) in favor of a radically egalitarian notion of personhood and a multilevel metaphysics or philosophy of being. This philosophy of being is not merely multidimensional at the level of the individual in isolation; rather, it articulates the individual or personal with the collective and political. Echoing Frances Harper's earlier expression of a Black feminist concept of collectivity in her 1857 speech before the New York Anti-Slavery Society, "We Are All Bound Up Together" (see Logan, *We* 44–97), Cooper stipulates that self-love and the quest for autonomy, whether pursued as a group or as an individual, do not require eradication of or domination over others, but mutuality and reciprocal recognition (*Voice* 168). This collective worldview, combined with a notion of a complex and reciprocal self, which stands in contradistinction to an atomized and individualist notion of agency and self-determination, can be found not only in Black feminist theory and politics but also in literary production. As Karla Holloway illustrates, "Instead of reflections that isolate and individuate, characters such as Gwendolyn Brooks' Maud Martha or Ntozake Shange's Sassafrass see themselves surrounded by a tradition of women like them" (619).

More sustained work is needed to uncover these earlier efforts to articulate a comparative and collective critical consciousness, in terms of both race and gender. Such inquiry not only necessitates a revolution in the operative methods of many traditional disciplines but also demands a considerable rethinking of the origins or beginning points of what many regard as "new" interdisciplinary fields that reject deficit models of ethnicity, race, culture, and/or gender in which the agency and intellect of marginalized groups is diminished, if not made entirely invisible. Over the past thirty years, fields such as women's studies, African American studies, ethnic studies, and queer studies have sought to document, through careful research across the bounds of disciplines and cultures, not merely histories of oppression and marginalization, but a dialectical "simultaneity of oppression and resistance" (Brewer 28).

Many of us who have worked to secure a place in the academy for these fields have presumed our critical, interdisciplinary methodologies to be fairly recent innovations, since the genesis of the interdisciplines is generally traced to the liberation movements of the second half of the twentieth century. But a closer look at earlier thinkers like Cooper belies this presumption. She crafted an overtly political, experientially informed, interrogative and interdisciplinary method, and contemporary students and scholars in the interdisciplines have much to learn from her techniques. Cooper developed this critical methodology not simply to leverage space within and across fields of inquiry but also to propel a sustained critique of supremacy in its many forms, whether physical, representational, epistemological, historical, theological, political, cultural, racial, or gendered.

It is unjustifiable to continue to downplay, even unwittingly, the longevity of critical, comparative methods grounded in a Black feminist "multiplicative theory and praxis of being" (Wing 27), which Cooper's work clearly is. Therefore, over and above the transformations of various historical and theoretical frameworks I have already mentioned, to do proper justice to the far-reaching implications of Cooper's ideas requires acknowledging, in a sustained rather than fleeting manner, the ways in which her methods and premises fit the parameters of what we would now call Black feminist theorizing. Furthermore, it requires recognizing more fully how Cooper's varied forms of work as an educator, community advocate, and scholar played a part in the development of Black feminist liberation movements.

In other words, to engage genuinely with the wider implications of Cooper's ideas, it is essential to take equally seriously Black feminist theorizing. That Cooper's contributions are consistent with many of the premises and methods of Black feminist theory and activism is not surprising: after all, she helped to shape this field of inquiry and to establish many of the key sites of organizing and activism at a local, national, and international level. This is not to suggest that African American feminist theory "begins" solely with Cooper or only among Cooper and her peers in the 1890s; her work must be understood as emerging from and belonging to a long-standing genealogy of resistance in the Americas by peoples of African descent. As Cooper implies, this legacy can be traced back to 1619 (in Hutchinson 3)[5] or even 1492 (*L'Attitude* 8).[6] In other words, since their moment of arrival in the Americas, Black women have "struggled with the multiple realities of gender, racial, and economic or caste oppression" (James and Sharpley-Whiting 1).

Moreover, although Cooper's *A Voice from the South* is the first book-length theoretical analysis written from a Black feminist standpoint (Guy-Sheftall, "Evolution" 19), Maria Stewart's speeches of the 1830s can be considered the beginning of a written African American feminist discourse (1), or even the eighteenth-century poetry of Phyllis Wheatley for at least keeping "alive … *the notion of song*" despite her poetry's "contrary instincts" (A. Walker 237, 236, italics original). Too often, however, the normative timelines of feminist resistance have ignored this legacy. While African American feminists' work can be found increasingly in major anthologies about the histories of feminist movements or "feminisms," even when included, Black women's contributions to work on "epistemologies," "subjectivities," and "visualities," for example, are still often minimized or overlooked (e.g., Kemp and Squires).

It is still routine to find little more than a token gesture toward African American feminists' praxis as, in fact, *theoretical* or philosophical in nature. This is not to deny the existence of recent anthologies such as Bhavnani's *Feminism & 'Race,'* Shohat's *Talking Visions,* and many others that are excellent; the point is to query how it is that the genesis of feminist theory is, more often than not, traced to twentieth-century thinkers such as Virginia Woolf or Simone de Beauvoir, while the ideas of women of color are regularly omitted and erased. For example, Cudd and Andreasen recently asserted that "Feminist theory ... begins as a self-consciously distinct field only in the latter part of the twentieth century, with the publication of Simone de Beauvoir's *The Second Sex*" (1).

Obviously, I am not repudiating the groundbreaking work done by Beauvoir, Woolf, or anyone else. However, genealogies such as these remain all too common, and they have led African American feminist scholars to call, time and again, for an alternative periodization of feminist thought and action, a revised origin story that recognizes heretofore hidden or obscured modes of Black women's resistance and cultural production: it is essential to understand how they kept things "rolling" (Weathers 161) in the twentieth century and "stirring" in the nineteenth (Truth, "When" 37). But further, these new genealogies would seek to understand this political and intellectual work on its own terms, not just as it matches up to extant unidimensional notions about women's agency, historical roles, methods of protest, or nascent feminism.[7] Whether we begin our timeline of African American feminist theorizing and organizing for liberation with the year 1619 or 1830, it is clear that neither of these activities are recent developments. Black women have long been "custodian[s] of a house of resistance" (Davis, "Reflections" 207) and architects of a "protest infrastructure" (Hine, "Rape" 386).

At minimum two hundred years in the making, African American feminism is not a new wave or late arrival on the scene of an ostensibly more universal women's movement, nor is Black feminist theory merely an appendage to, satellite of, mimetic reaction to, or subsidiary of a more general body of feminist thought.[8] It has often been relegated to such roles because of a prevailing "one-dimensional perspective on women's reality" (hooks, *Feminist* 3), an exclusionary way of thinking that Cooper challenged and sought to eradicate.[9] There has also been a concomitant narrow conceptualization of the locations and boundaries of feminist theorizing and activism (Lorde, *Sister* 116–17). As Elise Johnson McDougald would assert, echoing Cooper's earlier insights, Black women's issues, experiences, lives, and needs are "multiform" and "cannot be thought of in mass" (80).

Like many women before and after her, Cooper struggled against overly narrow and simplistic approaches to both intellectual and political work around issues of race, as if race as an identity, experience, lens, or politic were superordinate to gender. Cooper was not alone in this critique or struggle, of course. For example, Ida B. Wells also protested simplistic ways of addressing issues of domination, exploitation, and violence: she consistently argued for an understanding of lynching as an issue of race and gender politics simultaneously ("Lynch Law"). Before such declarations by Wells or Cooper, Sojourner Truth asserted that "it is hard for men to give up [their privilege] entirely" because they have a tendency to "run in the old track"; however, they must abandon the idea of "having" all the rights for themselves even if "it cuts like a knife" (38).

Unfortunately, single-axis models that inherently delegitimize African American feminisms by castigating them as secondary at best, betrayal at worst, would continue to prevail, provoking Toni Cade Bambara to exclaim almost a century after Cooper that Black feminism is, definitively, not "just honky horseshit" ("Roles" 102). Likewise, Audre Lorde would repeatedly contend that to be antisexist is not to be antiblack (*Sister* 120–1). Years later, in response to the appointment of Clarence Thomas to the Supreme Court "as an affront not only to African American women and men, but to all people concerned with social justice," the collective African American Women in Defense of Ourselves would write: "Many have erroneously portrayed the allegations against Clarence Thomas as an issue of either gender or race. As women of African descent, we understand sexual harrassment as both. ... In 1991, we cannot tolerate this type of dismissal of any one Black woman's experience or this attack upon our collective character without protest, outrage, and resistance" (271–2).

Cole and Guy-Sheftall contend that perhaps the most "stark illustration of the overall marginalization of Black women in the [contemporary] Black liberation struggle, despite their intense involvement, is manifest in the decision on the part of civil rights leaders not to allow a Black woman to speak at the March on Washington in 1963" (85). In other words, too frequently, radical Black men have "ignore[d] both the personhood and the contributions of Black women to the cause of human rights" (Murray 190). Thus, not only would the Combahee Collective be forced to reiterate what should be an obvious fact — "there have always been Black women activists" — they would also have to restate, both to feminists and civil rights leaders, that "our liberation is a necessity not as an adjunct to somebody else's but because of our need as human persons for autonomy" (274).

Clearly, it is both possible and necessary to trace philosophical and activist genealogies of African American feminisms that are at once distinctive and multiform; however, this is not to suggest that this discourse and movement have stood alone. There has been overlap and cross-fertilization among different sites of feminist and Black radical action and thought, and across different liberation movements, both within and outside the United States. As with the history and practice of any other political movement and area of critical inquiry, African American feminist theorizing and organizing should not be thought of as islands, historically or presently: they are, and have always been, dialectically engaged with a wide array of political, social, cultural, and intellectual realities. In fact, given this ongoing history of dialogue, exchange, and overlap, African American feminists have continuously highlighted the fundamentally intersubjective nature of reality and have issued calls for coalition (Combahee, B. Smith xxxii), for "a feminist articulation of diaspora" (Edwards 122), and for a "comparative study of women's roles" (Guy-Sheftall, "Evolution" 15).

Long harbingers of what Crenshaw would name "intersectionality" (see "Demarginalizing"), Black feminist theorists have consistently addressed the "interstructure of ... oppressions" (D. King 312). They have therefore maintained that to realize a radical humanism grounded in a politics of difference — to be, in other words, "pro-human for all peoples" (Weathers 159) — requires "destroy[ing] oppression of any type" rather than choosing to battle only one form of domination at a time as if they were discrete and separable (Beale 99). Unsettling normative hierarchies both of identities and politics, African American feminists have, in different ways, resolutely asserted that on account of the simultaneous and interlocking nature of forms of oppression, all efforts toward liberation must operate from a matrix perspective and toward an intersectional model of rights and freedom that does not presume any form of privilege as "given" in its foundational premises.[10]

Although there are consistent tenets that emerge from an historical overview of the work of Black feminist theorists, the various principles of African American feminist thought should not be thought of as monolithic in form, rigid in outlook, unanimous in assertions, or fixed in terms of methodology.[11] Rather than a "biologically grounded positionality" (Smith, Not Just xv) or a "transhistorical" ideology based on an unvarying, absolute essence, African American feminist theorizing is a situated and "multiaccented discourse" (E. White, "Africa" 510) that is both "plurisignant" and "polyphonic" (K. Holloway 618). This inherent diversity does not mean that there are no central beliefs or general themes to be traced; to the contrary, it signals a rejection of monolithic thinking. Thus the field's coherence lies not in homogeny or sameness, but in its fundamental engagement with multiplicity.

Though not uniformly articulated or identically conceived across time, space, and circumstance, several of the theoretical-political precepts that have emerged can certainly be said to have been shaped or informed by Cooper. From within the varied historical dimensions of African American feminist theory and action, some of the key principles in which Cooper clearly had a hand include the following[12]:

1. *Redefining what "counts" as a feminist/women's or a civil rights/race issue* by starting from the premise that race is gendered and gender is raced, and that both are shot through with the politics of class, sexuality, and nation.

   - In addition to evidence of this precept in her various activist contributions, Cooper makes a case for redefinition in her writings. In *A Voice*, see, for example, "Womanhood" (25, 28, 32, 42, 44), "Higher Education" (54, 61, 68–69, 73–79), "'Woman vs. The Indian'" (80–82, 88–89, 91, 94–95, 100–01, 108, 111–13), "Race Problem" 143, and "Worth" (208, 211, 251–52, 254–55). See also "Intellectual," "Wage Earners," "Ethics," "Equality" (294), and "On Education" (255).

   - For other examples of Black feminist theorists redefining political issues, see Toni Cade Bambara, "Roles"; Bernice McNair Barnett; Elsa Barkley Brown; Rudolph P. Byrd and Beverly Guy-Sheftall; Stephanie M. H. Camp; Johnetta Betsch Cole and Beverly Guy-Sheftall; Patricia Hill Collins; Angela Y. Davis, "Rape," "Reflections," and *Women*; Bonnie Thornton Dill, "Race"; Paula Giddings, *When*; Darlene Clark Hine, "Rape"; Darlene Clark Hine and Kate Wittenstein; bell hooks, *Ain't*; Harriet Jacobs; June Jordan; Audre Lorde, *Sister*; Wahneema Lubiano; Deborah McDowell; Pat Robinson et al., "Poor"; Ranu Samantrai; Kimberly Springer, *Still Lifting*; Sojourner Truth; Alice Walker; and Michele Wallace.

2. *Arguing for "both/and" thinking alongside sustained critiques of "either/or" dualisms* to show how false dichotomies (mind/body, self/other, reason/emotion, philosophy/politics, fact/value, science/society, metropole/colony, subject/object) have served to justify domination and reinforce hierarchy.

   - Cooper articulates a "both/and" view in *A Voice*. See, for example, "Womanhood" (44), "Higher" (50, 52–53, 59–61, 75, 78), "'Woman vs. The Indian'" (80, 96, 98, 115, 122–23, 134), "Race Problem" (163, 168), and "Gain" (294–5). She builds on this premise in later writings as well, including her speech at the World Columbian Exposition ("Intellectual"), in her doctoral exams ("Legislative," "Equality"), and in her dissertation, where she outlines a transatlantic dialectic between France and Haiti/Saint-Domingue (see chapter 4 in the present volume, as well as the text of *L'Attitude* or *Slavery*).

- For other arguments advancing a "both/and" dialectic framework, see Toni Cade Bambara; Frances Beale; Rose Brewer; Stephanie M. H. Camp; Devon Carbado; Kathleen Neal Cleaver; Patricia Hill Collins; the Combahee Collective; Angela Y. Davis, *Women*; Bonnie Thornton Dill, "Dialectics"; Beverly Guy-Sheftall, *Daughters* and *Words*; Calvin Hernton; Deborah K. King; Audre Lorde, *Sister*; Deborah McDowell; Nellie McKay; Pauli Murray; Barbara Smith; Valerie Smith; Rosalyn Terborg-Penn, "Discrimination"; Freida Tesfagiorgis; Michele Wallace, "Anger"; and E. Frances White.

3. *Naming multiple domains of power and illustrating how they interrelate* (these include economic or material, ideological, philosophical, emotional or psychological, physical, and institutional sites of power).

   - Cooper executes this multilevel analysis differently across her written work (including *Voice*, "Wage Earners," "Ethics," *L'Attitude/ Slavery*, "On Education," and others) as well as in her community activism. Rather than break down the specific domains of power by category, which would violate her argument for seeing them as interwoven and mutually reinforcing, see chapter 5, where I discuss in detail how Cooper identifies the workings of power on many levels simultaneously, and chapter 4, where I analyze how Cooper traces vectors of power in her doctoral thesis.

   - For more discussion of how different sites of power are connected, see also Stephanie M. H. Camp; Patricia Hill Collins, *Black Feminist, Fighting,* and *Sexual*; Anne duCille; Beverly Guy-Sheftall, *Daughters* and "Evolution"; Deborah K. King; Gail Lewis; Audre Lorde, *Sister*; Wahneema Lubiano; Elise Johnson McDougald; Helen Neville and Jennifer Hamer; Susan L. Smith; Hortense Spillers, "Mama's"; Gayle T. Tate, and Ida B. Wells.

4. *Advocating a multi-axis or intersectional approach to liberation politics* because domination is multiform and because different forms of oppression are simultaneous in nature.

   - In *Voice*, see for example "Womanhood" (32–3), "Higher" (78), "'Woman vs. The Indian'" (82, 94–7, 100, 108, 117–18, 121–5), "Status" (134), and "Race Problem" (164–5). See also "Intellectual," *Slavery* (especially 64, 78–9, 91, 105–6, 114), and "On Education" (252).

   - For more examples of theorists and activists calling for intersectional politics and liberation strategies, see Barbara Smith; Patricia Hill Collins, *Black* and *Fighting*; the Combahee Collective; Kimberlé Crenshaw; Beverly Guy-Sheftall; Calvin Hernton; Coretta Scott King; Deborah K. King; Pauli Murray; Bernice Johnson Reagon;

Amy Schulz and Leith Mullings; Filomina Chioma Steady; Julia Sudbury; Ida B. Wells; and Adrien K. Wing.

5. *Challenging hierarchical, top-down forms of knowing, leading, learning, organizing, and "helping" in favor of participatory, embodied, reflexive models.*

- In *Voice,* see: "Raison d'être" (i–ii), "Womanhood" (36–7, 39, 41), "Higher" (58), ""Woman vs. The Indian'" (118), "Race Problem" (155–6, 160–4), "Negro/Literature" (179, 219, 283), and "Gain" (291–3). See also "Ethics," "Equality" (291, 295), "Humor," "On Education" (251), "Angry Saxons," and "Hitler" (263).

- For more critiques of hierarchical models of leadership, knowledge, education, and/or organizing, see Patricia Hill Collins; the Combahee Collective; Lisa Delpit; Bonnie Thornton Dill; Anne duCille; bell hooks, *Teaching*; Coretta Scott King; Gloria Ladson-Billings; Rachel Lee; Jennifer L. Morgan; Leith Mullings; Bernice Johnson Reagon; Patricia Bell Scott; Julia Sudbury; Mary Ann Weathers; Aaronette M. White; E. Frances White; and Patricia J. Williams.

6. *Rejecting dehumanizing discourses, deficit models, biologistic/ determinist paradigms, and pathologizing approaches to culture or to individuals.*

- This theme is persistent across Cooper's body of work. In *Voice,* see "Womanhood" (26, 32, 37, 39, 41), "Higher" (51, 53, 65, 75, 79), "'Woman vs. The Indian'" (91–2, 96–7, 103, 109, 125), "Race Problem" (154), "Negro/Literature" (179, 185–9, 195–9, 202–8, 216, 222, 225), "Worth" (247–8, 253–5, 260, 270), and "Gain" (289, 291–3, 299–300). See also "Intellectual" (205), "Ethics," "Social Settlement" (217, 219), her dissertation as a whole (where she debunks the notion that the Haitian Revolution was merely mimetic), as well as specific references in *Slavery* (48, 75–6, 147 fn.102, 149 fn. 139), "Equality" (291–2, 298), "On Education" (250, 252), "Negro's," "Angry Saxons," and "Hitler."

- For other analyses of objectification and the politics of Black women's embodiment, see Emma Amos; Stephanie Athey; Roseanne P. Bell, Bettye J. Parker and Beverly Guy-Sheftall; Jacqueline Bobo; Johnetta Betsch Cole and Guy-Sheftall; Patricia Hill Collins, *Black Sexual*; Kimberlé Crenshaw, "Beyond"; Carole Boyce Davies; Beverly Guy-Sheftall, "Body"; Evelyn Hammonds; Trudier Harris Mammies and *Saints*; bell hooks, *Black Looks*; Tera Hunter; Terri Kapsalis; Jennifer L. Morgan; Toni Morrison; Patricia Morton; Lorraine O'Grady; Gwendolyn D. Pough; Barbara Ransby and Tracye Matthews; Marlon T. Riggs; Faith Ringgold; Dorothy Roberts; Patricia Bell Scott;

Hortense Spillers, "Mama's"; Freida Tesfagiorgis; Michele Wallace; Kimberly Wallace-Sanders.

7. *Crafting a critical interdisciplinary method* that crosses boundaries of knowledge, history, identity, and nation to reveal how these constructed divisions marginalize those whose lives and ways of knowing straddle borders and *modeling discursive/analytic techniques* that are flexible, kinetic, comparative, multivocal, and plurisignant.

- I discuss these aspects of Cooper's activism and theory in detail in chapters 2 and 3. Rather than point to specific moments in Cooper's scholarship where these qualities are present, I would argue that Cooper's multivalent and multivocal praxis emerges most fully when we take a comprehensive view of her life's work: the cumulative impact of her analyses and of her actions has a greater meaning than any individual example in isolation.

- For other examples of flexible, multivocal methods, see Elizabeth Alexander; Abena P. Busia; Hazel Carby; Barbara Christian; Patricia Hill Collins, *Black* and *Fighting*; Carole Boyce Davies; Kathy L. Glass; Paula Giddings; Beverly Guy-Sheftall; Mae Gwendolyn Henderson; Karla F. C. Holloway; Irma McClaurin; Helen Neville and Jennifer Hamer; Margo V. Perkins; Carla L. Peterson; Amy Schulz and Leith Mullings; Patricia Bell Scott; Valerie Smith; Cheryl Wall; Michele Wallace; and Patricia J. Williams.

8. *Using counter-memory and other insurgent methods to work against sanctioned ignorance* and to make visible the "undersides" of history as well as the shadows or margins of subjectivity.

- In addition to her entire doctoral thesis (see *L'Attitude/Slavery*), Cooper uses this tactic in her other writings. For example, in *Voice* see "Raison d'être" (i), "Womanhood" (9, 37), "'Woman vs. The Indian'" (90, 101–8, 111, 134–6), "Race Problem" (163), "Negro/Literature" (178–9, 193, 198), "Worth" (239, 251–5), "Gain" (299). See also "Intellectual" (202), "Ethics," "Equality" (293), "Legislative," and "Sketches" (226).

- For more examples of writers breaking silences, reframing the past, or using counter-memory as a political tactic, see Bernice McNair Barnett; Jennifer Anne Boittin; Rudolph P. Byrd and Beverly Guy-Sheftall; Stephanie M. H. Camp; Hazel Carby; Cheryl Clarke; Julie Dash; Anne duCille; Paula Giddings; Frances Smith Foster; Beverly Guy-Sheftall, *Daughters* and *Words*; Evelyn Hammonds; Trudier Harris; Darlene Clark Hine, *When*; Calvin Hernton; Karen Johnson; Jacqueline Jones; Terri Kapsalis; Shirley Logan; Jennifer Morgan; Pat Robinson et al., "Historical"; Loretta J. Ross; T. Denean

Sharpley-Whiting; Kimberly Springer; Judith L. Stephens; Claudia Tate; Gayle T. Tate; Rosalyn Terborg-Penn; Ula Taylor; Freida Tesfagiorgis; Alice Walker; and Margaret Walker.

9. *Stipulating as the precondition to systemic change the rejection of internalized oppression* alongside the development of a transformed self and critical consciousness.

- Cooper emphasizes this concept most overtly in her activism and in her educational leadership. In *Voice* see "'Woman vs. The Indian'" (102), "Status" (131), "Race Problem" (172), "Negro/Literature" (175–6, 223–6), and "Worth" (231). See also "Humor" (234–5), "Equality" (297), and her letters to Walter White in the NAACP Papers.

- For other theorists' insistence on self-transformation and self-definition, see Karen Baker-Fletcher; Toni Cade Bambara, "Roles;" Devon Carbado; Johnetta Betsch Cole and Beverly Guy-Sheftall; Carole Boyce Davies; Angela Y. Davis, "Conversation;" Philomena Essed; V. P. Franklin; bell hooks, *Teaching* and *Yearning*; June Jordan; Robin D. G. Kelley; Gloria Ladson-Billings; Audre Lorde, *Sister*; Gwendolyn D. Pough; and Ula Taylor.

10. *Arguing for the inherent philosophical relevance of and political need for theorizing from lived experience.*

- Cooper weaves this concept throughout *Voice*. See, for example, "Raison d'être" (ii–iii), "Womanhood" (30–1), "Higher" (73, 76–7), "'Woman vs. The Indian'" (89–90, 93–4, 96, 99, 134–9, 144–5), "Race Problem" (164, 167), "Negro/Literature" (176–7, 183, 185, 195, 201), "Worth" (234–8), and "Gain" (298). See also Cooper's two educational essays in which she builds upon her experiences as a teacher, "Sketches" and "Humor," as well as her doctoral exam, "Equality" (293–4).

- For other articulations of standpoint theory or advocacy of theorizing from experience, see Elizabeth Alexander; Toni Cade Bambara; Frances Beale; Dionne Brand; Katie Cannon; Devon Carbado; Johnetta Betsch Cole and Beverly Guy-Sheftall; Patricia Hill Collins; Angela Y. Davis, "Conversation;" Kathy L. Glass; Lorraine Hansberry, *To Be Young*; Calvin Hernton; bell hooks; Stanlie James and Abena Busia; June Jordan; Robin D. G. Kelley; Audre Lorde, *Sister*; Paule Marshall, "From;" Irma McClaurin; Leith Mullings; Gwendolyn D. Pough; Tracey Reynolds; Barbara Smith; and Patricia J. Williams.

11. *Conceptualizing the self as inherently connected to others, and therefore arguing for an ethic of reciprocity and collective accountability.*

  • In *Voice,* see "Womanhood" (23, 27, 29–30, 32), "'Woman vs. The Indian'" (86, 92, 100, 102, 122), "Race Problem" (165–8), "Worth" (282–5), and "Gain" (298–9, 303). See also "Equality" (298) and "On Education" (249–50).

  • For other theories of collective selfhood and intersubjective eth-ics, see African American Women in Defense of Ourselves; Karen Baker-Fletcher; Bernice McNair Barnett; Stephanie M. H. Camp; Katie Cannon; Patricia Hill Collins; the Combahee Collective; Kathy L. Glass; Frances Harper in Shirley Logan, *We*; Karla F. C. Holloway; Joyce Ladner; Robin D. G. Kelley; Bernice Johnson Reagon; Tracey Reynolds; Kimberly Springer; Julia Sudbury; Gayle Tate; Ula Taylor, "'Negro;'" and Aaronette White, "I Am."

Although I have summarized these premises in a linear fashion, the list, while fairly succinct and, I hope, useful as a resource, also has its limits. First, in offering a general summary, lists highlight the big picture over the specifics. Paradoxically, however, this emphasis can obfuscate even as it clarifies because details, nuances, and differences tend to be suppressed in favor of a broad overview. In other words, using a list risks oversimplify-ing a complex field of inquiry (i.e., Black feminist theorizing) or artificially reducing an individual's intellectual contributions (i.e., Cooper's). Second, and just as significant, is the fact that the linearity and the separation of the eleven points above artificially contain the give-and-take at work among these ideas, potentially obscuring sites of overlap and interconnection. For example, it is essential to note that the last concepts listed (the individual as inherently part of a self-other dynamic and an ethic of connectedness and accountability to others) lead back to the first premise identified (a "both/and" worldview and method of analysis that inherently refuses false divides between identities, ways of knowing and being, and politics). What this conceptual motif of the return reveals is a moving circuit of ideas, a recursive and nonlinear revolution: it does not signify circular logic or a closed theoretical system.

In other words, it is not just African American feminist theorists' anal-yses of identities, systems, knowledges, politics, and communities that are multidimensional and that delineate how various forms of power are interlocking; it is also the case that the various theoretical precepts, ana-lytic methods, political techniques, and genres are themselves interlaced and matric. I have sought to illustrate this fundamental recursiveness and intrinsic affinity between form and content, idea and action, self and other in Cooper's work. The diverse forms and manifold voices that emerge out of Cooper's theorizing correspond to the multidimensionality of her content and are informed by and relate to the range of her life's work as an intellectual and as a community activist. It is my sincerest hope that *Anna Julia Cooper, Visionary Black Feminist: A Critical Introduction* has brought to life Cooper's ideas and analyses in a way that honors her complexity of thought, highlights her continued relevance, and inspires other scholars and activists to rediscover Cooper's life work with renewed interest, or to encounter its many pleasures for the first time.

Notes

Foreword

1. See Elizabeth Alexander, "'We Must Be About Our Father's Business': Anna Julia Cooper and the In Corporation of the Nineteenth Century African American Woman Intellectual," *Signs* 20.2 (1995): 336–56; David W. H. Pellow, "Anna J. Cooper: The International Dimensions," in *Recovered Writers/Recovered Texts: Race, Class, and Gender in Black Women's Literature*, ed. Dolan Hubbard (Knoxville: University of Tennessee Press, 1997); Kathy L. Glass, "Tending to the Roots: Anna Julia Cooper's Sociopolitical Thought and Activism," *Meridians* 6.1 (2004): 23–55.
2. See Karen Baker-Fletcher, *'A Singing Something': Womanist Reflections on Anna Julia Cooper*. New York: Crossroads, 1994.

Introduction

1. Hundley 15.
2. For a succinct overview of Cooper's writings, organizational memberships, and employment history, see Cooper's Curriculum Vitae at the end of the Introduction.
3. Correspondence between Cooper and Sylvester Williams shows that the Executive Committee anticipated that the next meeting would be in Boston in 1902, followed by a third in Haiti, but they did not materialize (Hutchinson 111). The second was in Paris in February 1919, the third in London and Brussels in late August–early September 1921, and the fourth in London and Lisbon in November 1923. Note that when Black women became a larger force in organizing, the conference (the fifth in 1927 in New York) was held before the school year and more women participated (though sadly, many scholars dismiss the fifth as less significant than the four earlier ones).
4. "Toussaint Louverture savait voir et prévoir" (Cooper, *L'Attitude* 111).
5. I complied Cooper's CV from a wide range of sources: it is as complete as possible given the materials available.

Chapter 1: "A little more than ordinary interest in the underprivileged"

1. Cooper, 1934 letter to Dr. Mordecai Johnson, president of Howard University, in the NAACP Papers, Part 3: The campaign for educational equity. Series A. Legal Department and Central Office records (1913–1940): reel 21, "I-C-291" (hereafter referred to as the NAACP Papers).

2. The precise date of Cooper's birth is not known: it is variously reported as 1858, 1859, or 1860. Hutchinson deduced that 1858 was the most accurate, and I follow her lead here. However, Eva Semien Baham, Associate Professor of History at Southern University, who is working on a new biography of Cooper, has uncovered evidence suggesting that Cooper's year of birth may in fact be 1860.

3. Description of Cooper in a June 30, 1975 letter to Leona C. Gabel by the daughter of Lula Love (Lawson), one of Cooper's foster children (in Gabel 67).

4. This would be the younger Dr. Fabius J. Haywood, not his father. Mary Helen Washington identifies Fabius's brother, George Washington Haywood, as Cooper's father (xxxi). Since Cooper wrote that she "presumed" her father was her mother's master (Fabius), based on her mother's refusal to discuss the matter, her paternal lineage can only be surmised. Cooper also stated that her mother had spent her whole life in Raleigh; George Washington Haywood was state attorney for Wake County, North Carolina, and a plantation owner in Greene County, Alabama, and most of his time was thus spent outside Raleigh. Note that at the time Cooper was born, her mother had been hired out by the Haywoods to be a nurse to the family of Charles Busbee in Raleigh; "Annie" Cooper was named for Busbee's mother, Annie Busbee (Hutchinson 9).

5. Cooper wrote a short story of this struggle, "The Tie That Used to Bind" (Hutchinson 136).

6. By 1860, save for one, none of the 271 enslaved people on the Haywood holdings in the city of Raleigh had been manumitted by the family; thus, not until the Emancipation Proclamation of 1863 were Hannah Stanley Haywood and her children freed (Hutchinson 14).

7. These sacrifices within everyday life can be read as acts of a tacit feminism on Hannah Stanley's part. For a discussion of identifying, retroactively, instances of feminist, antiracist parenting and its political implications, see Cole and Guy-Sheftall, "The Personal Is Political," in *Gender Talk*, 1–30.

8. i.e., an unclassifiable or unknown third factor that fits neither side of a binary pair.

9. Today, Dillon's grandson Emile Dillon II is an artist who lives in New York.

10. For an image of the window, see Hutchinson (180) or St. Augustine's Web site, <http://www.st-aug.edu/chapel.htm>.

11. After researching Oberlin College's "Addendum to the 'Catalogue and Record of Colored Students,' 1862–99," it seems likely that the couple were Sallie (Sally) Constance Jordan, of Kansas City, Missouri, and John Lorenzo Love, of Asheville, North Carolina, both of whom attended Oberlin. See <http://www.oberlin.edu/archive/holdings/finding/RG5/SG4/S3/addendum.html>

12. See, for example, Cooper's 1926 lengthy letter of protest in Lemert and Bhan 332–35.
13 For Cooper's letter of application to Oberlin, see Hutchinson 32–34.
14. Oberlin's radical tradition does not mean that, over time, there was no backlash over race or gender politics. For example, in the 1920s Cooper would attempt to secure help distributing her French publications in the United States from a much-changed Oberlin — an institution that, as she would discover, sought to distance itself from its inclusive legacy rather than to embrace it (see Shilton). Moreover, several years before Cooper attended Oberlin, in 1859, the Chippewa-African American sculptor Edmonia Lewis had been enrolled. However, she was charged with witchcraft and poisoning two white students, beaten by a white mob, and taken to trial for her ostensible crimes; John Mercer Langston, the renowned African American lawyer and politician, successfully defended Lewis in court. She moved to Boston, then to Rome, where she lived in exile until her death. Given Cooper's reference to Lewis as her "friend" (*Voice* 113), Cooper may well have visited her while in Italy in 1900 after the Pan-African Congress in London.
15. Cooper did, however, belong to Oberlin's Ladies' Literary Society — a club that, despite its prim-sounding name, provided space for political discussion and social analysis.
16. Two of Bishop Delaney's daughters, Sadie and Elizabeth Delaney, would later publish *Having Our Say: The Delaney Sisters' First One Hundred Years* (1993).
17. The others were Hallie Quinn Brown, Frances Ellen Watkins Harper, Fannie Barrier Williams, Fanny Jackson Coppin, and Sarah J. Early. For all six speeches, see Sewall. Note that Ida B. Wells did not speak; instead, she protested the nation's racist and sexist politics, including lynching, and documented African Americans' progress since emancipation by handing out a booklet at the fair, *The Reason Why the Colored American Is Not in the World's Columbian Exposition.* The booklet contains five essays, including one by Frederick Douglass. See Wells.
18. Correspondence between Cooper and Anna M. Jackson and her daughter, Anna M. Theiss, Quaker activists involved in suffrage, prison reform, peace activism, and interracial alliances, can be found at Swarthmore College in the Branson-Jackson Family Papers.
19. Although both Gabel and Hutchinson suggest that Cooper was the only female member of the ANA, the current consensus is that the ANA was indeed exclusively male in membership. See, for instance, Alfred A. Moss, Jr.'s *The American Negro Academy: Voice of the Talented Tenth* (Baton Rouge: Louisiana State University Press, 1981).
20. For more information about Nannie Helen Burroughs's school and educational model, see K. Johnson and Gyant.
21. Harley, "For the Good" 346; Hutchinson 75; K. Johnson 80–84; Washington xxxvii.
22. It is not out of the question that Cooper and Love, who was an adult by this time, may have been fond of each other, or that Love may have once proposed to Cooper only to have her abruptly reject this idea (see Lemert, "Colored" 13, footnote 21). However, it is essentially futile to speculate as to whether the allegations were false and in some ways serves to distract us from what is most important: to recognize that the accusation, presented with no evidence, was a low and calculated attempt to get Cooper, ever reso-

lute, to back down, which she did not. Nor did she ever stoop to answer these unseemly charges against her person.

23. Actually, the April 4, 1952 Washington *Post* article (page C9) about a reunion of the three Oberlin graduates at Cooper's house suggests a rather jovial relationship between the women, despite the economic and age disparities among them — which Cooper was careful to point out to the reporter, remarking, for example, that she had remained poor, unlike her two colleagues. See "Reunited Trio."

24. For more information about the racial politics of the national YWCA movement and the ways African American women sought to organize Ys independent from the purview of white women, see Weisenfeld.

25. For a photograph of two of the Scottsboro mothers and Ruby Bates (the white woman who would retract her false accusation of rape and give new testimony before the Supreme Court) gathered together at the Wheatley YWCA, see the Scurlock Studio photograph in the online Smithsonian archive: <http://sirismm.si.edu/archivcenter/scurlock/618ps0227902-01pw.jpg >

26. For more information about Merritt, see E. Taylor and also Woodson, "Profile." For a photograph of Merritt, see Hutchinson 125.

27. As was her dear friend and Dunbar High colleague, Georgiana Simpson, who had earned her Ph.D. in German from the University of Chicago in 1921 at the age of fifty-five. The year 2008 marks the 100th year anniversary of AKA.

28. Bouglé believed in a supremacist approach to culture and race that Cooper obviously opposed and which she fought in her doctoral defense and in her dissertation.

29. In 1988 Frances Richardson Keller translated Cooper's thesis as *Slavery and the French Revolutionists (1788–1805)*. Keller recently published a second edition of her translation with the new title *Slavery and the French and Haitian Revolutionists*.

30. In 1924 Cooper's colleague and friend Georgiana Simpson edited and annotated Thomas Gragnon-Lacoste's biography of Toussaint L'Ouverture, entitled *Toussaint Louverture (surnommé le premier des noirs)*, for teaching French language and history at Dunbar. Like Cooper, Simpson was interested in culturally relevant teaching materials; we can speculate that the two must have enjoyed researching Haiti and the Revolution during the same time period. To read a review of Simpson's book, see the *Journal of Negro History* 10.3 (1925): 574.

31. Hurston completed her play in 1925 but could not get it published. Johnson wrote several lynching dramas, none of which were published in her lifetime. Cooper would not be the only African American woman unable to publish her work in the 1920s and 1930s, in other words.

32. By 1934, out of "the 117 Black colleges in the U.S. which attempted to gain" accreditation, "only twenty percent ... were accredited" (Chateauvert 268).

33. Burleigh, who had studied under Antonin Dvořák at the New York Conservatory of Music, was a composer and well-known arranger of African American spiritual and folk music; for instance, he arranged "Deep River," "Go Down, Moses," "Were You There?" and countless others he had learned from his grandfather, a former slave. The NAACP awarded Burleigh the

Spingarn Medal in recognition of his efforts to preserve African American culture and to counteract the minstrelsy tradition that made a mockery of spiritual music. Burleigh was a sought-after artist: he sang as a baritone soloist for St. George's Episcopal Church in New York City from 1894 to 1946, and there performed Cooper's "Paean" in 1942 in his annual concert of spirituals. He was also a soloist at Temple Emanuel in New York for 25 years.

34. To view an image of this painting, see the video about Amos, *Action Lines*, produced by Linda Freeman, written by David Irving, and hosted by Anna Deveare Smith (Chappaqua, NY: L & S Videos, 1996).

35. A first edition of *A Voice from the South* sold for $3,800 on February 28, 2006 at Swann Galleries (sale 2068, lot 184). Once notified of the errors, the auction house assured me that they would make corrections on the day of the auction (personal correspondence). Note that this instance of inaccuracy is just one example among many. Cooper's obituary in 1964 in the Washington *Post* incorrectly stated that her father was a slave and that she earned her M.A from Oberlin in 1884, for example. For a facsimile of the obituary, see Hutchinson 187.

Chapter 2: "Life must be something more than dilettante speculation"

1. Cooper, *Voice* 298.

2. I use the term "praxis" here and elsewhere to emphasize the reflective linking of theory and practice, a dialectic of critical thinking and social action.

3. See Cooper's correspondence with Walter White, chair of the NAACP, and Mordecai Johnson, president of Howard University, in the NAACP papers.

4. True Womanhood ideology grew out of both a "cult of domesticity" and separate spheres gender ideology in the nineteenth century: an ideal or "true" woman supposedly lived her life according to the tenets of purity, piety, submissiveness, and domesticity. Though ostensibly universal, this ideology was clearly based on idealized white, middle-class gender norms, family structures, and work roles. See Welter, *Dimity* and "Cult."

5. As Washington points out (xli), Du Bois wrote this famous book partly in response to Cooper's urging him to counter Claude G. Bowers's racist 1929 tract on Reconstruction, *The Tragic Era: The Revolution after Lincoln*. For Cooper's letter to Du Bois, see Lemert and Bhan 336.

6. The issue of Cooper's methodological innovations is explored in more detail in chapter 3.

7. See Integrated Public Use Microdata Series Census samples for 1900 for an overview of educational data: <http://www.ipums.umn.edu/usa/person. html#peducation>

8. Standpoint theorists, whether materialist, feminist, and/or Afrocentric, argue that the "outsider-within" viewpoint, an achieved (not given or innate) critical consciousness, offers a more dimensional understanding of the world and a different approach to the contexts of inquiry, false universals, and epistemic erasures (e.g., Bar On; Collins, *Black Feminist* 21–40 and 206–20; Harding "Rethinking"; Hartsock; Mills, "Alternative"; Reynolds; D. Smith; Whitten).

9. An androcentric interpretation of Cooper as mimic of Du Bois is particularly ironic in that she anticipated by a decade many of Du Bois's key ideas; see West and J. James, *Transcending*.

10. In contrast, Cooper's Oberlin classmate, fellow Washingtonian, and NACW president Mary Church Terrell, operating rhetorically from a charity model of activism, often disparaged poor Black women and distanced herself from them (Baker-Fletcher 172–75, Jones 144, Nash 129–32). Although both Terrell and Cooper were clubwomen and Oberlin graduates and had some of the same colleagues in Washington, there are important differences. Unlike Terrell, Cooper was not born free to middle-class parents. Cooper worked her way through her education, relying on scholarships and jobs, while Terrell's father paid her full tuition and board. Upon marriage, her husband, Judge Robert H. Terrell, supported her. They moved in the most elite social circles, far apart from the lives of most Black women and men in Washington. In contrast, Cooper's brief marriage ended when she was young; she did not share in the economic, social, or emotional benefits of the marriage contract. Nevertheless, she raised five adopted and two foster children, worked full-time, volunteered in her community, and pursued a doctorate simultaneously.

11. Bailey 59, 64; Harley, "Beyond" 260 and "For the Good" 247, 349; J. James, *Transcending* 45; K. Johnson 137; McCaskill 82; Terborg-Penn, "Discrimination" 21; Washington xlvi; West 83–85, 93; D. Williams 122–30.

12. For analysis of how discourses of race and disability overlap in education debates over desegregation and inclusion, see Ferri and Connor. For current data about educational segregation and inequality in terms of race and disability, see the Harvard Civil Rights Project: <http://www.civilrightsproject.harvard.edu>.

13. As Giddings points out, "Black women saw no contradiction between domesticity and political action" (*When* 52). Cooper's rhetorical claiming of domesticity is not equivalent to her accepting a limited gender role or narrow political agenda.

14. See R. Logan.

15. Her dissertation is discussed in detail in chapter 4.

16. Giddings, *When* 116; Guy-Sheftall, *Daughters* 161–2; Spillers, "Crisis" 90–92; Washington xxxiii-xxxv and xxxix-xlii; West 99.

17. Here Cooper anticipates hooks's analysis of the politics of Black women's speech. There hooks describes how she was "never taught absolute silence ... but to talk a talk that was in itself a silence." She therefore calls for Black women to "change the nature and direction of our speech, to make a speech that compels listeners, one that is heard" (*Talking* 7, 6).

Chapter 3: "If you object to imaginary lines — don't draw them!"

1. Cooper, *Voice* 300.

2. For a later example of this impossible rhetorical position, see her 1926 letter to Dr. Wilkinson (Lemert and Bhan 332–5) protesting her supposed failure to pass school district exams that would allow her a promotion in grade and a raise in salary. Her closing paragraph praising his fairness as a way to introduce her view illustrates the vicious circles of logic Cooper was forced to negotiate.

3. Like Cooper, contemporary Black feminists also document legacies of resistance by other Black women. See Guy-Sheftall "Evolution" and Combahee, for example.

4. Indeed, Cooper and others in her generation, including Pauline Elizabeth Hopkins, Ida B. Wells, Frances Ellen Watkins Harper, and Gertrude Bustill Mossell, were not "isolated figures of intellectual genius" (Carby, *Reconstructing* 115). See Carby, *Reconstructing*, Foster, and Guy-Sheftall, *Words* for more details about these and other political, literary, and philosophical allies.

5. Cooper's 1926 letter to George M. Jones, secretary of Oberlin (in Shilton), discussing her astute and, unfortunately, correct fear that racism would negatively affect perception of her *Le Pèlerinage de Charlemagne*.

6. It is unknown what became of this account (Lemert and Bhan 308). Fortunately, Lemert and Bhan fulfilled Cooper's wishes.

7. In 1951 Cooper self-published *The Life and Writings of the Grimké Family* and *Personal Recollections of the Grimké Family*, a two-volume set. For a brief excerpt from *Personal Recollections*, see Lemert and Bhan 310–17.

8. For instance, a 1925 letter of inquiry from faculty at Middlebury College to Oberlin College exclaims that Cooper's book was already "receiving much praise from Frenchmen" (Shilton).

9. For the 1933 letter to Cooper from Thomas R. Palfrey and William C. Holbrook of Northwestern University requesting permission to reprint, see Lemert and Bhan 337 and Shilton.

10. For example, a 1926 letter from T. A. Jenkins, president of the Modern Language Association and professor at the University of Chicago, disparages this translation by a "distinguished colored [Oberlin] graduate" as "pretty bad," although he bought a copy of the text for his own private library, suggesting that it had merit (Shilton).

11. Cooper 1926 letter to Wilkinson, in Lemert and Bhan 333.

12. This is a recurrent theme in the history of Black feminist thought. For example, in an 1833 speech Maria Stewart asserted, "God makes use of feeble means sometimes to bring about his most exalted purposes" ("What If").

13. Here, I build on Gayle Tate's analysis of how free and enslaved Black women appropriated "tools of oppression" into "instruments of resistance" (4). Specifically, she identifies slave women's dialectical claiming of "their labor power, despite its exploitation by slaveholders, as instruments in the protracted struggle of liberation" (11).

14. e.g., the conflicting debates, discussed in chapter 2, about Cooper — was she a eugenicist or existentialist, critic or advocate of "True Womanhood," an elitist or a radical thinker, and so on.

15. Cooper takes on Ingersoll's agnosticism, but he was also a lawyer for railroad magnates, for whom he negotiated predatory land contracts. He also opposed Black suffrage, proposing instead "relocation" for Black Americans. Cooper sees agnosticism, combined with objectivist positivism, as dangerous because together they lay the foundation for what she describes as heartless rule and ruthless greed. See "The Gain from a Belief" in *Voice* 286–304.

16. This generally known yet denied "discrepancy" is often characterized as a tragic error of an otherwise honorable system, rather than as part of the system's foundational logic. See Spelman, *Fruits*.

17. Note that Cooper refuses to characterize the Southern woman as a "lady" here, as she would in turn deny Cooper, a Black woman, this designation.

18. The prominent and powerful Harvard polygeneticist Agassiz was hired by the Lincoln administration as an advisor about "managing" the free Black population. Based on his supposedly scientific studies of racial differences, he warned that African Americans were inherently "incapable of living on a footing of social equality" and advised against "endangering" the progress and ascendancy of whites (Adelman, Episode 1 *Race*).

19. Cooper, *Voice* 176.

20. For a brief overview of this concept, see Collins, *Black Feminist* 225–6.

21. Two influential Black feminist essays on coalition politics are "Combahee" and Reagon.

22. To protect the rights of freed men and women, the 14th Amendment changed the definition of citizenship to include African Americans. It played a significant role in *Brown v. Board of Education* and in other civil rights legislation.

23. Technically, the 15th Amendment gives all men the right to vote (many white feminists fought it): "The right of citizens ... to vote shall not be denied or abridged by the United States or by any state on account of race, color, or previous condition of servitude." However, states still had the right to decide voter "qualifications," hence poll taxes, intimidation, and tests to restrict voting.

24. This is not to say that knowing from experience has no universal value, meaning, or relevance. It is to emphasize the philosophical and political salience of social identity and lived situation.

25. In *An Imperative Duty* (1891), the only one of his thirty-eight novels to focus on race relations, Howells writes about a white woman who discovers her Black lineage, but his descriptions of Black womanhood are filled with references to subhuman, ugly, animal natures. Many would have been familiar with this novel, as he was already a man of influence in American letters.

26. Note that Bouglé presumed a biased reading of the Haitian Revolution on Cooper's part, since she was Black, and also told her that her original dissertation topic was "too broad." In her oral defense, Cooper gives it back full force to Bouglé: she calls her *soutenance* topics "too broad" in scope and warns him of his own "preconceptions."

27. Cooper also shows how one's underlying assumptions affect perception of the "facts" of history. These issues are discussed in more detail in Chapter 4.

28. Nearly twenty years later, in "Hitler and the Negro," Cooper builds on her critique of supremacy to show how it rationalizes violent extermination of difference: "Elimination of the unfit ... [and] ultimate annihilation or enslavement, not of Jews alone, but of Frenchmen, Italians, all Mediterranean races and nations and finally the now courted and applauded Japanese. ... Such is Hitler's ideal ... and deliberate aim. ... No need of a prophet to tell what would befall the darker races of this hemisphere should Hitler triumph" ("Hitler" 264).

29. i.e., the rise of Lenin and the Bolshevik revolution.

30. i.e., the Nationalist movement under Sun Yat-sen's three principles of revolution (nationalism, democracy, and livelihood).

31. i.e., emergence of constitutional rule (1908) and establishment of the Turkish Republic (1923).

32. i.e., Egypt's anticolonial "first revolution" of 1919 against the British and the 1922 Egyptian liberation from the British Protectorate.
33. Here, Cooper is quoting from Lincoln's 1863 Gettysburg Address, although introducing quite a different historical narrative by juxtaposing her voice with his.
34. Code, "Rational" 278.
35. Cooper's interdisciplinary analysis of domination is discussed in more detail in Chapter 5.
36. In this chapter, for example, this is evident in the ways Cooper's ideas dovetail with analyses by Alcoff, Anzaldúa, Carby, Christian, Collins, Davies, Davis, Foster, Giddings, Guy-Sheftall, T. Harris, hooks, Lugones, Marshall, Mohanty, Morrison, Narayan, Peterson, Reagon, Samantrai, Schutte, V. Smith, Springer, Trinh, Wall, and P. Williams.

Chapter 4: " Failing at the most essential provision of the revolutionary ideal"

1. Cooper, *L'Attitude* 77, "faillir à la plus grande des tâches imposées par l'idéal révolutionnaire."
2. Note that unlike C. L. R. James (*The Black Jacobins*) or W. E. B. Du Bois (*Haiti: A Drama of the Black Napoleon*), Cooper's title does not frame the actions in Saint-Domingue as Black versions of "French" politics. In Cooper's dissertation title, as throughout her study, "the Revolution" is not explicitly limited to mean only the "French" Revolution: she leaves the referent open-ended. This sly technique would allow readers at the Sorbonne to *presume* she meant the French Revolution while, simultaneously, she creates space to argue for the viability of seeing the Haitian Revolution as much a part of the Age of Revolution as the political upheavals in the United States or in France.
3. In 1988 Keller published a translation of Cooper's thesis, entitled *Slavery and the French Revolutionists (1788–1805)*. She recently published a second edition, entitled *Slavery and the French and Haitian Revolutionists*. When citing Cooper's thesis in French, I refer to it as "Cooper, *L'Attitude*"; when citing Keller's translation (new edition), I refer to it as "Cooper, *Slavery*." When citing Cooper in English, the references to *Slavery* are Keller's translations, whereas the references to *L'Attitude* are my own translations.
4. Sharpley-Whiting has translated both essays into English ("Black Internationalism" and "Exotic Puppets"): see her *Negritude Women*, 105–13.
5. The NAACP and other anti-imperial groups opposed the occupation and objected to the use of the Monroe Doctrine to intervene in a sovereign nation. The occupation was fueled by the U.S. desire to control Haiti's customs house and banks and to alter the law so whites and foreigners could own property there, which was outlawed in Haiti's 1804 constitution. See James Weldon Johnson's "Self-Determining Haiti: The American Occupation."
6. For readers unfamiliar with the Haitian Revolution, there are several excellent overviews, including Laurent Dubois's *Avengers of the New World* and *A Colony of Citizens*, Sibylle Fischer's *Modernity Disavowed*, Michel-Rolph Trouillot's *Silencing the Past*, Aimé Césaire's *Toussaint Louverture*, and C. L. R. James's *The Black Jacobins*, among others.

7.   Although the *gens de couleur* were free (i.e., their "natural" rights were recognized), they did not have full rights of citizenship (i.e., "political" rights) despite being property owners. Like all nonwhites, their lives were circumscribed by the *Code Noir* or Black Codes, which regulated clothing, rules of social deference to be shown to whites of all classes (from the *petits blancs* or white workers to the *colons* and *grand blancs* or white colonists/big whites), shopping or market rules, housing segregation, and more (see Cooper, *L'Attitude* 22). For an overview of the Codes and their political, economic, and philosophical roles, see Dayan.

8.   Kaplan notes two citations of Cooper's thesis prior to 1982: Edward Derbyshire Seeber's 1937 *Anti-Slavery Opinion in France during the Second Half of the Eighteenth Century* and Carminella Biondi's 1979 *Ces esclaves sont des hommes: Lotta abolizionista e negrofila nella Francia del Settecento* (ix).

9.   Even after she received the Ph.D., it was not acknowledged in her contract, nor was she ever formally referred to as "Dr." Cooper by district officials.

10. For a facsimile of Cooper's 1924 letter in French naming her original topic, see Hutchinson 139. Her preferred topic was broader in scope: she had wanted to write about "L'Attitude de la France à l'égard de l'égalité des races" ("France's Attitudes toward Racial Equality") from the time of the French Revolution through to the present (i.e., 1925). Her study would have included the debates about slavery and race with regard to Saint-Domingue and the Amis des Noirs, but also two other areas: (1) current (1925) laws about the "droits de cité" in French colonies (examining the question of full citizenship rights and equal standing before the French constitution in all areas, including voting, housing, equal protection, etc.), and (2) current (1925) laws in France with regard to immigrant populations from Japan, Africa, and India.

11. "While the events of France had an effect on Saint-Domingue, those of Saint-Domingue had an effect on French public opinion and the Constituent Assembly."

12. "Qui n'avaient vu là qu'un problème á résoudre par l'humanité et par la théorie, alors qu'il y auraient fallue toute une préparation préalable."

13. The active role one plays in ignorance is emphasized more in the French with the reflexive verb *se refuser*: "se refusaient à faire face aux réalités" (*L'Attitude* 23).

14. *Marronage* refers to the ongoing armed conflict enacted by maroon (runaway slave) communities of Saint-Domingue to protect their freedom and independence. Their highly effective guerilla warfare increased during the eighteenth century as the slave/plantation economy expanded and became more entrenched.

15. Cooper was at *the* "bastion," the Sorbonne. Moreover, Fischer is describing circumstances today; her analysis helps us imagine what Cooper must have been up against in 1925.

16. Cooper, *L'Attitude* 77.

17. Literally, "all the spirits."

18. Theologically, Cooper is not suggesting passivity before a dominant divine being; her premises are in accord with what today would be characterized as a theology of liberation.

19. Fischer argues that this silencing occurred both in France and in the Carib-

bean (in Cuba and Santo Domingo in particular, as well as within Haiti itself). She finds that "The truncation of an emerging transnational and syncretistic modernity we have observed in the nineteenth-century Caribbean around the phenomenon of Haiti thus has an unexpected counterpart in the silences of the historiography of the metropolis" (226). See her *Modernity Disavowed*.

20. Generally preferring nonviolent solutions, Cooper does not tend to glorify violence in any form; she criticizes both whites and blacks for brutality. Although she deplores excessive violence, she frames it as an element of war and revolution — she contextualizes it.

21. For electronic access to many of Bouglé's works, see the University of Quebec at Chicoutimi Web site: <http://www.uqac.uquebec.ca/zone30/Classiques_des_sciences_sociales/>

22. Cooper refers (*L'Attitude* 61, fn. 1) to the successful revolts organized by maroon leader François Makandal ("Macaudal"). The French burned Makandal at the stake in 1758.

23. In addition to the presumption that the *noirs* would be easily defeated by Rochambeau, the irony here is that *gens de couleur* from Saint-Domingue had served in the American Revolution, helping the elder General Rochambeau fight the British in the Battle of Savannah. For more information on the role of *gens de couleur* in the American Revolution, see Dubois, *Avengers* 66.

24. Although Keller uses the term "easier," *douce* also means "sweeter."

25. Keller uses "Santo Domingo" which would more accurately refer to Spain's colony on Hispaniola (now the Dominican Republic), not the French colony of Saint-Domingue (now Haiti).

26. As with her dissertation title, the referent here to "the Revolution" is open-ended.

27. See Paul Robert's *Le Petit Robert 1: Dictionnaire de la langue française*. Rédaction dirigée par A. Rey et J. Rey-Debove. Paris: Le Robert, 1990.

28. Keller correctly uses "intend" here for the verb *destiner*, but the English usage does not communicate quite as strongly the overt biological determinism in Legorgne's statement about "Africans'" preordained "fate" as slaves, not equal persons. See Cooper, *L'Attitude* 91, fn. 3.

29. Raimond, a free man of color, was an outspoken planter on Saint-Domingue. He was part of a coalition of *gens de couleur* who addressed the French Assembly and sought the rights of citizenship for propertied men of color. He worked closely with the Friends of the Blacks and published many political pamphlets. Although abolition was not on his agenda at first, over time he came to advocate gradualist abolition. Raimond later returned to Saint-Domingue and allied with Toussaint L'Ouverture. Nevertheless, Cooper condemns his early shortsightedness.

30. Like Cooper, Mercer Cook (a graduate of Dunbar High who, in 1926, also earned a doctorate at the Sorbonne) argues that the "Wealthy Raimond was no radical demanding the abolition of slavery. As he himself stated: 'One could scarcely suppose that I should wish to ruin with one blow my entire family which possesses seven or eight millions [of francs] in property at Saint-Domingue'" ("Literary" 522). See Cook's "The Literary Contribution of the French West Indian" (1940) and his "Julien Raimond" (1941) — both in *The Journal of Negro History* — for more details.

31. "Equality of Races," one of Cooper's oral *soutenance* essays, 291.
32. *An Inquiry into the Causes of the Insurrection of the Negroes in the Island of St. Domingo to which are added Observations by M. Garran-Coulon on the Same Subject, Read in His Absence by M. Guadet, before the National Assembly, 29 February 1792.* London, 1792.
33. T. Lothrop Stoddard, *The French Revolution in San Domingo.* Boston: Houghton Mifflin, 1914. In 1920, Stoddard, a eugenicist, would publish another virulently racist book, *The Rising Tide of Color against White World-Supremacy.*
34. Although Keller uses "tend to prove that" for "tendent à prouver que," given the context of Cooper's overall argument, I would translate this phrase as "are predisposed toward proving that." See Cooper, *L'Attitude* 146.
35. L'Abbé Henri Grégoire was an influential Roman Catholic priest who was a member of the Friends of the Blacks. He advocated for limited rights for the *gens de couleur.*
36. Jacques Pierre Brissot de Warville helped to found the Friends of the Blacks.
37. Pétion de Villeneuve was also a member of the Friends of the Blacks.
38. Although Keller uses the word "occupation," which conveys invasion of a country by enemy forces, the word "conquest" would more accurately reflect Cooper's emphasis on ridding of all vestiges of European colonization and violent takeover: "afin que plus rien ne restât des souvenirs de la conquête européenne" (*L'Attitude* 124).
39. Cooper, "Souvenir" 339.

Chapter 5: Mapping Sites of Power

1. *Voice* 118.
2. *Voice* iii.
3. See chapter 4.
4. The massacre Cooper refers to occurred in the fall of 1898 in Wilmington, North Carolina. In backlash against Reconstruction, members of white supremacy organizations and of the Democratic Party allied forces to wage an ideological war, with racist cartoons and editorials in newspapers, against the "threat" of Black citizens before the November election to ensure the election of white supremacists. Following the election, on November 9, whites gathered at the city's courthouse to proclaim the "White Man's Declaration of Independence," decreeing that Black people's holding any political office was "unnatural" and contrary to the "original intent" of the Constitution (reminding us today how wary we must remain of "original intent" legal arguments). The next day, on November 10, whites took up arms and started mass violence, killing between 120 and 150 people, most of them Black. Then members of the Black middle class (ministers, lawyers, teachers, barbers, merchants) and their white sympathizers were rounded up by the police and banished from Wilmington, their properties seized and "given" to white supremacists. Charles Chestnutt's 1901 novel *The Marrow of Tradition* <http://www.gutenberg.org/etext/11228> deals with the massacre, as does Philip Gerard's 1994 novel *Cape Fear Rising.* Nonfiction sources include *Gender and Jim Crow* by Glenda Gilmore and *Democracy Betrayed: The Wilmington Race Riot of 1898 and Its Legacy,* edited by David S. Cecelski and Timothy B. Tyson.

5. Excerpted from Cooper's answer to Question 38 in Charles S. Johnson's "Negro College Graduates' Questionnaire," Moorland-Spingarn Research Center, Howard University. Today, with the rise of school testing at every level of education, we should heed Cooper's skepticism about the "Machine Method" of intelligence testing in the 1920s and 1930s (e.g., the Binet and the Stanford-Binet IQ tests).

6. "Angry Saxons and Negro Education" 259.

7. For some discussions in feminist epistemology about the implications of fact/value distinctions, see Code, "Rational" 261–3 and *Rhetorical* 24–9, 38–44; Collins, *Fighting* 106–7; Gannett 324–32; Grosz 189–92; and Harding, "Rethinking" 50, 69–70.

8. Hoffman was chief statistician for Prudential Life Insurance and published an influential study, *Race Traits and Tendencies of the American Negro*, in 1896, the same year the Supreme Court legalized Jim Crow. Kelly Miller, a well-known Howard University professor, *Crisis* columnist, and NAACP lawyer, wrote a critical review of Hoffman's work — the first paper published by the American Negro Academy (Hutchinson 110). However, Miller resorted to blaming Black women for the woes of the Black community. In "Colored Women as Wage Earners," Cooper takes on Miller's misogynist solution for "the race," suggesting that his proposal to eliminate or "kill off" Black women from the workforce and to reinstitute a middle-class, white-modeled separate-spheres ideology is a foolhardy and retrograde solution. For more about Hoffman, see Adelman's *Race: The Power of an Illusion*, Episode 1, "The Difference Between Us." See Episode 2, "The Story We Tell," for analysis of Thomas Jefferson's role in theories of race in the United States and for a discussion of the racist ideas of the prominent nineteenth-century scientists Samuel Morton and Louis Agassiz.

9. "Cur" is a derogatory term for a mutt or inferior mixed-breed dog, here treated with cruelty and whipped. Through metaphor, Cooper emphasizes the somatic feeling of constant subjugation and the risk of internalized oppression.

10. Here Cooper invokes Robert Burns's 1795 defiant song of Scottish liberty that affirms egalitarian ideals and speaks out against the ruling classes, "A Man's a Man for A' That."

11. Although Cooper critiques Orientalism and ethnocentrism elsewhere (e.g., *Voice* 52), here her examples lack nuance, reinforce Orientalist stereotypes, and play into Western ideologies of rescue and protection. For some current discussions of feminism and Islam, see Ahmed, Ali, Barazangi, and Bodman and Tohidi. For some analyses of foot binding and of Western feminism's ongoing fascination with it, see Ebrey, Ko, Teng, and Yu.

12. Although Lemert and Bhan suggest that the "Dr. Mayo" here is the medical doctor of Mayo clinic fame, I find it more likely, given the references to Black female teachers in Mayo's larger paragraph included in *A Voice*, that Cooper is citing the influential U.S. Commissioner of Education Amory Dwight Mayo, who was also a reverend. His lengthy 1892 study published by the federal government, *Southern Women in the Recent Educational Movement of the South*, was reprinted in 1978 by Louisiana State University Press with an introduction by Dan T. Carter and Amy Friedlander. There Mayo uses the phrase "slough of unchastity" (107), but I have not been able to track down

the source of the full paragraph Cooper cites; it is likely from another of the many pamphlets, books, and speeches Mayo published.

13. Here in Mayo's nineteenth-century federal pamphlet we find an "observation" that anticipates the "specious ideology" of Moynihan's "matriarchy thesis" and cruel theory of a "'tangle of pathology'" in the federal Moynihan Report of 1965. See Angela Davis, "Reflections."

14. Wells successfully filed a lawsuit against the Chesapeake & Ohio Railroad and was awarded damages in the amount of $500. However, the Tennessee State Supreme Court overturned the ruling in 1887.

15. Livermore, well known in her time, was an abolitionist, journalist, and leader in both the women's suffrage movement and the temperance movement. In this public censure of a prominent white feminist, Cooper underscores that she wants no part in an exclusionary feminism invested in perpetuating dominance: she seeks a radical transformation of the social and political order for all.

16. For some contemporary debates about sexism in Black popular culture, see Cole and Guy-Sheftall, "No Respect: Gender Politics and Hip-Hop" in *Gender Talk*; Collins, "Get Your Freak On: Sex, Babies, and Images of Black Femininity" in *Black Sexual Politics*; Crenshaw, "Beyond"; and Pough.

17. See Collins, *Black Feminist* 11–13, 201–2, 207–8 for a succinct discussion of the "outsider-within" concept in Black feminist theorizing.

18. Combahee 273–77; Davis, "Reflections"; hooks, *Feminist* 6–14; B. Smith xxxi–xxxiv.

19. *Voice* 51–55, 103–4, 143–44, 195–96; "Equality" 293, 295–6; "Third" 324.

Chapter 6: Tracing Resistant Legacies, Rethinking Intellectual Genealogies

1. When possible, I use the participial phrase to emphasize the action involved in theory-making (rather than the fixed, object-status implied by a noun) and simultaneously to highlight that Black feminist theories are varied and multiple: there is not one monolithic entity known as "Black feminist theory" or "African American Feminist Thought" (Christian, "Race" 336–41; V. Smith, *Not Just* xix). However, the rules and rhythms of syntax being what they are, I occasionally use the nominal phrase "Black feminist theory" in this chapter, but not to imply singularity or a homogenous, universal discourse of African American feminist thought.

2. Gordon, "Human", Hartman, K. Johnson, and Pitts are exceptions, but further inquiry is needed.

3. Cooper's use of the phrase is not determinist or condescending here, unlike W. E. B. Du Bois's use of it in *The Philadelphia Negro* in 1899 to characterize that part of the population he considered below economic viability and involved in criminal activity (which Du Bois blamed in part on Black female-headed households — see Hunter). Du Bois again used the term in *The Souls of Black Folk* in 1903 to discuss the "croppers and a few paupers" within African American class structures. Earlier, in 1891, William Booth, founder of the Salvation Army, used "the submerged tenth" to draw an analogy between the "masses" of urban poor in London — "Darkest England"

— and imperialist images of "savages" populating the jungles of Africa (see Booth). However, in addition to addressing Du Bois and possibly Booth, it is likely that Cooper is critiquing the American Eugenics movement's cooptation of the phrase and their hope to eradicate the "submerged tenth" who were considered "socially unfit" because of their "inferior" genes and "defective" lineages. The Eugenics Records Office, or ERO, was set up in Cold Spring Harbor for such purposes (see Black). In contrast, Cooper saw those who were most marginalized as *structurally* disenfranchised, not *biologically* deficient: as a critical educator, she rejected all forms of determinism, whether social or biological. Her fight to educate as equals (not as "hands" or machines) the "submerged tenth" must be understood as radical and outspoken, for she rejects entirely an "underclass" pathology thesis.

4. As discussed earlier, her comparisons do occasionally leave something to be desired in the ways she at times perpetuates Judeo-Christian, Western notions of progress and freedom. Nevertheless, the impetus toward a comparative rather than universalizing analysis of sexism is important.

5. See also Guy-Sheftall, "Evolution" 2; Hansberry, *To Be Young* 246; James and Sharpley-Whiting 1.

6. See also Gordon, *Existentia* 1.

7. Davis, "Reflections" 202, 204–7; Hine, "Rape" 380–6; Murray 187–8; Sandoval 47–63; V. Smith, *Not Just* xiv; Springer, *Living* 7.

8. Collins, *Black Feminist* 1–10; Combahee 273; Guy-Sheftall, "Evolution"; Lee 97; Sandoval 47–50; Shohat 17; Wallace, *Dark* 95.

9. See in particular her "'Woman vs. The Indian'" in *Voice* and "Intellectual."

10. Collins, *Black Feminist*; Combahee; Crenshaw, "Demarginalizing"; B. Smith.

11. Carby, *Reconstructing*, 16–17; Christian, "Race" 341; James and Sharpley-Whiting 6; Springer, *Living* 171; Tesfagiorgis 240; Weisenfeld 6–7; Wing 27–31.

12. To document where Cooper develops these concepts and to place her in dialogue with a wide range of scholars of African American feminist thought who also take up these ideas, references to Cooper's work are here juxtaposed with references to works by her compatriots, past and present. The goal of this juxtaposition is to make visible a contrapuntal give-and-take among these voices, not to suggest complete agreement in outlook or analysis or a tidy continuum of African American feminist thought and action. Because the field of Black feminist theorizing is large and varied, these lists are not intended to be comprehensive, but are included as a resource or starting point.

References

Adelman, Larry (executive producer). *Race: The Power of an Illusion.* 3 episodes, 56 mins. each. DVD. Episode producers: Christine Herbes-Sommers, Tracy Strain, Llewellyn Smith. Series co-producer: Jean Cheng. California Newsreel, 2003.

Ahmed, Leila. *Women and Gender in Islam: The Historical Roots of a Modern Debate.* New Haven: Yale University Press, 1992.

African American Women in Defense of Ourselves. In *The Black Feminist Reader.* Ed. Joy James and T. Denean Sharpley-Whiting. Malden, MA: Blackwell, 2000. 271-72.

Alarcón, Norma. "The Theoretical Subject(s) of This Bridge Called My Back and Anglo-American Feminism." In *Making Face, Making Soul Haciendo caras: Creative and Critical Perspectives by Feminists of Color.* Ed. Gloria Anzaldúa. San Francisco: Aunt Lute Books, 1990. 356–69.

Alcoff, Linda Martín. "On Judging Epistemic Credibility: Is Social Identity Relevant?" In *Women of Color and Philosophy: A Critical Reader.* Ed. Naomi Zack. Malden, MA: Blackwell, 2000. 235–62.

———. "The Unassimilated Theorist." *PMLA* 121.1 (2006): 255–59.

Alexander, Elizabeth. "'We Must Be about Our Father's Business': Anna Julia Cooper and the In-Corporation of the Nineteenth-Century African-American Woman Intellectual." *Signs* 20.2 (1995): 336–56.

Ali, Shaheen Sardar. *Human Rights and International Law: Equal before Allah, Unequal before Man?* The Hague: Kluwer Law, 2000.

Amos, Emma. *Work Suit.* 1994. Artist's private collection.

Anzaldúa, Gloria. *Borderlands/La frontera: The New Mestiza.* 2nd ed. San Francisco: Aunt Lute Books, 1999.

———. "Haciendo caras, una entrada." In *Making Face, Making Soul Haciendo caras.* xv–xxviii.

———. "Now Let Us Shift ... The Path of Conocimiento ... Inner Work, Public Acts." In *This Bridge We Call Home: Radical Visions for Transformation.* Ed. Gloria Anzaldúa and AnaLouise Keating. New York: Routledge, 2002. 540–75.

Athey, Stephanie. "Eugenic Feminism in Late Nineteenth-Century America: Reading Race in Victoria Woodhull, Francis Willard, Anna Julia Cooper, and Ida B. Wells." *Genders Online Journal* 31 (2000): <http://genders.org/g31/g31_athey.html>

Bailey, Cathryn. "Anna Julia Cooper: 'Dedicated in the Name of My Slave Mother to the Education of Colored Working People.'" *Hypatia* 19.2 (2004): 56–73.

Baker-Fletcher, Karen. *'A Singing Something': Womanist Reflections on Anna Julia Cooper.* New York: Crossroads, 1994.

Bakhtin, M. M. *Speech Genres and Other Late Essays: M. M. Bakhtin.* Ed. Carl Emerson and Michael Holquist. Trans. V. W. McGee. Austin, TX: University of Texas Press, 1986.

Baldwin, James. *The Evidence of Things Not Seen.* New York: Holt, Rinehart, and Winston, 1985.

Bambara, Toni Cade. "On the Issue of Roles." In *The Black Woman: An Anthology.* Ed. Toni Cade Bambara. New York: Mentor, 1970. 101–10.

———. "Preface." *The Black Woman.* 7–12.

Barazangi, Nimat Hafaz. *Woman's Identity and the Qur'an: A New Reading.* Gainesville, FL: University Press of Florida, 2004.

Barnett, Bernice McNair. "Invisible Southern Black Women Leaders in the Civil Rights Movement: The Triple Constraints of Gender, Race, and Class." *Gender & Society* 7.2 (1993): 162–82.

Bar On, Bat Ami. "Marginality and Epistemic Privilege." In *Feminist Epistemologies.* Ed. Linda Alcoff and Elizabeth Potter. New York: Routledge, 1993. 83–100.

Beale, Frances. "Double Jeopardy: To Be Black and Female." In *The Black Woman.* Ed. Toni Cade Bambara. New York: Mentor, 1970. 90–100.

Beauvoir, Simone de. *The Ethics of Ambiguity.* New York: Citadel, 1962.

Behling, Laura. "Reification and Resistance: The Rhetoric of Black Womanhood at the Columbian Exposition, 1893." *Women's Studies in Communication* 25.2 (2002): 173–95.

Bell, Roseanne P., Bettye J. Parker, and Beverly Guy-Sheftall. *Sturdy Black Bridges: Visions of Black Women in Literature.* Garden City, NY: Anchor, 1976.

Bell, Virginia E. "Counter-Chronicling and Alternative Mapping in *Memoria del fuego* and *Almanac of the Dead.*" *MELUS* 25.3–4 (2000): 6–30.

Bergin, Lisa A. "Testimony, Epistemic Difference, and Privilege: How Feminist Epistemology Can Improve Our Understanding of the Communication of Knowledge." *Social Epistemology* 16.3 (2002): 197–213.

Bhavnani, Kum-Kum, ed. *Feminism and 'Race'.* London: Oxford University Press, 2001.

Billington, Ray Allen, ed. *The Journal of Charlotte L. Forten: A Free Negro in the Slave Era.* 1953. Repr., New York: Collier, 1969.

Black, Edwin. *War against the Weak: Eugenics and America's Campaign to Create a Master Race.* New York: Four Walls Eight Windows, 2003.

Bobo, Jacqueline, ed. *Black Feminist Cultural Criticism.* Malden, MA: Blackwell, 2001.

———. *Black Women as Cultural Readers.* New York: Columbia University Press, 1995.

Bodman, Herbert L., and Nayereh Tohidi, eds. *Women in Muslim Societies: Diversity within Unity.* Boulder, CO: Lynne Rienner, 1998.

Bogues, Anthony. *Black Heretics, Black Prophets: Radical Political Intellectuals.* New York: Routledge, 2003.

———. *Caliban's Freedom: The Early Political Thought of C. L. R. James.* London and Chicago: Pluto, 1997.

Boittin, Jennifer Anne. "In Black and White: Gender, Race Relations, and the Nardal Sisters in Interwar Paris." *French Colonial History* 6 (2005): 120–35.

Bonner, Marita. "On Being Young -- A Woman -- and Colored." *The Norton Anthology of Literature by Women*. Ed. Sandra M. Gilbert and Susan Gubar. New York: Norton, 1996. 1577-81.

Booth, William. *In Darkest England, and the Way Out*. New York: Funk & Wagnalls, 1890.

Borchert, James. *Alley Life in Washington: Family, Community, Religion and Folklife in the City, 1850–1970*. Urbana: University of Illinois Press, 1980.

Bouglé, Célestin. *Les idées égalitaires; étude sociologique*. Paris: F. Alcan, 1899.

Brand, Dionne. *Bread out of Stone: Recollections, Sex, Recognitions, Race, Dreaming, Politics*. Toronto: Coach House, 1994.

Brewer, Rose M. "Theorizing Race, Class and Gender: The New Scholarship of Black Feminist Intellectuals and Black Women's Labor." In *Theorizing Black Feminisms: The Visionary Pragmatism of Black Women*. Ed. Stanlie M. James and Abena P. Busia. New York: Routledge, 1993. 13–30.

Brown, Elsa Barkley. "Negotiating and Transforming the Public Sphere: African American Political Life in the Transition from Slavery to Freedom." *Public Culture* 7.1 (1994): 107–46.

———. "'What Has Happened Here': The Politics of Difference in Women's History and Feminist Politics." *Feminist Studies* 18.2 (1992): 295–312.

Burton, Thomas William. *History of the Underground Railroad: American Mysteries and Daughters of Jerusalem*. Springfield, OH: Whyte Printing, 1925.

Busia, Abena P. "Performance, Transcription and the Languages of the Self: Interrogating Identity as a 'Post-Colonial' Poet." In *Theorizing Black Feminisms*. Ed. Stanlie M. James and Abena P. Busia. New York: Routledge, 1993. 203–13.

Byrd, Rudolph P. and Beverly Guy-Sheftall, eds. *Traps: African American Men on Gender and Sexuality*. Bloomington: Indiana University Press, 2001.

Camp, Stephanie M. H. "'I Could Not Stay There': Enslaved Women, Truancy and the Geography of Everyday Forms of Resistance in the Antebellum Plantation South." *Slavery and Abolition* 23.2 (2001): 1–20.

Cannon, Katie G. *Black Womanist Ethics*. Atlanta: Black Scholars, 1988.

Carbado, Devon W. "Epilogue: Straight Out of the Closet: Men, Feminism, and Male Heterosexual Privilege." In *Black Men on Race, Gender, and Sexuality*. Ed. Devon W. Carbado. New York: New York University Press, 1999. 417–48.

Carby, Hazel V. *Race Men*. Cambridge, MA: Harvard University Press, 1998.

———. *Reconstructing Womanhood: The Emergence of the Afro-American Woman Novelist*. Oxford: Oxford University Press, 1987.

Cecelski, David S., and Timothy B. Tyson, eds. *Democracy Betrayed: The Wilmington Race Riot of 1898 and Its Legacy*. Chapel Hill: University of North Carolina Press, 1998.

Césaire, Aimé. *Toussaint Louverture: La Révolution française et le problème colonial*. 1961. Repr. Paris: Présence Africaine, 1981.

Chateauvert, Melinda. "The Third Step: Anna Julia Cooper and Black Education in the District of Columbia, 1910–1960." In *Black Women in United States History, The Twentieth Century*. Vol. 5. Ed. Darlene Clark Hine. Brooklyn: Carlson, 1990. 261–76.

Chestnutt, Charles. *The Marrow of Tradition*. 1901. Project Gutenberg e-book: <http://www.gutenberg.org/etext/11228>

Christian, Barbara. "Images of Black Women in Afro-American Literature: From Stereotype to Character." (1975) In *Black Feminist Criticism: Perspectives on Black Women*. New York: Teachers College Press, 1997. 1–30.

———. "The Race for Theory." In *Making Face, Making Soul: Haciendo caras*. Ed. Gloria Anzaldúa. San Francisco: Aunt Lute Books, 1990. 335–45.

———. "'Somebody Forgot to Tell Somebody Something': African-American Women's Historical Novels." In *Feminism & 'Race'*. Ed. Kum-Kum Bhavnani. London: Oxford University Press, 2001. 220–32.

Clarke, Cheryl. "Living the Texts *Out*: Lesbians and the Uses of Black Women's Traditions." In *Theorizing Black Feminisms*. Ed. Stanlie M. James and Abena P. Busia. New York: Routledge, 1993. 214–27.

Cleaver, Kathleen Neal. "Racism, Civil Rights, and Feminism." In *Critical Race Feminism: A Reader*. Ed. Adrien Katherine Wing. New York: New York University Press, 1997. 35–43.

Code, Lorraine. "Rational Imaginings, Responsible Knowings." In *Engendering Rationalities*. Ed. Nancy Tuana and Sandra Morgen. Albany, NY: State University of New York Press, 2001. 125–50.

———. *Rhetorical Spaces: Essays on Gendered Locations*. New York: Routledge, 1995.

Cole, Johnnetta Betsch, and Beverly Guy-Sheftall. *Gender Talk: The Struggle for Women's Equality in African American Communities*. New York: Ballantine, 2003.

Collins, Patricia Hill. *Black Feminist Thought: Knowledge, Consciousness, and the Politics of Empowerment*. London: Unwin Hyman, 1990.

———. *Black Sexual Politics: African Americans, Gender, and the New Racism*. New York: Routledge, 2004.

———. *Fighting Words: Black Women and the Search for Justice*. Minneapolis: University of Minnesota Press, 1998.

Combahee River Collective. "The Combahee River Collective Statement." 1977. Repr. in *Home Girls: A Black Feminist Anthology*. Ed. Barbara Smith. New York: Kitchen Table Press, 1983. 272–82.

Cook, Mercer. "Julien Raimond." *Journal of Negro History* 26.2 (1941): 139–170.

———. "The Literary Contribution of the French West Indian." *Journal of Negro History* 25.4 (1940): 520–30.

Cooper, Anna Julia. "Angry Saxons and Negro Education." 1938. Repr. in *The Voice of Anna Julia Cooper*. Ed. Charles Lemert and Esme Bhan. Lanham, MD: Rowman & Littlefield, 1998. 259–61.

———. *L'Attitude de la France à l'égard de l'esclavage pendant la Révolution*. Paris: Impr. de la cour d'appel, L. Maretheux, 1925.

———. "Autobiographical Fragment." (n.d.) In *The Voice of Anna Julia Cooper*. 331. Also in Louise Daniel Hutchinson, *Anna J. Cooper: A Voice from the South*. Washington, D.C.: Smithsonian Press, 1981. 4.

———. "Colored Women as Wage Earners." Originally appeared in *Southern Workman*, August 1899. Reprinted in the *Washington Bee* 18 (Aug. 26, 1899). Available online at Moorland-Spingarn Research Center, Howard University: <http://www.huarchivesnet.howard.edu/9908huarnet/cooper1.htm>

———. "The Early Years in Washington: Reminiscences of Life with the Grimkés." 1951. In *The Voice of Anna Julia Cooper*. 310–19.

———. "Equality of Races and the Democratic Movement." 1925. In *The Voice of Anna Julia Cooper*. 291–98.

——. "The Ethics of the Negro Question." 1902. In *The Voice of Anna Julia Cooper*. 206–15.

——. "Foreword to *Le Pèlerinage de Charlemagne*." 1925. In *The Voice of Anna Julia Cooper*. 230–31.

——. Frelinghuysen University Flyer. Washington, D.C: 1930s. Accessed online 8/15/05 at Moorland-Spingarn Research Center, Howard University: <http://www.huarchivesnet.howard.edu/0005huarnet/cooper3.htm>

——. "Hitler and the Negro." c. 1942. In *The Voice of Anna Julia Cooper*. 262–65.

——. "The Humor of Teaching." 1930. In *The Voice of Anna Julia Cooper*. 232–35.

——. "The Intellectual Progress of the Colored Women in the United States since the Emancipation Proclamation: A Response to Fannie Barrier Williams." 1893. In *The Voice of Anna Julia Cooper*. 201–5.

——. "Legislative Measures Concerning Slavery in the United States: 1787–1850." 1925. In *The Voice of Anna Julia Cooper*. 299–304.

——. Letter to Mr. Wilkinson, 5/24/26. In *The Voice of Anna Julia Cooper*. 332–35.

——. Letter to W. E. B. Du Bois, 12/31/29. In *The Voice of Anna Julia Cooper*. 336.

——. "My Racial Philosophy." 1930. In *The Voice of Anna Julia Cooper*. 236–37.

——. "The Negro's Dialect." c. 1930s. In *The Voice of Anna Julia Cooper*. 238–47.

——. "On Education." c. 1930s. In *The Voice of Anna Julia Cooper*. 248–58.

——. *Le Pèlerinage de Charlemagne*. Paris: Lahure, 1925.

——. *Personal Recollections of the Grimke Family (Volume I)* and *The Life and Writings of Charlotte Forten Grimke (Volume II)*. Washington, D.C.: Privately printed, 1951.

——. "Sketches from a Teacher's Notebook: Loss of Speech Through Isolation." c. 1923. In *The Voice of Anna Julia Cooper*. 224–29.

——. *Slavery and the French and Haitian Revolutionists*. Trans. Frances Richardson Keller. Lanham, MD: Rowman and Littlefield, 2006.

——. "The Social Settlement: What It Is, and What It Does." 1913. In *The Voice of Anna Julia Cooper*. 216–23.

——. "Souvenir." In *The Voice of Anna Julia Cooper*. 339–41.

——. "The Third Step" (privately printed autobiographical booklet). c. 1945–1951. In *The Voice of Anna Julia Cooper*. 320–30.

——. *A Voice from the South by a Black Woman of the South*. 1892. Repr. New York: Oxford University Press, 1988.

Corbett, Bob. Review of *Slavery and the French Revolutionists (1788–1805)* by Frances Richardson Keller (Mellen Press, 1988). Online at Hartford Web Publishing: <http://www.hartford-hwp.com/archives/43a/082.html>

Crenshaw, Kimberlé. "Beyond Racism and Misogyny: Black Feminism and 2 Live Crew." *Boston Review* 16.6 (1991): 6–33.

——. "Demarginalizing the Intersection of Race and Sex: A Black Feminist Critique of Antidiscrimination Doctrine, Feminist Theory, and Antiracist Politics." In *The Black Feminist Reader*. Ed. Joy James and T. Denean Sharpley-Whiting. Malden, MA: Blackwell, 2000. 208–38.

Cudd, Anne E. and Robin O. Andreasen, eds. *Feminist Theory: A Philosophical Anthology*. Malden, MA: Blackwell, 2004.

Cullen, Countee. *Color.* New York: Harper, 1925.

Cuthbert, Marion Vera. *Education and Marginality: A Study of the Negro Woman College Graduate.* Dissertation, Columbia University. New York: Stratford, 1942.

Dash, Julie. Dir. *Daughters of the Dust.* Kino International, 1992.

Davies, Carole Boyce. "Other Tongues: Gender, Language, Sexuality and the Politics of Location." In *Women, Knowledge, and Reality: Explorations in Feminist Philosophy.* Ed. Ann Garry and Marilyn Pearsall. New York: Routledge, 1996. 339–52.

Davis, Angela Y. "Conversation." In *African-American Philosophers: 17 Conversations.* Ed. George Yancy. New York: Routledge, 1998. 13–30.

———. "Reflections on the Black Woman's Role in the Community of Slaves." In *Words of Fire: An Anthology of African-American Feminist Thought.* Ed. Beverly Guy-Sheftall. New York: New Press, 1995. 200–218.

———. *Women, Race, and Class.* New York: Random House, 1981.

Dayan, Joan. "Codes of Law and Bodies of Color." *New Literary History* 26.2 (1995): 283–308.

Delaney, Lucy A. *From the Darkness Cometh the Light, or, Struggles for Freedom.* St. Louis, MO: J. T. Smith, 1892.

Delaney, Sarah L., A. Elizabeth Delaney, and Amy Hill Hearth. *Having Our Say: The Delaney Sisters' First 100 Years.* New York: Dell, 1993.

Delpit, Lisa. "The Silenced Dialogue: Power and Pedagogy in Educating Other People's Children." *Harvard Educational Review* 58 (Aug. 1988): 280–98.

Dennis, Rutledge M. "Social Darwinism, Scientific Racism, and the Metaphysics of Race." *Journal of Negro Education* 64.3 (1995): 243–52.

Dill, Bonnie Thornton. "The Dialectics of Black Womanhood." *Signs* 4.2 (1979): 543–55.

———. "Race, Class, and Gender: Prospects for an All-Inclusive Sisterhood." *Feminist Studies* 9.2 (1983): 131–50.

Dubois, Laurent. *Avengers of the New World: The Story of the Haitian Revolution.* Cambridge, MA: Harvard University Press, 2004.

———. *A Colony of Citizens: Revolution and Slave Emancipation in the French Caribbean, 1787–1804.* Chapel Hill: University of North Carolina Press, 2004.

———. "*La République Métissée*: Citizenship, Colonialism, and The Borders of French History." *Cultural Studies* 14.1 (2000): 15–34.

Du Bois, W. E. B. *Black Reconstruction in America, 1860–1880.* Intro. David Levering Lewis. New York: Free Press, 1992.

———. *Haiti: A Drama of the Black Napoleon.* New York: Lafayette Theatre (sponsored by the Federal Theatre Project), 1938.

———. *The Philadelphia Negro.* (1899) Intro. Herbert Aptheker. Millwood, NY: Kraus-Thomson, 1973.

———. *The Souls of Black Folk.* Intro. Donald B. Gibson. Notes, Monica M. Elbert. New York: Penguin, 1996.

duCille, Anne. *The Coupling Convention: Sex, Text, and Tradition in Black Women's Fiction.* New York: Oxford University Press, 1993.

———. "The Occult of True Black Womanhood: Critical Demeanor and Black Feminist Studies." In *Feminism and 'Race'.* Ed. Kum-Kum Bhavnani. London: Oxford University Press, 2001. 233–60.

Ebrey, Patricia. "Gender and Sinology: Shifting Western Interpretations of Footbinding, 1300–1890." *Late Imperial China* 20.2 (1999): 1–34.

Edwards, Brent Hayes. *The Practice of Diaspora: Literature, Translation, and the Rise of Black Internationalism*. Cambridge, MA: Harvard University Press, 2003.

Ellsworth, Elizabeth. "The U.S. Holocaust Museum as a Scene of Pedagogical Address." *Symploke* 10.1–2 (2002): 13–31.

Essed, Philomena. *Understanding Everyday Racism: An Interdisciplinary Theory*. Newbury Park, CA: Sage, 1991.

Fausto-Sterling, Anne. "Refashioning Race: DNA and the Politics of Health Care." *Differences* 15.3 (2004): 1–37.

Ferri, Beth A. and David J. Connor. *Reading Resistance: Discourses of Exclusion in Desegregation and Inclusion Debates*. New York: Peter Lang, 2006.

Fischer, Sybille. *Modernity Disavowed: Haiti and the Cultures of Slavery in the Age of Revolution*. Durham, NC: Duke University Press, 2004.

Foster, Frances Smith. *Written by Herself: Literary Production by African American Women, 1746–1892*. Bloomington: Indiana University Press, 1993.

Franklin, V. P. *Black Self-Determination: A Cultural History of African-American Resistance*. Chicago: Lawrence Hill, 1992.

Freeman, Linda, producer. *Action Lines*. Writer: David Irving; Host: Anna Deveare Smith. L & S Videos, 1996.

Freire, Paulo. *Letters to Cristina: Reflections on My Life and Work*. Trans. Donaldo Macedo et al. New York: Routledge, 1996.

———. *Pedagogy of the Oppressed*. New York: Continuum, 1970.

Fusco, Coco. *English Is Broken Here: Notes on Cultural Fusion in the Americas*. New York: New Press, 1990.

Gabel, Leona C. *From Slavery to the Sorbonne and Beyond: The Life & Writings of Anna J. Cooper*. Intro. Sidney Kaplan. Northampton, MA: Smith College Dept. of History, 1982.

Gaines, Kevin K. *Uplifting the Race: Black Leadership, Politics, and Culture in the Twentieth Century*. Chapel Hill: University of North Carolina Press, 1996.

Gannett, Lisa. "The Biological Reification of Race." *British Journal for the Philosophy of Science* 55 (2004): 323–45.

Garrigus, John D. "Blue and Brown: Contraband Indigo and the Rise of a Free Colored Planter Class in French Saint-Domingue." *Americas* 50.10 (1993): 233–63.

———. "Colour, Class and Identity on the Eve of the Haitian Revolution: Saint-Domingue's Free Coloured Elite as *Colons Américains*." *Slavery & Abolition* 17.1 (1996): 20–43.

———. "White Jacobins/Black Jacobins: Bringing the Haitian and French Revolutions Together in the Classroom." *French Historical Studies* 23.2 (2000): 260–75.

Garvey, Amy Jacques. "Women as Leaders." In *Words of Fire*. Ed. Beverly Guy-Sheftall. New York: New Press, 1995. 93–4.

Gates, Henry Louis. "'Writing 'Race' and the Difference it Makes': 'Race,' Writing, and Difference." In *Feminist Literary Theory: A Reader*. 2nd ed. Ed. Mary Eagleton. Malden, MA: Blackwell, 1996. 46–48.

Gayle, Addison. *The Way of the New World: The Black Novel in America*. Garden City, NJ: Doubleday, 1976.

Gerard, Philip. *Cape Fear Rising*. Winston-Salem, NC: Blair Press, 1994.

Giddings, Paula. "Missing in Action: Ida B. Wells, the NAACP, and the Historical Record." *Meridians: feminism, race, transnationalism* 1.2 (2001): 1–17.

————. *When and Where I Enter: The Impact of Black Women on Race and Sex in America*. New York: William Morrow, 1984.

Gilmore, Glenda Elizabeth. *Gender and Jim Crow: Women and the Politics of White Supremacy in North Carolina, 1896–1920*. Chapel Hill: University of North Carolina Press, 1996.

Glass, Kathy L. "Tending to the Roots: Anna Julia Cooper's Sociopolitical Thought and Activism." *Meridians: feminism, race, transnationalism* 6.1 (2004): 23–55.

Goldberg, David Theo. "Racial Knowledge." In *Theories of Race and Racism: A Reader*. Ed. Les Back and John Solomos. New York: Routledge, 2000. 154–80.

Gordon, Lewis R. "African-American Existential Philosophy." In *A Companion to African-American Philosophy*. Ed. Tommy L. Lott and John P. Pittman. Malden, MA: Blackwell, 2003. 33–47.

————. "Conversation." In *African-American Philosophers*. Ed. George Yancy. New York: Routledge, 1998. 95–118.

————. *Existentia Africana: Understanding Africana Existential Thought*. New York: Routledge, 2000.

————. "The Human Condition in an Age of Disciplinary Decadence: Thoughts on Knowing and Learning." Phil Smith Lecture, Ohio Valley Philosophy of Education Society: 27 September, 2002.

————. "Introduction: Black Existential Philosophy." In *Existence in Black: An Anthology of Black Existential Philosophy*. Ed. Lewis R. Gordon. New York: Routledge, 1997. 1–10.

Gould, Stephen Jay. *The Mismeasure of Man*. New York: Norton, 1981.

Greene, Maxine. *Variations on a Blue Guitar: The Lincoln Center Institute Lectures on Aesthetic Education*. New York: Teachers College Press, 2001.

Grosz, Elizabeth. "Bodies and Knowledges: Feminism and the Crisis of Reason." In *Feminist Epistemologies*. Ed. Linda Alcoff and Elizabeth Potter. New York: Routledge, 1993. 187–216.

Gutman, Herbert G. *The Black Family in Slavery and Freedom, 1750–1925*. New York: Pantheon, 1976.

Guy-Sheftall, Beverly. "The Body Politic: Black Female Sexuality and the Nineteenth-Century Euro-American Imagination." In *Skin Deep, Spirit Strong: The Black Female Body in American Culture*. Ed. Kimberly Wallace–Sanders. Ann Arbor: University of Michigan Press, 2002. 13–36.

————. *Daughters of Sorrow: Attitudes toward Black Women, 1880–1920*. Brooklyn, NY: Carlson, 1990.

————. "The Evolution of Feminist Consciousness Among African American Women." In *Words of Fire*. Ed. Beverly Guy-Sheftall. New York: New P, 1995. 1–22.

————. "Preface." In *Still Lifting, Still Climbing: African American Women's Contemporary Activism*. Ed. Kimberly Springer. New York: New York University Press, 1999. xix–xxiii.

————, ed. *Words of Fire: An Anthology of African-American Feminist Thought*. New York: New Press, 1995.

Gyant, LaVerne. "Educating Head, Hand, and Heart: Anna Cooper and Nannie Burroughs." *Thresholds in Education* 22.1 (1996): 3–9.

Hammonds, Evelyn. "Black (W)holes and the Geometry of Black Female Sexuality." *differences: A Journal of Feminist Cultural Studies* 6.2-3 (1994): 126–46.

———. "Missing Persons: African American Women, AIDS, and the History of Disease." In *Words of Fire*. Ed. Beverly Guy–Sheftall. New York: New Press, 1995. 434–49.

Hansberry, Lorraine. "Simone de Beauvoir and *The Second Sex*: An American Commentary." In *Words of Fire*. Ed. Beverly Guy–Sheftall. New York: New Press, 1995. 128–42.

———. *To Be Young, Gifted, and Black: An Informal Autobiography*. Adapted by Robert Nemiroff. Intro. James Baldwin. New York: Signet, 1969.

Haraway, Donna. "Situated Knowledges: The Science Question in Feminism as a Site of Discourse on the Privilege of Partial Perspective." *Feminist Studies* 14.3 (1988): 575–99.

Harding, Sandra G. "Introduction." In *The 'Racial' Economy of Science: Toward a Democratic Future*. Ed. Sandra Harding. Bloomington: Indiana University Press, 1993. 1–29.

———. "Rethinking Standpoint Epistemology: 'What is Strong Objectivity?'" In *Feminist Epistemologies*. Ed. Linda Alcoff and Elizabeth Potter. New York: Routledge, 1993. 49–82.

———. "A Socially Relevant Philosophy of Science? Resources from Standpoint Theory's Controversiality." *Hypatia* 19.1 (2004): 25–47.

———. *Whose Science? Whose Knowledge? Thinking from Women's Lives*. Ithaca, NY: Cornell University Press, 1991.

Harley, Sharon. "Anna J. Cooper: A Voice for Black Women." In *The Afro-American Woman: Struggles and Images*. 1978. Ed. Sharon Harley and Rosalyn Terborg-Penn. Repr. Baltimore: Black Classic Press, 1997. 87–96.

———. "Beyond the Classroom: The Organizational Lives of Black Female Educators in the District of Columbia, 1890–1930." *Journal of Negro Education* 51.3 (1982): 254–65.

———. "For the Good of Family and Race: Gender, Work, and Domestic Roles in the Black Community, 1880–1930." *Signs* 15.2 (1990): 336–49.

Harper, Frances Ellen Watkins. *Iola Leroy, or Shadows Uplifted*. Boston: James H. Earle, 1892.

Harris, Leonard. *The Philosophy of Alain Locke, Harlem Renaissance and Beyond*. Philadelphia: Temple University Press, 1989.

Harris, Robert L. Jr. "The Intellectual and Institutional Development of Africana Studies." In *The Black Studies Reader*. Ed. Jacqueline Bobo, Cynthia Hudley, and Claudine Michel. New York: Routledge, 2004. 15–20.

Harris, Trudier. *Exorcising Blackness: Historical and Literary Lynchings and Burning Rituals*. Bloomington: Indiana University Press, 1984.

———. *From Mammies to Militants: Domestics in Black American Literature*. Philadelphia: Temple University Press, 1982.

———. *Saints, Sinners, Saviors: Strong Black Women in African American Literature*. New York: Palgrave, 2001.

———. *South of Tradition: Essays on African American Literature*. Athens: University of Georgia Press, 2002.

Hartman, Andrew. "The Social Production of American Identity: Standardized Testing Reform in the United States." *Socialism and Democracy Online* 17.2 (Issue 34): <http://www.sdonline.org/34/andrew_hartman.htm> (accessed 4/10/05).

Hartsock, Nancy. "The Feminist Standpoint: Developing the Ground for a Specifically Feminist Historical Materialism." In *Discovering Reality: Feminist Perspectives on Epistemology, Metaphysics, Methodology, and Philosophy of Science*. Eds. Sandra Harding and Merrell Hintikka. Boston: D. Reidel, 1983. 283–310.

Hein, Hilde. "Liberating Philosophy: An End to the Dichotomy and Spirit of Matter." In *Women, Knowledge, and Reality*. Ed. Ann Garry and Marilyn Pearsall. New York: Routledge, 1996. 437–53.

Henderson, Mae Gwendolyn. "Speaking in Tongues: Dialogism and the Black Woman Writer's Literary Tradition." In *Changing Our Own Words: Essays on Criticism, Theory, and Writing by Black Women*. Ed. Cheryl A. Wall. New Brunswick: Rutgers University Press, 1989. 16–37.

Henry, Paget. *Caliban's Reason: Introducing Afro-Caribbean Philosophy*. New York: Routledge, 2000.

Hernton, Calvin. "Breaking Silences." In *Traps: African American Men on Gender and Sexuality*. Ed. Rudolph P. Byrd and Beverly Guy–Sheftall. Bloomington, IN: Indiana University Press, 2001. 153–57.

Hine, Darlene Clark. "Rape and the Inner Lives of Black Women in the Middle West: Preliminary Thoughts on the Culture of Dissemblance." In *Words of Fire*. Ed. Beverly Guy–Sheftall. New York: New Press, 1995. 380–87.

———. *When the Truth Is Told: A History of Black Women's Culture and Community in Indiana, 1875–1950*. Indianapolis: National Council of Negro Women, 1981.

Hine, Darlene Clark, and Kate Wittenstein. "Female Slave Resistance: The Economics of Sex." *Western Journal of Black Studies* 3 (1983): 123–7.

Holloway, Jonathan Scott. *Confronting the Veil: Abram Harris Jr., E. Franklin Frazier, and Ralph Bunche, 1919–1941*. Chapel Hill: University of North Carolina Press, 2002.

Holloway, Karla F. C. "Revision and (Re)membrance: A Theory of Literary Structures in Literature by African-American Women Writers." *Black American Literature Forum* 24.4 (1990): 617–31.

hooks, bell. *Ain't I a Woman? Black Women and Feminism*. Boston: South End, 1981.

———. *Black Looks: Race and Representation*. Boston: South End, 1992.

———. "Black Women: Shaping Feminist Theory." In *Feminist Theory: From Margin to Center*. Boston: South End, 1984. 1–15.

———. *Feminist Theory: From Margin to Center*. Boston: South End, 1984.

———. *Talking Back: Thinking Feminist, Thinking Black*. Boston: South End Press, 1989.

———. *Teaching to Transgress: Education as the Practice of Freedom*. New York: Routledge, 1994.

———. *Yearning: Race, Gender, and Cultural Politics*. Toronto: Between the Lines P, 1990.

Howells, William Dean. *An Imperative Duty*. New York: Harper, 1891.

Hull, Gloria T., Patricia Bell Scott, and Barbara Smith, eds. *All the Women Are White, All the Men Are Black, But Some of Us Are Brave: Black Women's Studies*. New York: Feminist Press, 1982.

Hundley, Mary Gibson. *The Dunbar Story*. New York: Vantage, 1965.

Hunter, Tera W. "'The "Brotherly Love" for Which This City Is Proverbial Should Extend to All': The Everyday Lives of Working-Class Women in Philadelphia and Atlanta in the 1890s." In *W.E.B. Dubois, Race, and the City: The Philadelphia Negro and Its Legacy.* Ed. Michael B. Katz and Thomas J. Sugrue. Philadelphia: University of Pennsylvania Press, 1998. 127–52.

Hurston, Zora Neale. *Color Struck.* (1925). *In Black Female Playwrights: An Anthology of Plays before 1950.* Ed. Kathy A. Perkins. Bloomington, IN: Indiana University Press, 1989. 89–102.

Hutchinson, Louise Daniel. *Anna J. Cooper: A Voice from the South.* Washington, D.C.: Smithsonian Institution Press, 1981.

Jacobs, Harriet. *Incidents in the Life of a Slave Girl.* Ed. Jean Fagan Yellin. Cambridge, MA: Harvard University Press, 1987.

James, C. L. R. *The Black Jacobins: Toussaint L'Ouverture and the San Domingo Revolution.* New York: Vintage, 1963.

James, Joy. *Transcending the Talented Tenth: Black Leaders and American Intellectuals.* New York: Routledge, 1997.

James, Joy and T. Denean Sharpley-Whiting. "Editors' Introduction." In *The Black Feminist Reader.* Malden, MA: Blackwell, 2000. 1–7.

James, Stanlie M. and Abena P. Busia. *Theorizing Black Feminisms: The Visionary Pragmatism of Black Women.* New York: Routledge, 1993.

Johnson, Georgia Douglas. *A Sunday Morning in the South.* (1925) In *Black Female Playwrights.* 31–37.

Johnson, James Weldon, ed. *The Book of American Negro Spirituals.* New York: Viking, 1925.

———. "Self-Determining Haiti: The American Occupation." *The Nation,* August 28, 1920. See *The Nation* digital archives: <http://www.thenation.com/doc/19200828/johnson>

Johnson, Karen A. *Uplifting the Women and the Race: The Educational Philosophies and Social Activism of Anna Julia Cooper and Nannie Helen Burroughs.* New York: Garland, 2000.

Jones, Jacqueline. *Labor of Love, Labor of Sorrow: Black Women, Work and the Family, from Slavery to the Present.* New York: Vintage, 1985.

Jordan, June. *Civil Wars.* Boston: Beacon, 1981.

———. *Some of Us Did Not Die.* New York: Basic/Civitas, 2002.

———. *Technical Difficulties: African-American Notes on the State of the Union.* New York: Pantheon, 1992.

Kaplan, Sydney. "Introduction." In *From Slavery to the Sorbonne and Beyond: The Life & Writings of Anna J. Cooper.* Ed. Leona C. Gabel. Northampton, MA: Smith College Dept. of History, 1982. ix–xiii.

Kapsalis, Terri. "Mastering the Female Pelvis: Race and the Tools of Reproduction." In *Skin Deep, Spirit Strong: The Black Female Body in American Culture.* Ed. Kimberly Wallace-Sanders. Ann Arbor: University of Michigan Press. 263–300.

Keller, Frances Richardson. "An Educational Controversy: Anna Julia Cooper's Vision of Resolution." *NWSA Journal* 11.3 (1999): 49–67.

———. "The Perspective of a Black American on Slavery and the French Revolution: Anna Julia Cooper." In *Slavery and the French and Haitian Revolutionists* by Anna Julia Cooper (1925). Trans. Frances Richardson Keller. Lanham, MD: Rowman & Littlefield, 2006. 11–26.

————, ed. and trans. *Slavery and the French and Haitian Revolutionists* by Anna Julia Cooper, 1925. Lanham, MD: Rowman & Littlefield, 2006.

Kelley, Robin D. G. *Freedom Dreams: The Black Radical Imagination.* Boston: Beacon, 2002.

Kelly, Dierdre M. "Practicing Democracy in the Margins of School: The Teen-age Parents Program as Feminist Counterpublic." *American Education Research Journal* 40.1 (2003): 123–46.

Kemp, Sandra and Judith Squires, eds. *Feminisms.* New York: Oxford University Press, 1997.

King, Coretta Scott. "The Right to a Decent Life and Human Dignity." January 1971 speech to Chicano farm workers after King's December 1970 visits with Cesar Chavez in prison. Performed by Ruby Dee: Side 2, Band 2. *What If I Am A Woman* (Album no. FH 5538). New York: Folkways Records, 1977.

King, Deborah K. "Multiple Jeopardy, Multiple Consciousness: The Context of a Black Feminist Ideology." *Signs* 14.1 (1988): 88–111.

Klein, Félix. *Au pays de "La vie intense."* 6th ed. Paris: Plon–Nourrit, 1905.

Ko, Dorothy. "The Body as Attire: The Shifting Meanings of Footbinding in Seventeenth-Century China." *Journal of Women's History* 8.4 (1997): 8–27.

Ladner, Joyce. "Black Women as Doers: The Social Responsibility of Black Women." *Sage: A Scholarly Journal on Black Women* 6.1 (1989): 87–88.

Ladson–Billings, Gloria. *The Dreamkeepers: Successful Teachers of African American Children.* San Francisco: Jossey–Bass, 1994.

Lee, Rachel. "Notes from the (Non)Field: Teaching and Theorizing Women of Color." In *Women's Studies on Its Own.* Ed. Robyn Wiegman. Durham, NC: Duke University Press, 2002. 82–105.

Lemert, Charles. "Anna Julia Cooper: The Colored Woman's Office." In *The Voice of Anna Julia Cooper.* Ed. Charles Lemert and Esme Bhan. Lanham, MD: Rowman & Littlefield, 1998. 1–43.

Lemert, Charles and Esme Bhan, eds. *The Voice of Anna Julia Cooper.* Lanham, MD: Rowman & Littlefield, 1998.

Lewis, Gail. "Black Women's Employment and the British Economy." In *Inside Babylon: The Caribbean Diaspora in Britain.* Ed. Winston James and Clive Harris. London: Verso, 1993. 73–96.

Locke, Alain LeRoy. Ed. *The New Negro: An Interpretation.* New York: Albert and Charles Boni, 1925.

Logan, Rayford. *The Negro in American Life and Thought: The Nadir, 1877–1901.* New York: Dial, 1954.

Logan, Shirley. *'We Are Coming': The Persuasive Discourse of Nineteenth–Century Black Women.* Carbondale and Edwardsville: Southern Illinois University Press, 1999.

————. ed. and intro. *With Pen and Voice: A Critical Anthology of Nineteenth-Century African-American Women.* Carbondale and Edwardsville: Southern Illinois University Press, 1995.

Lorde, Audre. "The Brown Menace or Poem to the Survival of Roaches." In *The Collected Poems of Audre Lorde.* New York: Norton, 1997. 149.

————. *Sister Outsider: Essays and Speeches.* Freedom, CA: Crossing Press, 1984.

Losen, Daniel J. and Gary Orfield, eds. *Racial Inequity in Special Education.* Cambridge, MA: Harvard Education Press, 2002.

Lott, Tommy L. and John P. Pittman, eds. *A Companion to African-American Philosophy*. Malden, MA: Blackwell, 2003.

Lubiano, Wahneema. "Black Ladies, Welfare Queens, and State Minstrels: Ideological War by Narrative Means." In Toni Morrison, ed. *Race-ing Justice, En-gendering Power: Essays on Anita Hiill, Clarence Thomas and the Construction of Social Reality*. New York: Pantheon, 1992. 323–63.

———. "Talking about the State and Imagining Alliances." In *Talking Visions: Multicultural Feminism in a Transnational Age*. Ed. Ella Shohat. New York and Cambridge, MA: New Museum of Contemporary Art and MIT Press, 1998. 441–49.

Lugones, María. "Hablando cara a cara/Speaking Face to Face: An Exploration of Ethnocentric Racism." In *Making Face, Making Soul Haciendo caras*. Ed. Gloria Anzaldúa. San Francisco: Aunt Lute Books, 1990. 46–64.

———. "Playfulness, 'World'-Traveling and Loving Perception." In *Making Face, Making Soul: Haciendo caras*. 390–402.

Marshall, Paule. "The Making of a Writer: From the Poets in the Kitchen." In *Reena and Other Stories*. New York: Feminist Press, 1983. 1–12.

———. "The Negro Woman in American Literature." *Freedomways* 6 (1966): 8–25.

Martin, Emily. "Anthropology and the Cultural Study of Science." *Science, Technology, & Human Values* 23.1 (1998): 24–44.

May, Vivian M. "Thinking from the Margins, Acting at the Intersections: Anna Julia Cooper's *A Voice from the South*." *Hypatia* 19.2 (2004): 74–91.

Mayo, Amory Dwight. *Southern Women in the Recent Educational Movement in the South*. 1892. Ed. with intro by Dan T. Carter and Amy Friedlander. Baton Rouge: Louisiana State University Press.

McCaskill, Barbara. "Anna Julia Cooper, Pauline Elizabeth Hopkins, and the African American Feminization of Du Bois's Discourse." In *The Souls of Black Folk: One Hundred Years Later*. Ed. and intro. Donald Hubbard. Columbia, MO: University of Missouri Press, 2003. 70–84.

McClaurin, Irma. "Theorizing a Black Feminist Self in Anthropology: Toward an Autoethnographic Approach." In *Black Feminist Anthropology: Theory, Politics, Praxis, and Poetics*. Ed. Irma McClaurin. New Brunswick, NJ: Rutgers University Press, 2001. 49–76.

McDougald, Elise Johnson. "The Struggle of Negro Women for Sex and Race Emancipation." In *Words of Fire*. Ed. Beverly Guy-Sheftall. New York: New P, 1995. 80–83.

McDowell, Deborah. *'The Changing Same': Black Women's Literature, Criticism, and Theory*. Bloomington: Indiana University Press, 1995.

McIntosh, Peggy. "White Privilege and Male Privilege: A Personal Account of Coming to See Correspondences through Work in Women's Studies." 1988. Repr. in *Race, Class, and Gender: An Anthology*. 4th ed. Ed. Margaret L. Anderson and Patricia Hill Collins. Belmont, CA: Wadsworth, 2001. 95–105.

McKay, Nellie. "Remembering Anita Hill and Clarence Thomas: What Really Happened When One Black Woman Spoke Out." In *Race-ing Justice, En-gendering Power*. Ed. Toni Morrison. New York: Pantheon, 1992. 269–89.

Menard, William T. Letter. *Washington Post*, 1 Sept. 1905: 13.

Mills, Charles W. "Alternative Epistemologies." *Social Theory and Practice* 14 (1988): 237–63.

———. *Blackness Visible: Essays on Philosophy and Race.* Ithaca, NY: Cornell University Press, 1998.

———. *The Racial Contract.* Ithaca, NY: Cornell University Press, 1997.

———. "White Supremacy." In *A Companion to African-American Philosophy.* Ed. Tommy L. Lott and John P. Pittman. Malden, MA: Blackwell, 2003. 269–81.

Mohanty, Chandra Talpade. "Crafting Feminist Geneaologies: On the Geography and Politics of Home, Nation, and Community." In *Talking Visions.* Ed. Ella Shohat. New York and Cambridge, MA: New Museum of Contemporary Art and MIT Press, 1998. 485–500.

Moody, Shirley C. "Anna Julia Cooper, Charles Chestnutt and the Hampton Folklore Society — Constructing a Black Folk Aesthetic through Folklore and Memory." Presented at conference "Celebrating the African American Novel." State College, PA: Penn State, April 1–2, 2005.

Moore, Jacqueline M. "Bethel Literary and Historical Association." In *Organizing Black America: An Encyclopedia of African American Organizations.* Ed. Nina Mjagkij. New York: Garland, 2001. 93–94.

Morgan, Jennifer L. "'Some Could Suckle over Their Shoulder': Male Travelers, Female Bodies, and the Gendering of Racial Ideology, 1500–1770." In *Skin Deep, Spirit Strong.* Ed. and Intro. Kimberly Wallace-Sanders. Ann Arbor: University of Michigan Press, 2002. 37–65.

Morrison, Toni. *Playing in the Dark: Whiteness and the Literary Imagination.* New York: Vintage, 1992.

———. "Unspeakable Things Unspoken: The Afro-American Presence in American Literature." In *The Black Feminist Reader.* Ed. Joy James and T. Denean Sharpley-Whiting. Malden, MA: Blackwell, 2000. 24–56.

Morton, Lena Beatrice. *Negro Poetry in America.* Boston: Stratford, 1925.

Morton, Patricia. *Disfigured Images: The Historical Assault on Afro-American Women.* New York: Praeger, 2001.

Mullings, Leith. *On Our Own Terms: Race, Class and Gender in the Lives of African American Women.* New York: Routledge, 1997.

Munro, Martin. "Can't Stand Up for Falling Down: Haiti, Its Revolutions, and Twentieth-Century Negritudes." *Research in African Literatures* 35.2 (2004): 1–17.

Murray, Pauli. "The Liberation of Black Women." In *Words of Fire.* Ed. Beverly Guy-Sheftall. New York: New Press, 1995. 186–97.

NAACP Papers, Part 3: The campaign for educational equity. Cooper Correspondence, 1934. Series A. Legal Department and Central Office records (1913–1940): reel 21, "I-C-291," fr. 0879-0893. Frederick, MD: University Publications of America.

Narayan, Uma. *Dislocating Cultures: Identities, Traditions, and Third-World Feminism.* New York: Routledge, 1997.

Nash, Margaret. "'Patient Persistence': The Political and Educational Values of Anna Julia Cooper and Mary Church Terrell." *Educational Studies* 35.2 (2004): 122–36.

Neverdon-Morton, Cynthia. *Afro-American Women of the South and the Advancement of the Race, 1895–1925.* Knoxville: University of Tennessee Press, 1989.

Neville, Helen A., and Jennifer Hamer. "'We Make Freedom': An Exploration of Revolutionary Black Feminism." *Journal of Black Studies* 31.4 (2001): 437–61.

"Not Entitled to Pay." *Washington Post*, 5 Jan. 1907: 14.

Oberlin College. "Addendum to the 'Catalogue and Record of Colored Students,' 1862–99." 2001. <http://www.oberlin.edu/archive/holdings/finding/RG5/SG4/S3/addendum.html>. Accessed 3/24/06.

O'Grady, Lorraine. "Olympia's Maid: Reclaiming Black Female Sexuality." *Afterimage* 20.1 (1992): 14–15.

Payne, Charles. "Men Led, but Women Organized: Movement Participation of Women in the Mississippi Delta." In *Women in the Civil Rights Movement*. Ed. Vicki L. Crawford, Jacqueline Anne Rouse, and Barbara Woods. Brooklyn, NY: Carlson, 1990. 1–11.

Pellow, David W. H. "Anna Julia Cooper: The International Dimensions." In *Recovered Writers/Recovered Texts: Race, Class, and Gender in Black Women's Literature*. Ed. Dolan Hubbard. Knoxville: University of Tennessee Press, 1997. 60–74.

Perkins, Margo V. *Autobiography as Activism: Three Black Women of the Sixties*. Jackson: University Press of Mississippi, 2000.

Peterson, Carla L. *'Doers of the Word': African-American Women Speakers and Writers in the North (1830–1880)*. New York: Oxford University Press, 1995.

Philip, M. Nourbese. "Songlines of Memory." Public lecture, Syracuse University, Syracuse, NY, March 24, 2006.

Pitts, Nicole. "Anna Julia Cooper: 'Not the Boys Less, but the Girls More.'" In *Women's Philosophies of Education: Thinking Through Our Mothers*. Ed. Connie Titone and Karen Maloney. Upper Saddle River, NJ: Prentice Hall, 1999. 73–96.

Pough, Gwendolyn. *Check It While I Wreck It: Black Womanhood, Hip-Hop Culture, and the Public Sphere*. Boston: Northeastern University Press, 2004.

Ransby, Barbara and Tracye Matthews. "Black Popular Culture and the Transcendence of Patriarchal Illusions." In *Words of Fire*. Ed. Beverly Guy-Sheftall. New York: New Press, 1995. 526–35.

Reagon, Bernice Johnson. "Coalition Politics: Turning the Century." In *Home Girls: A Black Feminist Anthology*. Ed. Barbara Smith. New York: Kitchen Table, 1983. 356–69.

Reinhardt, Catherine A. "Forgotten Claims to Liberty: Free Coloreds in St. Domingue on the Eve of the First Abolition of Slavery." *Colonial Latin American Review* 10.1 (2001): 105–24.

"Reunited Trio Blazed a Trail." *Washington Post* 4 April, 1952: C9.

Reynolds, Tracey. "Re-thinking a Black Feminist Standpoint." *Ethnic and Racial Studies* 25.4 (2002): 591–606.

Rich, Adrienne. *On Lies, Secrets, and Silence*. New York: Norton, 1979.

Riggs, Marlon. Producer/Director. *Ethnic Notions*. VHS: 56 mins. California Newsreel: 1987.

———. "Unleash the Queen." In *Black Popular Culture*. Ed. Michele Wallace and Gina Dent. Seattle: Bay, 1992. 99–105.

Ringgold, Faith. *Faith Ringgold: Twenty Years of Painting, Sculpture and Performance (1963–1983)*. Ed. Michele Wallace. New York: Studio Museum of Harlem, 1984.

Roberts, Dorothy. *Killing the Black Body: Race, Reproduction, and the Meaning of Liberty.* New York: Pantheon, 1997.

Robinson, Pat and Group. "A Historical and Critical Essay for Black Women in the Cities, June 1969." In *The Black Woman.* Ed. Toni Cade Bambara. New York: Mentor, 1970. 198–210.

———. "Poor Black Women's Study Papers by Poor Black Women of Mount Vernon, New York." In *The Black Woman.* 189–97.

Roediger, David R. *The Wages of Whiteness: Race and the Making of the American Working Class.* 1991. Rev. ed. New York: Verso, 1998.

Ross, Loretta J. "African-American Woman and Abortion: 1800–1970." In *Theorizing Black Feminisms: The Visionary Pragmatism of Black Women.* Ed. Stanlie M. James and Abena P. Busia. New York: Routledge, 1993. 141–59.

Samantrai, Ranu. *AlterNatives: Black Feminism in the Postimperial Nation.* Stanford, CA: Stanford University Press, 2002.

Sandoval, Chela. *Methodology of the Oppressed.* Minneapolis: University of Minnesota Press, 2000.

Schulz, Amy and Leith Mullings, eds. *Gender, Race, Class and Health: Intersectional Approaches.* San Francisco: Jossey-Bass, 2005.

Schutte, Ofelia. "Cultural Alterity: Cross-Cultural Communication and Feminist Theory in North–South Contexts." In *Women of Color and Philosophy: A Critical Reader.* Ed. Naomi Zack. Malden, MA: Blackwell, 2000. 44–68.

Scott, Patricia Bell. "Debunking Sapphire: Toward a Non-Racist and Non-Sexist Social Science." In *All the Women Are White, All the Blacks are Men, But Some of Us Are Brave: Black Women's Studies.* Ed. Gloria T. Hull, Patricia Bell Scott, and Barbara Smith. Old Westbury, NY: Feminist Press, 1982. 85–92.

Scruggs, Lawson A. *Women of Distinction: Remarkable in Works and Invincible in Character.* Raleigh, NC: E. M. Uzzeli, 1892. Accessed electronically at <http://aabd.chadwyck.com>

Sewall, May Wright, ed. *World's Congress of Representative Women.* Chicago: Rand McNally, 1894.

Sharpley-Whiting, T. Denean. *Negritude Women.* Minneapolis: University of Minnesota Press, 2002.

Shilton, Katherine. "'This Scholarly and Colored Alumna': Anna Julia Cooper's Troubled Relationship with Oberlin College.". <http://www.oberlin.edu/external/EOG/History322/AnnaJuliaCooper/AnnaJuliaCooper.htm> accessed 9/8/05.

Shohat, Ella. "Preface." In *Talking Visions: Multicultural Feminism in a Transnational Age.* Ed. Ella Shohat. New York and Cambridge, MA: New Museum of Contemporary Art and MIT Press, 1998. 1–62.

Simpson, Georgiana Rose, ed. *Toussaint Louverture (surnommé le premier des noirs),* by Thomas Gragnon-Lacoste. Washington, DC: Associated Press, 1924.

Smith, Barbara. "Introduction." In *Home Girls: A Black Feminist Anthology.* Ed. Barbara Smith. New York: Kitchen Table, 1983. xix–lvi.

Smith, Dorothy. *The Everyday World as Problematic: A Feminist Sociology.* Boston: Northeastern University Press, 1987.

Smith, Susan L. *Sick and Tired of Being Sick and Tired: Black Women's Health Activism in America, 1890–1950.* Philadelphia: University of Pennsylvania Press, 1995.

Smith, Valerie. "Black Feminist Theory and the Representation of the 'Other.'" In *The Woman That I Am: The Literature and Culture of Contemporary Women of Color*. Ed. D. Soyini Madison. New York: St. Martin's, 1994. 671–87.

———. *Not Just Race, Not Just Gender: Black Feminist Readings*. New York: Routledge, 1998.

Sowards, Stacey K. and Valerie R. Renegar. "Reconceptualizing Rhetorical Activism in Contemporary Feminist Contexts." *Howard Journal of Communications* 17 (2006): 57–74.

Spelman, Elizabeth V. *Fruits of Sorrow: Framing Our Attention to Suffering*. Boston: Beacon, 1997.

———. *Inessential Woman: Problems of Exclusion in Feminist Thought*. Boston: Beacon, 1988.

Spillers, Hortense. "The Crisis of the Black Intellectual." In *A Companion to African-American Philosophy*. Ed. Tommy L. Lott and John P. Pittman. Malden, MA: Blackwell, 2003. 87–104.

———. "Mama's Baby, Papa's Maybe: An American Grammar Book." In *The Black Feminist Reader*. Ed. Joy James and T. Denean Sharpley-Whiting. Malden, MA: Blackwell, 2000. 57–87.

Springer, Kimberly. "Being the Bridge: A Solitary Black Woman's Position in the Women's Studies Classroom as a Feminist Student and Professor." In *This Bridge We Call Home: Radical Visions for Transformation*. Ed. Gloria E. Anzaldúa and Analouise Keating. New York: Routledge, 2002. 381–89.

———. Black History Commemorative Lecture, Syracuse University, Syracuse, NY, February 13, 2006.

———. "The Interstitial Politics of Black Feminist Organizations." *Meridians: feminism, race, transnationalism* 1.2 (2001): 155–91.

———. *Living for the Revolution: Black Feminist Organizations, 1968–1980*. Durham, NC: Duke University Press, 2005.

———, ed. *Still Lifting, Still Climbing: African American Women's Contemporary Activism*. New York: New York University Press, 1999.

Stanfield, John H., II. "The Myth of Race and the Human Sciences." *Journal of Negro Education* 64.3 (1995): 218–31.

Steady, Filomina Chioma, ed. *The Black Woman Cross-Culturally*. Cambridge, MA: Schenkman, 1981.

Stephens, Judith L. "Art, Activism, and Uncompromising Attitude in Georgia Douglas Johnson's Lynching Plays." *African American Review* 39.1–2 (2005): 87–102.

Stewart, Maria. "Religion and the Pure Principles of Morality, the Sure Foundation on Which We Must Build." In *Words of Fire*. Ed. Beverly Guy-Sheftall. New York: New Press, 1995. 26–29.

———. "What If I Am A Woman?" Speech delivered September 21, 1833, Boston, MA. Performed by Ruby Dee. Track # 1. *What If I Am A Woman* (Album no. FH 5537). New York: Folkways Records, 1977.

Stubblefield, Anna. "Meditations on Postsupremacist Philosophy." In *White on White/Black on Black*. Ed. George Yancy. Lanham, MD: Rowman and Littlefield, 2005. 71–81.

Sudbury, Julia. *Other Kinds of Dreams: Black Women's Organisations and the Politics of Transformation*. London: Routledge, 1998.

Sullivan, Shannon W. and Nancy Tuana, eds. *Race and Epistemologies of Igno-rance*. Albany, NY: SUNY Press, 2007.

Tanesini, Allessandra. *An Introduction to Feminist Epistemologies*. Malden, MA: Blackwell, 1999.

Tate, Claudia. *Domestic Allegories of Political Desire: The Black Heroine's Text at the Turn of the Century.* Oxford: Oxford University Press, 1992.

Tate, Gayle T. *Unknown Tongues: Black Women's Political Activism in the Antebellum Era, 1830–1860.* East Lansing, MI: Michigan State University Press, 2003.

Taylor, Estelle W. "Emma Frances Grayson Merritt: Pioneer in Negro Education." *Negro History Bulletin* (1975). Repr. Jan.–Sept (1996): 3–4.

Taylor, Ula Y. "Intellectual Pan-African Feminists: Amy Ashwood-Garvey and Amy Jacques-Garvey." In *Time Longer than Rope: A Century of African American Activism, 1850–1950.* Ed. Charles M. Payne and Adam Green. New York: New York University Press, 2003. 179–95.

———. "'Negro Women Are Great Thinkers as well as Doers': Amy Jacques-Gar-vey and Community Feminism in the United States, 1924–1927." *Journal of Women's History* 12.2 (2000): 104–26.

Tejeda, Carlos, Manuel Espinoza, and Kris Gutierrez. "Toward a Decoloniz-ing Pedagogy: Social Justice Reconsidered." In *Pedagogies of Difference: Rethinking Education for Social Change.* Ed. Peter Pericles Trifonas. New York: Routledge Falmer, 2003. 10–40.

Teng, Jinhua Emma. "The Construction of the 'Traditional Chinese Woman' in the Western Academy: A Critical Review." *Signs* 22.1 (1996): 115–51.

Terborg-Penn, Rosalyn. "Black Male Perspectives on the Nineteenth–Century Woman." In *The Afro-American Woman: Struggles and Images.* Ed. Sharon Harley and Rosalyn Terborg-Penn. 1978. Repr. Baltimore: Black Classic Press, 1997. 28–42.

———. "Discrimination against Afro-American Women in the Women's Move-ment, 1830–1920." In *The Afro-American Woman.* Ed. Sharon Harley and Rosalyn Terborg-Penn. 1978. Repr. Baltimore: Black Classic Press, 1997. 17–27.

Tesfagiorgis, Freida High W. "In Search of a Discourse and Critique/s that Center the Art of Black Women Artists." In *Theorizing Black Feminisms.* Ed. Stanlie M. James and Abena P. Busia. New York: Routledge, 1993. 228–66.

Thiong'o, Ngugi Wa. *Moving the Centre: The Struggle for Cultural Freedom.* Lon-don: James Currey, 1993.

Trinh T. Minh-ha. *Cinema Interval.* New York: Routledge, 1999.

———. "Commitment from the Mirror-Writing Box." In *Woman, Native, Other.* Bloomington and Indianapolis: Indiana University Press, 1989. 5–46.

Trouillot, Michel-Rolph. *Silencing the Past: Power and the Production of History.* Boston: Beacon, 1995.

Truth, Sojourner. "When Woman Gets Her Rights Man Will Be Right." In *Words of Fire.* Ed. Beverly Guy-Sheftall. New York: New Press, 1995. 37–38.

Tuana, Nancy and Shannon Sullivan. "Introduction." *Hypatia* 21.3 (2006): vii–ix.

Vogel, Todd. *ReWriting White: Race, Class, and Cultural Capital in Nineteenth-Century America.* New Brunswick, NJ: Rutgers University Press, 2004.

Walker, Alice. *In Search of Our Mother's Gardens: Womanist Prose.* New York: Harcourt Brace, 1983.

Walker, Margaret. *How I Wrote Jubilee.* Chicago: Third World, 1972.

Wall, Cheryl A. "Poets and Versifiers, Singers and Signifiers: Women Writers of the Harlem Renaissance." In *Women, the Arts, and the 1920s in Paris and New York*. Ed. Kenneth W. Wheeler and Virginia Lee Lussier. New Brunswick, NJ: Transaction, 1982. 74–98.

———. *Worrying the Line: Black Women Writers, Lineage, and Literary Tradition*. Chapel Hill: University of North Carolina Press, 2005.

Wallace, Michele. "Anger in Isolation: A Black Feminist's Search for Sisterhood." *Village Voice* 28 (1975): 6–7.

———. *Dark Designs and Visual Culture*. Durham, NC: Duke University Press, 2004.

Wallace-Sanders, Kimberly, ed. *Skin Deep, Spirit Strong: The Black Female Body in American Culture*. Ann Arbor: University of Michigan Press, 2002.

Walters, Alexander. "Chapter XX: The Pan-African Conference." In *My Life and Work*. New York: Fleming H. Revell, 1917. 253–64. Available in an electronic edition published by the University of North Carolina Chapel Hill, 1999. <http://docsouth.unc.edu/neh/walters/menu.html>

Washington, Mary Helen. "Introduction." In *A Voice from the South by a Black Woman of the South*. Anna Julia Cooper. New York and Oxford: Oxford University Press, 1988. xxvii–liv.

Watson, Hilbourne. "Theorizing the Racialization of Global Politics and the Caribbean Experience." *Alternatives: Global, Local, Political* 26.4 (2001): 449–84.

Weathers, Mary Ann. "An Argument for Black Women's Liberation as a Revolutionary Force." In *Words of Fire*. Ed. Beverly Guy-Sheftall. New York: New Press, 1995. 158–61.

Weisenfeld, Judith. *African American Women and Christian Activism: New York's Black YWCA, 1905–1945*. Cambridge, MA: Harvard University Press, 1997.

Wells, Ida B. "Lynch Law in America." In *Words of Fire*. Ed. Beverly Guy-Sheftall. New York: New P, 1995. 70–76.

———. *Southern Horrors: Lynch Law in All Its Phases*. 1892. Available as a Project Gutenberg e-text. <http://www.gutenberg.org/etext/14975>

———. *The Reason Why the Afro-American is Not at the World's Columbian Exposition: The Afro-American's Contribution to Columbian Literature*. Chicago: Privately published, 1893.

Welter, Barbara. "The Cult of True Womanhood, 1820–1860." *American Quarterly* 18 (1966): 151–74.

———. *Dimity Convictions: The American Woman in the Nineteenth Century*. Athens: Ohio University Press, 1976.

West, Elizabeth. "Cooper and Crummell: Dialogics of Race and Womanhood." In *Rhetorical Women: Roles and Representations*. Eds. Hildy Miller and Lillian Bridwell-Bowles. Tuscaloosa, AL: University of Alabama Press, 2005. 81–102.

White, Aaronette M. "I Am Because We Are: Combined Race and Gender Political Consciousness among African American Women and Men Anti-Rape Activists." *Women's Studies International Forum* 24.1 (2001): 11–24.

———. "Talking Black, Talking Feminist: Gendered Micromobilization Processes in a Collective Protest against Rape." In *Still Lifting, Still Climbing: African American Women's Contemporary Activism*. Ed. Kimberly Springer. New York: New York University Press, 1999. 189–218.

White, E. Frances. "Africa on My Mind: Gender, Counterdiscourse, and African American Nationalism." In *Words of Fire*. Ed. Beverly Guy-Sheftall. New York: New Press, 1995. 504–24.

———. *Dark Continent of Our Bodies: Black Feminism and the Politics of Respectability*. Philadelphia: Temple University Press, 2001.

Whitten, Barbara L. "Standpoint Epistemology in the Physical Sciences: The Case of Michael Faraday." In *Engendering Rationalities*. Ed. Nancy Tuana and Sandra Morgen. Albany, NY: State University of New York Press, 2001. 361–80.

Williams, Delores. *Sisters in the Wilderness*. Maryknoll, NY: Orbis, 1993.

Williams, Patricia J. *The Alchemy of Race and Rights: Diary of a Law Professor*. Cambridge, MA: Harvard University Press, 1991.

Williams-Myers, A.J. "Slavery, Rebellion, and Revolution in the Americas: A Historiographical Scenario on the Theses of Genovese and Others." *Journal of Black Studies* 26.4 (1996): 381–400.

Wing, Adrien Katherine. "Brief Reflections toward a Multiplicative Theory and Praxis of Being." In *Critical Race Feminism*. Ed. Adrien Katherine Wing. New York: New York University Press, 1997. 27–34.

Woodson, Carter G. *A Brief Treatment of the Free Negro*. Washington, DC: Associated Press, 1925.

———. "Emma Merritt" (Profile). *Opportunity* 8 (1930): 244–45.

———. *Free Negro Heads of Families in the United States in 1830*. Washington, DC: Association for the Study of Negro Life and History, 1925.

———. *Negro Orators and Their Orations*. Washington, DC: Associated Press, 1925.

Wright, Richard. *Native Son*. New York: Harper, 1940.

Yancy, George. "Introduction: Philosophy and Moving the Center of Conversation." In *African-American Philosophers: 17 Conversations*. Ed. George Yancy. New York: Routledge, 1998. 1–12.

Young, Iris Marion. *Inclusion and Democracy*. Oxford and New York: Oxford University Press, 2000.

Yu, Su-lin. "Reconstructing Western Female Subjectivity: Between Orientalism and Feminism in Julia Kristeva's *About Chinese Women*." *Jouvert* 7.1 (2002): online journal. <http://social.chass.ncsu.edu/jouvert> Accessed 1/3/06 and 2/1/06.

Index

A

Abstract generalization, 163
Activism
  activities, 48
  biased view, 47–48
  collective accountability and, 64
  description of, 75–76
  forms of, 50–51
  gendered division of labor in, 47, 75
  involvement in, 18, 45
  oversight of, 45
  reductive ideas about, 46–47
Adoptions, 16
African American(s)
  caricatures of, 96
  character of, 153–154
  dehumanizing of, 157
  domination by, 71–72
  persistent poverty for, 152
  political rights of, 135
  stereotyped representations of, 97,
    156, 159
  struggles for, 101
African American feminists, 178–180
African American men
  cultural objectification of, 154
  depiction of, 156–157
  inequalities faced by, 55
  self-love by, 161
  stereotypes of, 156, 159
African American women, *See also*
    Women
  cultural objectification of, 154
  depiction of, 157
  economic burdens, 16
  education of, 65, 67–68
  labor by, 56
  marginalization of, 180
  politics of speech by, 89
  prostitute depiction of, 157–158
  rape of, 146
  reproductive labor of, 55–56
  sexual violence against, 146
  stereotypes of, 154–155
  undertheorizing of, 39
  unnamable burden for, 88
  virtue of, 155
Africana philosophy, 175
Agassiz, Louis, 92, 154
Age of Revolution, 119, 138, 171
Alley Sanitation Committee, 23–24
Alpha Kappa Alpha, 33
American Negro Academy, 21
Amis des Noirs, 113, 117
"Angry Saxons," 149–150

.